The Idries Shah
Anthology

The Idries Shah Anthology

ISF PUBLISHING

BOOKS BY IDRIES SHAH

SUFI STUDIES AND MIDDLE EASTERN LITERATURE
The Sufis
Caravan of Dreams
The Way of the Sufi
Tales of the Dervishes: *Teaching-stories Over a
Thousand Years*
Sufi Thought and Action

TRADITIONAL PSYCHOLOGY,
TEACHING ENCOUNTERS AND NARRATIVES
Thinkers of the East: *Studies in Experientialism*
Wisdom of the Idiots
The Dermis Probe
Learning How to Learn: *Psychology and Spirituality
in the Sufi Way*
Knowing How to Know
The Magic Monastery: *Analogical and Action Philosophy*
Seeker After Truth
Observations
Evenings with Idries Shah
The Commanding Self

UNIVERSITY LECTURES
A Perfumed Scorpion (Institute for the Study of
Human Knowledge and California University)
Special Problems in the Study of Sufi Ideas
(Sussex University)
The Elephant in the Dark: *Christianity, Islam
and the Sufis* (Geneva University)
Neglected Aspects of Sufi Study: *Beginning to Begin*
(The New School for Social Research)
Letters and Lectures of Idries Shah

To be a Sufi is to detach from fixed
ideas and from preconceptions; and
not to try to avoid what is your lot.

Abu-Said, son of Abi-Khair
From *The Way of the Sufi*

Contents

The Tale of The Sands

A STREAM, FROM its source in the faraway mountains, at last reached the sands of a desert. Just as it had crossed every other barrier, the stream tried to cross this one, but it found that as fast as it ran into the sands, its waters disappeared.

It was convinced that its destiny was to cross this desert, yet how was this to be achieved?

All at once, a voice came from the sands: "The wind crosses the desert. Allow yourself to be absorbed by the wind, and it will carry you across in its arms."

This was not acceptable to the stream. It feared it would lose its individuality. Once having lost it, what guarantee was there it could ever be regained?

The voice of the sands said: "You cannot in any case remain the same stream you are today. If you allow the wind to take you, your essential part will be carried away and will form a stream again."

When it heard this, certain echoes began to arise in the thoughts of the stream. Dimly it remembered a state in which it, or some part of it, had been held in the arms of a wind. It raised its vapor to the welcoming arms of the breeze, which carried it gently above the desert and dropped it as rain upon the roof of a mountain, many miles away.

And because it had had its doubts, the stream was able to remember the details of the experience more strongly. It reflected: "Yes, now I have found my identity."

But the sands whispered: "We know, because we see it happen day after day and because we, the sands, extend all the way from the desert to the mountains."

And that is why it is said the way in which the stream of life is to continue on its journey is written in the sands.

From *Tales of the Dervishes*

Editor's Note

Sufis say that we are being constantly bombarded by the "spiritual impulse," the "source of being" – that without this permeating us, we would simply not exist. It is an influence on all our lives, part of the fabric of existence, and it may be recognized by everybody at times as "something other."

Sufism is concerned with the attunement of the individual to perceive this impulse.

To hear this subtle whisper, they say, we need to still the babble of what Sufis term our secondary selves, the bundle of conditioned impulses and instilled beliefs that we think of as our personalities, but that are very far from being so.

I am not a Sufi (the term Sufi is considered to describe the human being who has undergone a process of "perfection") but my father, Idries Shah, was one.

According to Shah:

"Sufism has two main technical objectives: 1) to show the man himself as he really is; and 2) to help him develop his real, inner self, his permanent part" (*Thinkers of the East*).

In his writing about Sufism, Idries Shah did some revolutionary things. Critically, and almost alone, he said that it was possible to divorce the essence of Sufi philosophy from what he insisted were secondary accretions of Islamic culture and religion.

Moreover, he said, in making this material available to the West, you not only could do this, you must do it.

This is because, he believed, you can only absorb materials that are designed for your own time and place. Sufism as an essence may be "truth without form" but, in order to penetrate into the human mind, it must be delivered in a package shaped to fit the receiving culture.

Sufism, he said, has existed over the millennia within a number of hosts. It originally resided within all religions and great philosophical systems. But it is so delicate and indefinable that it invariably becomes fossilized – mere mimetic ritual. Its worn-out accretions litter the world: the whirling dervishes of Turkey, traditionalist Sufi schools, and so on.

This is the point when somebody who has made the Sufi journey must excavate it and present it to a new generation. In a secular age, some aspects of Sufism may slot better into psychology than religion.

These views made him unpopular in some quarters, both in the East (among some traditionalist Sufi schools and orthodox Muslims alike) and in the West.

Another of his assertions – that "he who tastes knows," and that therefore Sufism may only really be studied from within – earned him the enmity of many academics.

His radical approach also brought him followers – over fifteen years, his mailbox averaged ten thousand letters a year – yet these overexcited devotees appeared not to have read his warnings that people often claim they want spiritual learning when they really only want emotional stimulus, attention, reassurance, etc.

As a child, I witnessed many of these would-be acolytes quite literally beating a path to his door and the frustrated disappointment with which they departed when they realized he was not interested in running a cult, in giving them dervish exercises, and the like.

So what were the key teachings of Idries Shah that earned him such fanatical adoration and vituperative hatred alike?

He argued that human beings, while capable of the most sublime capacities, choose to live on a plane far below their potential. Chained by the commanding self – a mixture of laziness, greed, fear and prejudice – they are driven on, harnessed and shackled by their own lower nature, fleeing from truth, from the exaltation and beauty that should be theirs.

Yet, his was no gloom-ridden moralizing. He held an optimistic message that it is possible for humans to develop, to reach our destiny.

He turned morality on its head; vices, he argued, are not morally loaded, but are veils that conceal our potential. Virtues are not remote wonders to be aspired to, but practical prescriptions for human progress. The virtues he emphasized were: generosity, humor, kindness, clear-thinking and common sense, to name but a few.

While insisting that the human tendency to emote, to feel special, to yearn for ritual or hierarchy has nothing to do with Sufism, he did not demand an obsessive denial of any of these things. They are necessary for the smooth running of society, and anybody wishing to approach Sufism should get them elsewhere.

He spent much of his time trying to help people "learn how to learn": how to put away the part of themselves that prevents them from learning. For instance, he pointed out that most approaches to spirituality are actually disguised consumerism, like the man who wrote to the mail order fitness program: "I've done the exercises, now send me the muscles!"

"If your desire for good is based on greed, it is not good but greed," he said (*Learning How to Learn*).

He is the only person I know to have pointed out the invisible attention-seeking factor in many human activities. People in our culture, he said, are starving for attention, although it is not acceptable to acknowledge this. So it becomes disguised. He demonstrated this again and again: when he provided attention, their desire for spiritual fulfillment, urgent answers to their questions and so on disappeared.

Similarly, he argued that much of our thinking is based upon conditioned impulses and beliefs, assumptions and automatic thinking. Sufism is not. This is not to say you should live without conditioning – you can't – but before approaching Sufism, the student must become more flexible.

He used traditional Sufic techniques, including humor and the "shock" of materials that deliberately clash with current cultural prejudices, to encourage flexibility of outlook.

Another unpopular assertion of his was that Sufism can't be profitably studied by anybody at any time or place that suits them. Time, place and people have to be right.

His writings, he believed, were a halfway house between mere literature and active teaching. There is a point beyond which a student needs a teacher. But first, one needs to absorb the materials in the books as a process of familiarization with the unaccustomed Sufic way of thinking. Few, if any, of the people who flocked to him, he said, had ever asked him a question that hadn't already been answered in his books.

Which brings us back to another Sufi claim, hinted at earlier. Sufi materials, said Shah, can only really be effective teaching aids when selected by a Sufi.

As such, this anthology is a mere collection of fragments of his work; the more than thirty books where all this material appeared in context are still in print, and the serious student is advised to read them.

So why assemble this collection at all?

As Shah pointed out, our culture is not always good at making use of the information it already has. In the past ten years or so, while the internet and other means of mass communication have fostered much speculative debate about Idries Shah himself, they have not resulted in a corresponding increase in people actually reading what he had to say.

This is a pity, not least because – even on the level of entertainment – his material is of such high quality. For over forty years, he mined the treasures of Oriental literature and surfaced bearing beautiful stories, sublime poetry, witty aphorisms, mental gymnastics and jokes. To these he added his own stories, sayings and fables.

He himself enjoyed all this material and wished others to do so, whether they were interested in its Sufic origin or not. To those who did wish to extract more than just enjoyment, he would say: "Look at these stories and be amused, laugh at their jokes. Then put that aside. After that look at their moral, at what a story appears to you to mean – then put that aside as well. Only then can you begin to benefit from their real impact – and remember that this could be a long time after you have read it."

A mystic, genius, madman, con artist – he has been called all these and more. During his lifetime he accepted the huge fuss surrounding him philosophically, even though it sometimes interfered in the time he had available to work.

"When something new enters a culture, there is a period where, like a new object being thrown into the chimpanzee pen at the zoo, all the chimps rush to touch it, throw it on the floor, fight over it and so on," he told me once. "We must wait until the dust settles; only then will people be in a position to assess this material."

My father died in 1996 and the dust is settling fast. He leaves a body of work behind and, on this work alone, he believed, he should and would be judged.

This anthology is intended to provide a basic sample of his work, an essential reader, to allow people to do exactly what he would have wished them to do: to think for themselves and to make up their own minds.

Saira Shah

1

On Sufism

Sufism is truth without form.
Ibn el-Jalali

From *The Way of the Sufi*

Becoming What One Can Become
To BE A Sufi is to become what you can become,
and not to try to pursue what is, at the wrong stage,
illusion.

It is to become aware of what is possible to you,
and not to think that you are aware of that of which
you are heedless.

Sufism is the science of stilling what has to be
stilled, and alerting what can be alerted; not thinking
that you can still or alert where you cannot, or that
you need to do so when you do not need it.

The following of the Dervish Path is pursuing a
concealed Unity in spite of, and not by means of, the
claims of diversity.

It is taking into account the means which are
presented in diversity, without thinking that the
externals of diversity are important in themselves.

It is approached by studying the factors of learning how to learn; not by trying to gain knowledge without correct practice in approaching it.

You come closer to being a Sufi through realizing that habit and preconception are essentials only in some studies; not by forming habits and judging by means of unsuitable preconceptions.

You must become as aware of insignificance as you think you are of significance; not seek feelings of significance alone.

The humble are so because they must be so; and worst of all men or women are those who practice humility for the purpose of pride, not as a means of travel.

The method of Sufism is as it always has been, to adopt that which is of value, when and where it is of value, and with whom it is of value; not to imitate because of awe, or to copy because of imitativeness.

The success of man in raising himself higher comes through the right effort and the right method, not merely by concentrating upon the right aspiration or upon the words of others directed to yet others.

It is as it were a trap laid for the ignoble element in you when a man, a book, a ceremonial, an organization a method, appears, directly or by recommendation, to have something which is applicable to all, or attracts you strongly though incorrectly.

Sayed Imam Ali Shah
From *The Way of the Sufi*

Confessions of John of Antioch

REPUTED TO HAVE lived in the thirteenth century, Yahya (John) of Antioch lived, worked and traveled in Syria, Palestine, Egypt and India. He may also have visited Central Asia. Though well known in oral tradition for his "Sayings," very few written records of his life survive. They have never been collected.

Quite early in my youth I noticed, provoked by what I do not know, that the beliefs and the loves and hatreds of people seemed to originate with the teachings of their parents and the community to which they belonged. The Mandeans, for instance, hated the Christians, although they knew little about them, and did not want to increase their knowledge. And the Christians believed preposterous things about the Muslims, in spite of living among them and having a daily refutation of their prejudices, which they were unprepared to accept. Again, philosophers debated doctrines and arrived at answers which were profoundly affected by the quantity and nature of the knowledge with which they started their exercises, and their pre-judgments about the world, life and people.

I was for these reasons attracted to the people of the Sufi thought, although, aware that I was myself greatly affected by changes in mood, in speculation which was a mental habit with me, and by hope and fear, I doubted whether I could reach the understanding of humanity which these marvelous people exhibited.

At first, because of these shortcomings, I found myself attracted by the assurance which came, as I saw, to many, by the repeated affirmation by teachers of all kinds that their own path, and theirs alone, led to salvation. I saw that it did, indeed, lead to a stilling of the searching and uncertainties of life. Again, because of the same reasons, I was at one time powerfully moved by the expedient devised by the Hindus, which consisted mainly in removing oneself, by an effort of the will, from the need to dwell upon human problems at all.

At length, I became a follower of the Sufis, because in my intercourse with them I discovered that they invariably helped protect me from the consequences of my selfishness, and seemed to help grow in me that part which could assent to the need to regard my fellow man as my brother, and my brother as myself. All religions preserved, it seemed to me, the indications of what should be attempted. None of them preserved the means by which a man could make his way from where he received the message up to the point where he practiced the message and became whole.

I understood, long after I first started to follow the Sufi people, that entry into the body of the Sufis is possible in truth only after one has passed beyond the "entry with the tongue" and the "entry with the heart" alike.

The Sufis, by accepting and passing on the capacity of guides in this way between where man finds himself to be and where he wants to be, made themselves knowing mediums fully sensitized, so that a certain high power could move through them.

They did this only at the risk of loss of personal repute (for men did not understand them), and by shunning the customary attachments of the world until they could truly resist them (and thereby often forswore the great dignities which they could otherwise have had), and they also took as their watchword the most courageous contract: "We can help you to help yourself, and we must discharge our duty setting aside whether we are understood by the generality of people, and our help to you is at whatever cost to our potential achievements in the superficial world."

These are the men who love man, and whose love enables him to find the road to his own home.

From *Caravan of Dreams*

Entry into a Sufi Circle

IF YOU READ, if you practice, you may qualify for a Sufi circle. If you only read, you will not. If you think you have had experiences upon which you can build, you may not qualify.

Words alone do not communicate; there must be something prepared, of which the words are a hint.

Practice alone does not perfect humanity. Man needs the contact of the truth, initially in a form which will help him.

What is suitable and unexceptionable for one time and place is generally limited, unsuitable or a hindrance in another time and place. This is true in the search and also in many fields of ordinary life.

Hope and work so that you may be acceptable to a Sufi circle. Do not try to judge it or its members unless you are free from greed. Greed makes you believe things you would not normally believe. It makes you disbelieve things you should ordinarily believe.

If you cannot overcome greed, exercise it only where you can see it working, do not bring it into the circle of the initiates.

(Nazir el Kazwini, "The Solitary Remarks")
From *Wisdom of the Idiots*

Source of Being

ALLOW THE SOURCE of Being to maintain contact with you; ignore the impressions and opinions of your customary self. If this self were of value in your search, it would have found realization for you. But all it can do is to depend upon others.

Amin Suhrawardi
From *Wisdom of the Idiots*

The Travelers and the Grapes

> There are three forms of culture: worldly
> culture, the mere acquisition of information;
> religious culture, following rules; elite
> culture, self-development.
>
> (The master Hujwiri,
> *Revelation of the Veiled*)

A Sufi, the Sufis, cannot be defined by any single set of words or ideas. Rumi, one of the greatest mystical masters, tells us in a famous passage that the Sufi is:

> Drunk without wine; sated without food;
> distraught; foodless and sleepless; a king
> beneath a humble cloak; a treasure within
> a ruin; not of air and earth; not of fire and
> water; a sea without bounds. He has a hundred
> moons and skies and suns. He is wise through
> universal truth – not a scholar from a book.

Is he a man of religion? No, he is far, far more: "He is beyond atheism and faith alike – what are merit and sin to him? He is hidden – seek him!"

The Sufi, as we are told in these most famous words from the thirteenth-century *Diwan of Shams of Tabriz*, is hidden – hidden more deeply than the practitioner of any secret school. Yet, individual Sufis are known in their thousands, throughout the East. Settlements of Sufis are found in the lands of the Arabs, the Turks, the Persians, Afghans, Indians, Malays.

The more the dogged searchers of the Western world have tried to dig out the secrets of the Sufi, the more hopelessly complex the task has seemed to be. Their work thus litters the fields of mysticism, Arabism, Orientalism, history, philosophy and even general literature. "The secret," in the Sufi phrase, "protects itself. It is found only in the spirit and the practice of the Work."

No investigation into the reality of Sufism can be made entirely from the outside, because Sufism includes participation, training and experience.

In ordinary life, certain forms of understanding become possible because of experience. The human mind is what it is partly because of the impacts to which it has been exposed, and its ability to use those impacts. The interaction between impact and mind determines the quality of the personality. In Sufism this normal physical and mental process is engaged in consciously. The result is felt to be more efficient; and "wisdom," instead of being a matter of time, age and accident, is regarded as inevitable. Sufis liken this process to the analogy between a savage who eats everything and a discriminating man who eats what is good for him as well as tasty.

Metaphysically minded people, and especially those who feel that they are comfortable in the domain of mysticism or "inner perception," have no greater start on the generality of humanity where the acceptance of Sufism is concerned. Their subjectivity, especially where it is linked with a strong sense of personal uniqueness "caught" from other people, can in fact be a serious disability.

Anyone who says, "It is all so indescribable, but I just *feel* what you mean," is unlikely to be able to profit by Sufism. For Sufis are working, are carrying out an effort to awaken a certain field of consciousness by means of an approach which is specialized, not fortuitous. Sufism does not trade in airy-fairiness, mutual admiration, or lukewarm generalities. When the "bite" disappears, so, too, does the Sufic element from a situation.

Sufism is not directed to a section of the community – for no such section exists – but to a certain faculty within individuals. Where this faculty is not activated, there is no Sufism. It contains "hard" as well as "soft" realities, discord as well as harmony, the sharp brightness of awakening as well as the gentle dark of a lulling to sleep.

There are imitation Sufis, who try to benefit from the prestige which attaches to the name. Some of them have written books, which only add to a general perplexity among outsiders.

Much of the Sufic spirit may be transmitted in writing. However, if one accepts the fact that Sufism has to be experienced, it does not depend upon the impact only of artistic forms, but of life upon life.

Sufism, in one definition, *is* human life. It is axiomatic that the attempt to become a Sufi through a desire for personal power will not succeed. Only the search for truth is valid, the desire for wisdom the motive. The method is assimilation, not study.

I report a glimpse of Sufis in a circle (*halka*), the basic unit and very heart of active Sufism. A group of seekers is attracted to a teaching master, and attends his Thursday evening assembly. The first part of the proceedings is the less formal time, when questions are asked, and students received.

On this occasion, a newcomer had just asked our teacher, the Agha, whether there was a basic urge toward mystical experience, shared by all humanity.

"We have a word," replied the Agha, "which sums all this up. It describes what we are doing, and it summarizes our way of thinking. Through it you will understand the very reason for our existence, and the reason why mankind is generally speaking at odds. The word is *Anguruzuminabstafil*." And he explained it in a traditional Sufi story.

Four men – a Persian, a Turk, an Arab, and a Greek – were standing in a village street. They were traveling companions, making for some distant place; but at this moment they were arguing over the spending of a single piece of money which was all that they had among them.

"I want to buy *angur*," said the Persian.

"I want *uzum*," said the Turk.

"I want *inab*," said the Arab.

"No!" said the Greek, "we should buy *stafil*."

Another traveler passing, a linguist, said, "Give the coin to me. I undertake to satisfy the desires of all of you."

At first they would not trust him. Ultimately, they let him have the coin. He went to the shop of a fruit-seller and bought four small bunches of grapes.

"This is my *angur*," said the Persian.

"But this is what I call *uzum*," said the Turk.

"You have brought me *inab*," said the Arab.

"No!" said the Greek, "this in my language is *stafil*."

The grapes were shared out among them, and each realized that the disharmony had been due to his faulty understanding of the language of the others.

"The travelers," said the Agha, "are the ordinary people of the world. The linguist is the Sufi. People know that they want something, because there is an inner need existing in them. They may give it different names, but it is the same thing. Those who call it religion have different names for it, and even different ideas as to what it might be. Those who call it ambition try to find its scope in different ways. But it is only when a linguist appears, someone who knows what they really mean, that they can stop the struggling and get on with the eating of the grapes."

The group of travelers which he had been describing, he continued, were more advanced than most, in that they actually had a positive idea of what they wanted, even though they could not communicate it. It is far more common for the individual to be at an earlier stage of aspiration than he thinks. He wants something but does not know what it is – though he may think that he knows.

The Sufic way of thinking is particularly appropriate in a world of mass communication, when every effort is directed toward making people believe that they want or need certain things; that they should believe certain things; that they should as a consequence do certain things that their manipulators want them to do.

The Sufi speaks of wine, the product of the grape, and its secret potential, as his means of attaining "inebriation." The grape is seen as the raw form of the wine. Grapes, then, mean ordinary religion, while wine is the real essence of the fruit. The travelers are therefore seen to be four ordinary people, differing in religion. The Sufi shows them that the basis of their religions is in fact the same. He does not, however, offer them wine, the essence, which is the inner doctrine waiting to be produced and used in mysticism, a field far more developed than mere organized religion. That is a further stage. But the Sufi's role as a servant of humanity is brought out by the fact that, although he is operating on a higher level, he helps the formal religionist as far as he can, by showing him the fundamental identity of religious faith. He might, of course, have gone on to a discussion of the merits of wine; but what the travelers wanted was grapes, and grapes they were given. When the wrangling over smaller issues subsides, according to the Sufi, the greater teaching may be imparted. Meanwhile, some sort of primary lesson has been given.

The basic urge toward mysticism is never, in the unaltered man, clear enough to be recognized for what it is.

Rumi, in his version of this story (*Mathnawi*, Bk II), alludes to the Sufi training system when he says that the grapes, pressed together, produce one juice – the wine of Sufism.

The Sufis often start from a nonreligious viewpoint.[1] The answer, they say, is within the mind of mankind. It has to be liberated, so that by self-knowledge the intuition becomes the guide to human fulfillment. The other way, the way of training, suppresses and stills the intuition. Humanity is turned into a conditioned animal by non-Sufi systems, while being told that it is free and creative, has a choice of thought and action.

The Sufi is an individual who believes that by practicing alternately detachment and identification with life, he becomes free. He is a mystic because he believes that he can become attuned to the purpose of all life. He is a practical man because he believes that this process must take place within normal society. And he must serve humanity because he is a part of it.

In order to succeed in this endeavor, he must follow the methods which have been devised by earlier masters, methods for slipping through the complex of training which makes most people prisoners of their environment and of the effect of their experiences.

The exercises of the Sufis have been developed through the interaction of two things – intuition and the changing aspects of human life. Different

---

1   "Words cannot be used in referring to religious truth, except as analogy" (Hakim Sanai, *The Walled Garden of Truth*).

methods will suggest themselves intuitively in different societies and at various times. This is not inconsistent, because real intuition is itself always consistent.

The Sufi life can be lived at any time, in any place. It does not require withdrawal from the world, or organized movements, or dogma. It is coterminous with the experience of humanity. It cannot, therefore, accurately be termed an Eastern system. It has profoundly influenced both the East and the very bases of the Western civilization in which many of us live – the mixture of Christian, Jewish, Muslim and Near Eastern or Mediterranean heritage commonly called "Western."

Mankind, according to the Sufis, is infinitely perfectible. The perfection comes about through attunement with the whole of existence. Physical and spiritual life meet, but only when there is a complete balance between them. Systems which teach withdrawal from the world are regarded as unbalanced.

Abridged from *The Sufis*

2

The Subtleties of Mulla Nasrudin

WHEN YOU ARRIVE at the sea, you do not talk of the tributary.

Hakim Sanai, The Walled Garden of Truth

From *The Sufis*

STORIES FEATURING MULLA Nasrudin are a hugely popular part of oral folk-culture from Turkey to Afghanistan. Idries Shah collected hundreds of these tales and published them in the West. Superficially, most are in the form of jokes and, even in the East, are generally considered of little importance.

Yet Shah maintained that they may also be used in higher studies, where they "halt for a moment situations in which certain states of mind are made clear."

Nasrudin tales, he says, "bridge the gap between mundane life and a transmution of consciousness in a manner which no other literary form yet produced has been able to attain" (The Sufis).

The stories, like most Sufic material, have no didactic morals, and people are encouraged to look at them from different angles, and even to return to them over a period of years, extracting different nourishment from them at different times. The Mulla himself plays different parts, sometimes the adept, sometimes the unthinking part of the brain.

"*The intention of the corpus,*" continues Shah in The Sufis, "*is to provide a basis for making available the Sufi attitude toward life and for making possible the attainment of Sufic realization and mystical experience.*"

Because they are mostly in the form of jokes, he says, they are able to slip under the barrier of the "Old Villain" – the complex of assumptions and automatic thinking in which most of us live.

This concept is itself encapsulated in a story – the legend of Nasrudin. It is told that Hussein, the founder of the system, searched for a teacher to bear his message.

One day, he heard the sound of riotous laughter. The Old Villain was chastising one of his students for telling jokes.

"*Nasrudin!*" *thundered the Villain,* "*for your irreverent attitude I condemn you to universal ridicule. From now on, when one of your absurd stories is told, six more will have to be heard in succession, until you are clearly seen as a figure of fun.*"

Seizing this opportunity, Hussein imparted to Nasrudin a portion of his baraka, *his Sufi power. The mere repetition of a Nasrudin story, the Sufis believe, carries with it some* baraka; *pondering over it carries more.*

In this way, the teachings were preserved forever within a vehicle that could not be utterly distorted.

Editor's note

Costly

NASRUDIN OPENED A booth with a sign above it:

TWO QUESTIONS ON ANY SUBJECT
ANSWERED FOR $50

A man who had two very urgent questions handed over his money, saying:
"Five pounds is rather expensive for two questions, isn't it?"
"Yes," said Nasrudin, "and the next question, please?"

From *The Subtleties of the Inimitable Mulla Nasrudin*

How to Keep It Going

MULLA NASRUDIN USED to stand in the street on market days, to be pointed out as an idiot.
No matter how often people offered him a large and a small coin, he always chose the smaller piece.
One day a kindly man said to him:

"Mulla, you should take the bigger coin. Then you will have more money and people will no longer be able to make a laughingstock of you."

"That might be true," said Nasrudin, "but if I always take the larger, people will stop offering me money to prove that I am more idiotic than they are. Then I would have no money at all."

From *The Subtleties of the Inimitable Mulla Nasrudin*

How to Get Out of Trouble

A MAN HAD fallen between the rails in an Underground station when Nasrudin came along one afternoon. People were crowding around, all trying to get him out before a train ran him over.

They were shouting, "Give me your hand!" But the man would not reach up.

The Mulla elbowed his way through the crowd and leaned over to the man. "Friend," he said, "what is your profession?"

"I am an income tax inspector," gasped the man.

"In that case," said Nasrudin, "*take* my hand!" The man immediately grasped the Mulla's hand and was hauled to safety.

Nasrudin turned to the open-mouthed audience. "Never ask a tax man to *give* you anything, you fools," he said, and walked away.

From *The Subtleties of the Inimitable Mulla Nasrudin*

The Trip

NASRUDIN'S FRIEND WALI slipped and fell from the immense height of the Post Office Tower in London.

The following night, Nasrudin dreamed that he was visiting Heaven when he ran across Wali.

"What was it like, Wali?"

"The impact was terrible, but the trip – the trip was terrific!"

From The Subtleties of the Inimitable Mulla Nasrudin

The Cat and the Meat

NASRUDIN GAVE HIS wife some meat to cook for guests. When the meal arrived, there was no meat. She had eaten it.

"The cat ate it, all three pounds of it," she said.

Nasrudin put the cat on the scales. It weighed three pounds.

"If this is the cat," said Nasrudin, "where is the meat? If, on the other hand, this is the meat – where is the cat?"

From The Exploits of the Incomparable Mulla Nasrudin

Cooking by Candle

NASRUDIN MADE A wager that he could spend a night on a nearby mountain and survive, in spite of ice and snow. Several wags in the teahouse agreed to adjudicate.

Nasrudin took a book and a candle and sat through the coldest night he had ever known. In the morning, half-dead, he claimed his money.

"Did you have nothing at all to keep you warm?" asked the villagers.

"Nothing."

"Not even a candle?"

"Yes, I had a candle."

"Then the bet is off."

Nasrudin did not argue.

Some months later, he invited the same people to a feast at his house. They sat down in his reception room, waiting for the food. Hours passed.

They started to mutter about food.

"Let's go and see how it is getting on," said Nasrudin.

Everyone trooped into the kitchen. They found an enormous pot of water, under which a candle was burning. The water was not even tepid.

"It is not ready yet," said the Mulla. "I don't know why – it has been there since yesterday."

From *The Exploits of the Incomparable
Mulla Nasrudin*

Caught

THE KING SENT a private mission around the countryside to find a modest man who could be appointed a judge. Nasrudin got wind of it.

When the delegation, posing as travelers, called on him, they found that he had a fishing net draped over his shoulders.

"Why, pray," one of them asked, "do you wear that net?"

"Merely to remind myself of my humble origins, for I was once a fisherman."

Nasrudin was appointed judge on the strength of this noble sentiment.

Visiting his court one day, one of the officials who had first seen him asked: "What happened to your net, Nasrudin?"

"There is no need of a net, surely," said the Mulla-Judge, "once the fish has been caught."

From *The Exploits of the Incomparable
Mulla Nasrudin*

I'll Take the Nine

IN A DREAM Nasrudin saw himself being counted out coins. When there were nine silver pieces in his hand, the invisible donor stopped giving them.

Nasrudin shouted, "I must have ten!" so loudly that he woke himself up.

Finding that all the money had disappeared, he closed his eyes again and murmured, "All right, then, give them back – I'll take the nine."

From *The Exploits of the Incomparable
Mulla Nasrudin*

Happiness is Not Where You Seek It

NASRUDIN SAW A man sitting disconsolately at the wayside, and asked what ailed him.

"There is nothing of interest in life, brother," said the man; "I have sufficient capital not to have to work, and I am on this trip only in order to seek something more interesting than the life I have at home. So far I haven't found it."

Without another word, Nasrudin seized the traveler's knapsack and made off down the road with it, running like a hare. Since he knew the area, he was able to outdistance him.

The road curved, and Nasrudin cut across several loops, with the result that he was soon back on the road ahead of the man whom he had robbed. He put the bag by the side of the road and waited in concealment for the other to catch up.

Presently the miserable traveler appeared, following the tortuous road, more unhappy than ever because of his loss. As soon as he saw his property lying there, he ran toward it, shouting with joy.

"That's one way of producing happiness," said Nasrudin.

From *The Exploits of the Incomparable Mulla Nasrudin*

The Majesty of the Sea

REGALLY THE WAVES were hurling themselves upon the rocks, each deep-blue curve crested by whitest foam. Seeing this sight for the first time, Nasrudin was momentarily overwhelmed.

Then he went near to the seashore, took a little water in his cupped hand and tasted it.

"Why," said the Mulla, "to think that something with such pretensions is not worth drinking."

From *The Exploits of the Incomparable Mulla Nasrudin*

Moment in Time

"WHAT IS FATE?" Nasrudin was asked by a scholar.

"An endless succession of intertwined events, each influencing the other."

"That is hardly a satisfactory answer. I believe in cause and effect."

"Very well," said the Mulla, "look at that." He pointed to a procession passing in the street.

"That man is being taken to be hanged. Is that because someone gave him a silver piece and enabled him to buy the knife with which he committed the murder; or because someone saw him do it; or because nobody stopped him?"

From *The Exploits of the Incomparable Mulla Nasrudin*

All I Needed was Time

THE MULLA BOUGHT a donkey. Someone told him that he would have to give it a certain amount of food every day. This he considered to be too much. He would experiment, he decided, to get it used to less food. Each day, therefore, he reduced its rations.

Eventually, when the donkey was reduced to almost no food at all, it fell over and died.

"Pity," said the Mulla. "If I had had a little more time before it died, I could have got it accustomed to living on nothing at all."

From *The Exploits of the Incomparable Mulla Nasrudin*

At Court

NASRUDIN APPEARED AT Court one day with a magnificent turban on his head.

He knew that the King would admire it, and that as a consequence he might be able to sell it to him.

"How much did you pay for that wonderful turban, Mulla?" the King asked.

"A thousand gold pieces, Majesty."

A Vizier who saw what the Mulla was trying to do whispered to the King, "Only a fool would pay that much for a turban."

The King said: "Why ever did you pay that amount? I have never heard of a turban at a thousand gold pieces."

"Ah, Your Majesty, I paid it because I knew that

there was in the whole world only one king who would buy such a thing."

The King ordered Nasrudin to be given two thousand pieces of gold, and took the turban, pleased by the compliment.

"You may know the value of turbans," the Mulla told the Vizier later, "but I know the weaknesses of kings."

From *The Exploits of the Incomparable
Mulla Nasrudin*

The Omen

THE KING WAS in a bad mood. As he left the palace to go hunting, he saw Nasrudin.

"It is bad luck to see a Mulla on the way to a hunt," he shouted to his guards. "Don't let him stare at me – whip him out of the way!"

They did so.

As it happened, the chase was successful.

The King sent for Nasrudin.

"I am sorry, Mulla. I thought you were a bad omen. You were not, it transpires."

"YOU thought *I* was a bad omen!" said Nasrudin. "YOU look at *me* and get a full game-bag. *I* look at YOU, and I get a whipping. Who is a bad omen for whom?"

From *The Exploits of the Incomparable
Mulla Nasrudin*

The Rope and the Sky
A SUFI MYSTIC stopped Nasrudin in the street. In order to test whether the Mulla was sensitive to inner knowledge, he made a sign, pointing at the sky.

The Sufi meant, "There is only one truth, which covers all."

Nasrudin's companion, an ordinary man, thought: "The Sufi is mad. I wonder what precautions Nasrudin will take?"

Nasrudin looked in a knapsack and took out a coil of rope. This he handed to his companion.

"Excellent," thought the companion, "we will bind him up if he becomes violent."

The Sufi saw that Nasrudin meant: "Ordinary humanity tries to find truth by methods as unsuitable as attempting to climb into the sky with a rope."

From *The Exploits of the Incomparable Mulla Nasrudin*

Eating his Money
MULLA NASRUDIN, AS everyone knows, comes from a country where fruit is fruit, and meat is meat, and curry is never eaten.

One day he was plodding along a dusty Indian road, having newly descended from the high mountains of Kafiristan, when a great thirst overtook him. "Soon," he said to himself, "I must come across somewhere that good fruit is to be had."

No sooner were the words formed in his brain

than he rounded a corner and saw sitting in the shade of a tree a benevolent-looking man, with a basket in front of him.

Piled high in the basket were huge, shiny red fruits. "This is what I need," said Nasrudin. Taking two tiny coppers from the knot at the end of his turban, he handed them to the fruit-seller.

Without a word the man handed him the whole basket, for this kind of fruit is cheap in India, and people usually buy it in smaller amounts.

Nasrudin sat down in the place vacated by the fruiterer, and started to munch the fruits. Within a few seconds, his mouth was burning. Tears streamed down his cheeks, fire was in his throat. The Mulla went on eating.

An hour or two passed, and then an Afghan hillman came past. Nasrudin hailed him. "Brother, these infidel fruits must come from the very mouth of Sheitan!"

"Fool!" said the hillman. "Hast thou never heard of the chilis of Hindustan? Stop eating them at once, or death will surely claim a victim before the sun is down."

"I cannot move from here," gasped the Mulla, "until I have finished the whole basketful."

"Madman! Those fruits belong in curry! Throw them away at once."

"I am not eating fruit any more," croaked Nasrudin; "I am eating my money."

From *The Pleasantries of the Incredible Mulla Nasrudin*

Assumptions

"WHAT IS THE meaning of fate, Mulla?"

"Assumptions."

"In what way?"

"You assume things are going to go well, and they don't – that you call bad luck. You assume things are going to go badly and they don't – that you call good luck. You assume that certain things are going to happen or not happen – and you so lack intuition that you don't *know* what is going to happen. You assume that the future is unknown.

"When you are caught out – you call that Fate."

From *The Pleasantries of the Incredible Mulla Nasrudin*

Whose Servant am I?

MULLA NASRUDIN HAD become a favorite at Court. He used his position to show up the methods of courtiers.

One day the King was exceptionally hungry. Some eggplants had been so deliciously cooked that he told the palace chef to serve them every day.

"Are they not the best vegetables in the world, Mulla?" he asked Nasrudin.

"The very best, Majesty."

Five days later, when the eggplants had been served for the tenth meal in succession, the King roared: "Take these things away! I HATE them!"

"They are the worst vegetables in the world, Majesty," agreed Nasrudin.

"But Mulla, less than a week ago you said that they were the very best."

"I did. But I am the servant of the King, not of the vegetable."

From *The Pleasantries of the Incredible Mulla Nasrudin*

How Foolish can a Man Be?

THE MULLA WAS found pouring wheat from the jars of his neighbors into his own, at the communal wheat store. He was taken before the judge.

"I am a fool, I don't know their wheat from mine," he stated.

"Then why did you not pour any wheat from your own jars into theirs?" demanded the judge.

"Ah, but I know *my* wheat from *theirs* – I am not such a fool as that!"

From *The Pleasantries of the Incredible Mulla Nasrudin*

Which is My Half?

NASRUDIN AND A friend were thirsty, and stopped at a café for a drink. They decided to share a glass of milk.

"You drink your half first," said the friend, "because I have some sugar here, just enough for one. I shall add this to my share of the milk and drink it."

"Add it now," said the Mulla, "and I will drink only my half."

"Certainly not. There is only enough sugar to sweeten half a glass of milk."

Nasrudin went to the owner of the café, and came back with a large packet of salt.

"Good news, friend," he said, "I am drinking first, as agreed, and I want my milk with salt."

From *The Pleasantries of the Incredible Mulla Nasrudin*

Dry in the Rain

A MAN INVITED Nasrudin to go hunting with him, but mounted him on a horse which was too slow. The Mulla said nothing. Soon the hunt outpaced him and was out of sight. It began to rain heavily, and there was no shelter. All the members of the hunt got soaked through. Nasrudin, however, as soon as the rain started, took off all his clothes and folded them. Then he sat down on the pile. As soon as the rain stopped, he dressed himself and went back to his host's house for lunch. Nobody could work out why he was dry. With all the speed of their horses they had not been able to reach shelter on that plain.

"It was the horse you gave me," said Nasrudin.

The next day he was given a fast horse and his host took the slow one. Rain fell again. The horse was so slow that the host got wetter than ever, riding at a snail's pace to his house. Nasrudin carried out the same procedure as before.

When he got back to the house, he was dry.

"It is all your fault!" shouted his host. "You made me ride this terrible horse."

"Perhaps," said Nasrudin, "you did not contribute anything of your own to the problem of keeping dry?"

From *The Pleasantries of the Incredible Mulla Nasrudin*

The Yogi, the Priest and the Sufi

NASRUDIN PUT ON a Sufi robe and decided to make a pious journey. On his way he met a priest and a yogi, and they decided to team up together. When they got to a village, the others asked him to seek donations while they carried out their devotions. Nasrudin collected some money and bought halwa with it.

He suggested that they divide the food, but the others, who were not yet hungry enough, said that it should be postponed until night. They continued on their way; and when night fell, Nasrudin asked for the first portion "because I was the means of getting the food." The others disagreed: the priest on the grounds that he represented a properly organized hierarchical body, and should therefore have preference; the yogi because, he said, he ate only once in three days and should therefore have more.

Finally, they decided to sleep. In the morning, the one who related the best dream should have first choice of the halwa.

In the morning the priest said: "In my dreams I saw the founder of my religion, who made a sign of benediction, singling me out as especially blessed."

The others were impressed, but the yogi said: "I dreamed that I visited Nirvana, and was utterly absorbed into nothing."

They turned to the Mulla. "I dreamed that I saw the Sufi teacher Khidr, who appears only to the most sanctified.

"He said: 'Nasrudin, eat the halwa – now!' And, of course, I had to obey."

From *The Pleasantries of the Incredible Mulla Nasrudin*

Truth

"WHAT IS TRUTH?" a disciple asked Nasrudin.

"Something which I have never, at any time, spoken – nor shall I."

From *The Pleasantries of the Incredible Mulla Nasrudin*

Remembering

THERE IS A game called "I remember," which has been the cause of greater suffering than almost anything else. It illustrates how difficult it is to remember even a simple thing for any length of time.

Two people make a pact to practice "I remember." Thenceforward, every time one of them hands anything to the other, the recipient must say "I remember!" when he accepts the object.

The first person to forget to say this phrase under these circumstances loses the game and pays a forfeit.

Nasrudin had an "I remember" duel with his wife. The honors were even, and they almost lost their reason, passing objects back and forth, until neither could stand the pace much longer. The Mulla devised a plan. He went on a pilgrimage to Mecca.

When he came back several months later, armed with a gift to hand his wife, finally to win the game in the excitement of the reunion, she met him at the gate.

In her arms was a bundle. "I am not going to take it," said the Mulla to himself. But, as soon as he was within a few paces of her, she said: "Here is your new son."

The Mulla, overcome with joy, took the child into his arms – and forgot to say: "I remember."

From *The Pleasantries of the Incredible Mulla Nasrudin*

A Word for It

HEARING THAT A man wanted to learn the Kurdish language, Nasrudin offered to teach him. Nasrudin's own knowledge of Kurdish was limited to a few words.

"We shall start with the word for 'hot soup,'" said the Mulla. "In Kurdish, this is Aash."

"I don't quite understand, Mulla. How would you say 'cold soup'?"

"You never say 'cold soup.' The Kurds like their soup hot."

From *The Pleasantries of the Incredible Mulla Nasrudin*

Repetitiousness

PROFITING BY THE immense reputation which Sufis have as teachers of special insight, a group of robbers settled in an abandoned monastery on a highway, pretending to be Sufi dervishes.

Nasrudin and his small son were traveling on a long journey when they were espied by a lookout man among the robbers. They immediately started to carry out a rhythmic dance, with a great deal of noise.

As they approached, Nasrudin said to his son: "Night will fall soon, and this seems to be a monastery of advanced dervishes. Let us seek their hospitality."

The false dervishes welcomed them heartily, and even asked the Mulla to join their special exercises.

These took the form of a rapid circular movement, with the repetition of phrases which were changed from time to time by the leader.

Presently Nasrudin was whirling with the best of them, taking up the repetitious cries and in a near-hysterical frame of mind. Now the leader of the "dervishes" started to call: "I give you my donkey! I give you my donkey!"

Obediently, Nasrudin echoed the refrain, and the tempo was increased until he fell unconscious.

When he awoke with the dawn, Nasrudin found the robbers – and the donkey – gone. "I thought I left you in charge of the animal!" he roared at his son.

"Yes, Father. But when one of the dervishes came and took the donkey I ran to you, and you were shouting 'I give you my donkey!' so often and in front of so many witnesses that I realized that you had given him away."

From *The Pleasantries of the Incredible Mulla Nasrudin*

Allah will Provide

"ALLAH WILL PROVIDE," said Nasrudin one day to a man who was complaining that someone had stolen some cash from his house.

The man expressed doubt.

Nasrudin took him to the mosque, and rolled on the ground, calling upon Allah to restore the man's twenty silver coins.

Annoyed by his presence, the congregation made a collection and the sum was handed to the surprised loser.

"You may not understand the means which operate in this world," said the Mulla, "but I trust that you understand the end when it is handed to you in such a concrete form."

From *The Pleasantries of the Incredible Mulla Nasrudin*

Where I Sit

AT A GATHERING of divines, Nasrudin was seated right at the end of the room, farthest from the place of honor. Presently he began to tell jokes, and soon people were crowded around him, laughing and listening. Nobody was taking any notice of the graybeard who was giving a learned discourse. When he could no longer hear himself speak, the president of the assembly roared out:

"You must be silent! Nobody may talk unless he sits where the Chief sits."

"I don't know how you see it," said Nasrudin, "but it strikes me that where I sit *is* where the Chief sits."

From *The Pleasantries of the Incredible Mulla Nasrudin*

The School

ONE OF THE boys at the Mulla's school asked:

"Which was the greatest achievement, that of the man who conquered an empire, the man who could have but did not, or the man who prevented another from doing so?"

"I don't know about any of that," said the Mulla, "but I do know a more difficult task than any of those."

"What is that?"

"Trying to teach you to see things as they really are."

From The Pleasantries of the Incredible Mulla Nasrudin

There is More Light Here

SOMEONE SAW NASRUDIN searching for something on the ground.

"What have you lost, Mulla?" he asked. "My key," said the Mulla. So they both went down on their knees and looked for it.

After a time the other man asked: "Where exactly did you drop it?"

"In my own house."

"Then why are you looking here?"

"There is more light here than inside my own house."

From The Exploits of the Incomparable Mulla Nasrudin

How Nasrudin Created Truth

"Laws as such do not make people better," said Nasrudin to the King; "they must practice certain things, in order to become attuned to inner truth. This form of truth resembles apparent truth only slightly."

The King decided that he could, and would, make people observe the truth. He could make them practice truthfulness.

His city was entered by a bridge. On this he built a gallows. The following day, when the gates were opened at dawn, the Captain of the Guard was stationed with a squad of troops to examine all who entered.

An announcement was made: "Everyone will be questioned. If he tells the truth, he will be allowed to enter. If he lies, he will be hanged."

Nasrudin stepped forward.

"Where are you going?"

"I am on my way," said Nasrudin slowly, "to be hanged."

"We don't believe you!"

"Very well, if I have told a lie, hang me!"

"But if we hang you for lying, we will have made what you said come true!"

"That's right: now you know what truth is – YOUR truth!"

From *The Exploits of the Incomparable Mulla Nasrudin*

Never Know When it Might Come in Useful

NASRUDIN SOMETIMES TOOK people for trips in his boat. One day a fussy pedagogue hired him to ferry him across a very wide river.

As soon as they were afloat, the scholar asked whether it was going to be rough.

"Don't ask me nothing about it," said Nasrudin.

"Have you never studied grammar?"

"No," said the Mulla.

"In that case, half your life has been wasted."

The Mulla said nothing.

Soon a terrible storm blew up. The Mulla's crazy cockleshell was filling with water.

He leaned over toward his companion.

"Have you ever learned to swim?"

"No," said the pedant.

"In that case, schoolmaster, ALL your life is lost, for we are sinking."

From *The Exploits of the Incomparable
Mulla Nasrudin*

The Smuggler

TIME AND AGAIN Nasrudin passed from Persia to Greece on donkeyback. Each time he had two panniers of straw, and trudged back without them. Every time the guard searched him for contraband. They never found any.

"What are you carrying, Nasrudin?"

"I am a smuggler."

Years later, more and more prosperous in appearance, Nasrudin moved to Egypt. One of the customs men met him there.

"Tell me, Mulla, now that you are out of the jurisdiction of Greece and Persia, living here in such luxury – what was it that you were smuggling when we could never catch you?"

"Donkeys."

From *The Exploits of the Incomparable Mulla Nasrudin*

Duck Soup

A KINSMAN CAME to see Nasrudin from the country, and brought a duck. Nasrudin was grateful, had the bird cooked and shared it with his guest.

Presently another visitor arrived. He was a friend, as he said, "of the man who gave you the duck." Nasrudin fed him as well.

This happened several times. Nasrudin's home had become like a restaurant for out-of-town visitors. Everyone was a friend at some removes of the original donor of the duck.

Finally Nasrudin was exasperated. One day there was a knock at the door and a stranger appeared. "I am the friend of the friend of the friend of the man who brought you the duck from the country," he said.

"Come in," said Nasrudin.

They seated themselves at the table, and Nasrudin asked his wife to bring the soup.

When the guest tasted it, it seemed to be nothing more than warm water. "What sort of soup is this?" he asked the Mulla.

"That," said Nasrudin, "is the soup of the soup of the soup of the duck."

From *The Exploits of the Incomparable Mulla Nasrudin*

Facts are Facts

WHEN THE MULLA was made a Cadi [magistrate], he was faced with a difficult problem.

In an assault case, the plaintiff said that the defendant had bitten his ear. The defense was that the plaintiff had bitten it himself.

"This is a clear conflict of evidence, because there are no witnesses," said the Mulla. "There is only one way to decide this. I therefore adjourn the Court for half an hour."

He went into a room attached to the courthouse, and spent the time trying to bite his own ear. Every time he tried, he lost his balance and fell over, bruising his head.

When the Court reassembled, the Mulla said: "Examine the head of the plaintiff. If it is bruised, he bit his own ear, and I find for the defendant. If, on the other hand, there is no bruise, the other man bit his ear, and that is assault."

From *The Pleasantries of the Incredible Mulla Nasrudin*

Why Don't You?

NASRUDIN WENT TO the shop of a man who stocked all kinds of bits and pieces.

"Have you got nails?" he asked.

"Yes."

"And leather, good leather?"

"Yes."

"And twine?"

"Yes."

"And dye?"

"Yes."

"Then why, for Heaven's sake, don't you make a pair of boots?"

From *The Pleasantries of the Incredible Mulla Nasrudin*

Why We are Here

WALKING ONE EVENING along a deserted road, Mulla Nasrudin saw a troop of horsemen coming toward him.

His imagination started to work; he saw himself captured and sold as a slave, or impressed into the army.

Nasrudin bolted, climbed a wall into a graveyard, and lay down in an open tomb.

Puzzled at his strange behavior, the men – honest travelers – followed him.

They found him stretched out, tense and quivering.

"What are you doing in that grave? We saw you run away. Can we help you?"

"Just because you can ask a question does not mean that there is a straightforward answer to it," said the Mulla, who now realized what had happened. "It all depends upon your viewpoint. If you must know, however: *I* am here because of *you*, and *you* are here because of *me*."

From *The Exploits of the Incomparable
Mulla Nasrudin*

The Use of a Light

"I CAN SEE in the dark," boasted Nasrudin one day in the teahouse.

"If that is so, why do we sometimes see you carrying a light through the streets?"

"Only to prevent other people from colliding with me."

From *The Pleasantries of the Incredible
Mulla Nasrudin*

See What I Mean?

NASRUDIN WAS THROWING handfuls of crumbs around his house.

"What are you doing?" someone asked him.

"Keeping the tigers away."
"But there are no tigers in these parts."
"That's right. Effective, isn't it?"

From *The Exploits of the Incomparable
Mulla Nasrudin*

There is a Different Time scale

NASRUDIN WENT TO a Turkish bath. As he was poorly dressed, the attendants treated him in a casual manner, gave him only a scrap of soap and an old towel.

When he left, Nasrudin gave the two men a gold coin each. He had not complained, and they could not understand it. Could it be, they wondered, that if he had been better treated he would have given an even larger tip?

The following week the Mulla appeared again. This time, of course, he was looked after like a king. After being massaged, perfumed and treated with the utmost deference, he left the bath, handing each attendant the smallest possible copper coin.

"This," said Nasrudin, "is for last time. The gold coins were for this time."

From *The Pleasantries of the Incredible
Mulla Nasrudin*

Eating-Matter and Reading-Matter

NASRUDIN WAS CARRYING home some liver which he had just bought. In the other hand he had a recipe for liver pie which a friend had given him.

Suddenly a buzzard swooped down and carried off the liver.

"You fool!" shouted Nasrudin, "the meat is all very well – but I still have the recipe!"

From *The Exploits of the Incomparable Mulla Nasrudin*

The High Cost of Learning

NASRUDIN DECIDED THAT he could benefit by learning something new.

He went to see a master musician. "How much do you charge to teach lute-playing?"

"Three silver pieces for the first month; after that, one silver piece a month."

"Excellent!" said Nasrudin. "I shall begin with the second month."

From *The Pleasantries of the Incredible Mulla Nasrudin*

The Mulla's Tomb

NASRUDIN'S TOMB WAS fronted by an immense wooden door, barred and padlocked. Nobody could get into it, at least through the door. As his last joke, the Mulla decreed that the tomb should have no walls around it...

The date inscribed on the tombstone was 386. Translating this into letters by substitution, a common device on Sufi tombs, we find the word SHWF. This is a form of the word for "seeing," especially for "making a person see."

Perhaps it is for this reason that for many years the dust from the tomb was considered to be effective in curing eye troubles...

From *The Pleasantries of the Incredible Mulla Nasrudin*

3

Fables

The Mouse and the Elephant

AN ELEPHANT AND a mouse who were in love decided to get married.

On their wedding night, the elephant keeled over and died.

The mouse said: "O Fate! I have bartered one moment of pleasure for a lifetime of digging a grave!"

From *The Commanding Self*

IDRIES SHAH HAD at the tip of his tongue a dazzling array of fables, collected from a wide array of sources in three or four languages.

He himself used fables as a sort of Sufic toolbox, often answering a question in the form of a short tale, sometimes one made up for the occasion.

In so doing, he claimed to be continuing a long-standing tradition – Aesop, for instance, is considered by Sufis to be one of their teachers.

As with much of his other written material, Shah advised readers to familiarize themselves with these fables without trying to tease meanings out of them. *They are, rather, he said, templates designed to pop into one's head when accompanied by a corresponding experience.*

As with much other Sufi material, many of the tales are humoros – Sufis have long claimed that anyone without a sense of humor has a deficiency in their soul. Their entertainment-value is also the outer packaging that allows them to survive.

But, say the Sufis, why would you merely smell and chew a peach, without swallowing and digesting as well?

Editor's note

The Blind Ones and the Matter of the Elephant

BEYOND GHOR THERE was a city. All its inhabitants were blind. A king with his entourage arrived nearby; he brought his army and camped in the desert. He had a mighty elephant, which he used in attack and to increase the people's awe.

The populace became anxious to see the elephant, and some sightless from among this blind community ran like fools to find it.

As they did not even know the form or shape of the elephant, they groped sightlessly, gathering information by touching some part of it.

Each thought that he knew something, because he could feel a part.

When they returned to their fellow-citizens, eager groups clustered around them. Each of these was anxious, misguidedly, to learn the truth from those who were themselves astray.

They asked about the form, the shape of the elephant, and listened to all that they were told.

The man whose hand had reached an ear was asked about the elephant's nature. He said: "It is a large, rough thing, wide and broad, like a rug."

And the one who had felt the trunk said: "I have the real facts about it. It is like a straight and hollow pipe, awful and destructive."

The one who had felt its feet and legs said: "It is mighty and firm, like a pillar."

Each had felt one part out of many. Each had perceived it wrongly. No mind knew all; knowledge is not the companion of the blind. All imagined something, something incorrect.

The created is not informed about divinity. There is no Way in this science by means of the ordinary intellect.

Point of View

SAADI OF SHIRAZ, in his *Bostan*, stated an important truth when he told this miniature tale:

A man met another, who was handsome, intelligent and elegant. He asked him who he was. The other said: "I am the Devil."

"But you cannot be," said the first man, "for the devil is evil and ugly."

"My friend," said Satan, "you have been listening to my detractors."

From *Reflections*

How to Catch Monkeys

ONCE UPON A time there was a monkey who was very fond of cherries. One day he saw a delicious-looking cherry, and came down from his tree to get it. But the fruit turned out to be in a clear glass bottle. After some experimentation, the monkey found that he could get hold of the cherry by putting his hand into the bottle by way of the neck. As soon as he had done so, he closed his hand over the cherry; but then he found that he could not withdraw his fist holding the cherry, because it was larger than the internal dimension of the neck.

Now all this was deliberate, because the cherry in the bottle was a trap laid by a monkey-hunter who knew how monkeys think.

The hunter, hearing the monkey's whimperings, came along and the monkey tried to run away. But, because his hand was, as he thought, stuck in the bottle, he could not move fast enough to escape.

But, as he thought, he still had hold of the cherry. The hunter picked him up. A moment later he tapped the monkey sharply on the elbow, making him suddenly relax his hold on the fruit.

The monkey was free, but he was captured. The hunter had used the cherry and the bottle, but he still had them.

From *Tales of the Dervishes*

The Golden Fly

THERE WAS ONCE a man called Salar, who knew right from wrong, and who knew what should be done and what should not be done, and who knew much of book-learning. He knew so much, in fact, that he had been appointed to be the personal assistant to the Mufti Zafrani, an eminent jurisconsult and judge.

But Salar did not know everything; and even in the things he did know, he did not always act in accordance with his knowledge.

One day, when he had set aside his glass of sweet juice, a tiny, shimmering golden fly settled on the rim and took a sip. Then the same thing happened the next day, and the next, until the fly grew in size and Salar could easily see him. But the fly had grown so slowly that Salar hardly noticed him at all.

Finally, after several weeks, Salar had been deep in study of a knotty legal problem when he looked up and realized that the fly seemed much larger than it should be. He brushed it away. The fly at once rose into the air, circled the grass, and flew away.

But it came back. When Salar's vigilance was relaxed, the fly would swoop down, sit on the rim of the glass, and drink as much as it could. As the days went by, the fly became larger and larger, and as it drank more and more, it also started to look different.

First, Salar flicked it away. Then he found that he had to take a stick to hit it with. Sometimes, too, the fly started to look to him like something with a semi-human form. It was, of course, a Jinn, and not a fly at all.

Finally, Salar shouted at the fly; and, lo, it answered, saying: "I do not take so very much of your drink, and besides, I am beautiful, am I not?"

Salar was first amazed, then afraid, and in the end completely confused.

He started to derive some pleasure from the visits of the fly, even though it was drinking some of his sherbet. He watched as the fly danced, he thought about it a great deal, he did less and less work, and – as the fly became larger, he found himself feeling weaker and weaker.

Salar was often in trouble with the Mufti, and so he pulled himself together and decided to make an end of the fly. Summoning up all his resolution, he hit it a violent blow, and it flew away, saying, "You have wronged me, for I only wanted to be your friend, but I shall go, if that is what you want."

Salar at first felt that he had got rid of the fly for good and all. He said to himself: "I have beaten it, and that proves that I am more powerful than it, be it man or Jinn, fly or not."

Then, when Salar had convinced himself that the whole matter was at an end, the fly appeared again. It had grown to an enormous size, and it descended from the ceiling like a shimmering lake in the form of a man.

Two huge hands reached out and grasped Salar's throat.

When the Mufti came to look for his assistant, he was lying strangled on the floor. The side wall of the house had collapsed with the Jinn's passing, and all that was there to mark his enormousness was a handprint on the whitewash, as large as the side of an elephant.

From *Wisdom of the Idiots*

The Ancient Coffer of Nuri Bey

Nuri Bey was a reflective and respected Albanian, who had married a wife much younger than himself.

One evening when he had returned home earlier than usual, a faithful servant came to him and said:

"Your wife, our mistress, is acting suspiciously.

"She is in her apartments with a huge chest, large enough to hold a man, which belonged to your grandmother.

"It should contain only a few ancient embroideries.

"I believe that there may now be much more in it.

"She will not allow me, your oldest retainer, to look inside."

Nuri went to his wife's room, and found her sitting disconsolately beside the massive wooden box.

"Will you show me what is in the chest?" he asked.

"Because of the suspicion of a servant, or because you do not trust me?"

"Would it not be easier just to open it, without thinking about the undertones?" asked Nuri.

"I do not think it possible."

"Is it locked?"

"Yes."

"Where is the key?"

She held it up, "Dismiss the servant and I will give it to you."

The servant was dismissed. The woman handed over the key and herself withdrew, obviously troubled in mind.

Nuri Bey thought for a long time. Then he called four gardeners from his estate. Together they carried the chest by night unopened to a distant part of the grounds, and buried it.

The matter was never referred to again.

From *Tales of the Dervishes*

The Camel and the Tent

THIS TALE IS *handed down from the Sufi Sheikh, Abdul-Aziz of Mecca, who died in the seventh century. He is said to have been given the "elixir of life" by Muhammad, whose companion he was, and to be still alive, in one sense or another, nourished by this magical potion.*

Other versions say that the "potion" was in fact an exercise called "imprisoning the breath" which – although dangerous for those who do not know how to use it – enables one to put the body into a state of suspended animation.

The method is used by the followers of several Sufi Orders; though Abul-Aziz's affiliation was with the Qalandari (whom some say he founded) and the Chishtis.

A bedouin, making a long desert trek, pitched his small black tent and lay down to sleep. As the night grew colder, his camel woke him up with a nudge. "Master, it is cold. May I put my nose inside the tent to warm it?" The traveler agreed, and settled down to sleep again. Scarcely an hour had passed, however, before the camel began to feel colder. "Master, it is much colder. Can I put my head inside the tent?"

First, his head was admitted to the tent, then, on the same argument, his neck. Finally, without asking, the camel heaved his whole bulk under the cloth. When he had, as he thought, settled himself, the bedouin was lying beside the camel, with no covering at all. The camel had uprooted the tent, which hung, totally inadequately, across his hump.

"Where has the tent gone?" asked the confused camel.

From *Caravan of Dreams*

The Horseman and the Snake

A HORSEMAN FROM his point of vantage saw a poisonous snake slip down the throat of a sleeping man. The horseman realized that if the man were allowed to sleep, the venom would surely kill him.

Accordingly he lashed the sleeper until he was awake. Having no time to lose, he forced this man to a place where there were a number of rotten apples lying upon the ground and made him eat them. Then he made him drink large gulps of water from a stream. All the while, the other man was trying to get away, crying: "What have I done, you enemy of humanity, that you should abuse me in this manner?"

Finally, when he was near to exhaustion, and dusk was falling, the man fell to the ground and vomited out the apples, the water and the snake. When he saw what had come out of him, he realized what had happened, and begged the forgiveness of the horseman.

This is our condition. In reading this, do not take history for allegory, nor allegory for history. Those who are endowed with knowledge have responsibility. Those who are not, have none beyond what they can conjecture.

The man who was saved said: "If you had told me, I would have accepted your treatment with a good grace."

The horseman answered: "If I had told you, you would not have believed. Or you would have been paralyzed by fright. Or run away. Or gone to sleep again, seeking forgetfulness. And there would not have been time."

Spurring his horse, the mysterious rider rode away.

From *Tales of the Dervishes*

In the Street of the Perfume-Sellers

A SCAVENGER, WALKING down the street of the perfume-sellers, fell down as if dead. People tried to revive him with sweet odors, but he only became worse.

Finally a former scavenger came along, and recognized the situation. He held something filthy under the man's nose, who immediately revived, calling out: "This is indeed perfume!"

You must prepare yourself for the transition in which there will be none of the things to which you have accustomed yourself. After death your identity will have to respond to stimuli of which you have a chance to get a foretaste here.

If you remain attached to the few things with which you are familiar, it will only make you miserable, as the perfume did the scavenger in the street of the perfume-makers.

This parable explains itself. Ghazali uses it in the eleventh-century *Alchemy of Happiness* to underline the Sufi teaching that only some of the things of familiar existence have affinities with the "other dimension."

From *Tales of the Dervishes*

The Aim

IT IS RELATED that the object of Alexander the Great's Eastern expedition was to find the Water of Eternal Life.

They tell of the occasion when the great conqueror entered the cave in which the spring of life was gushing.

Just as he stooped to swallow a mouthful of that liquid, he heard a strange sound from the roof of the cavern.

Alexander looked up, to see a crow perched in the gloom.

The crow was saying:

"Stop, for God's sake, stop!"

The king asked him why he should not taste of that miraculous water. "I have suffered much in order to be here today," he said.

The crow answered:

"Great king, look at me! I, too, sought and found the Water of Life. As soon as I saw it, I ran to the spring and drank my fill. Now, a thousand years later, without the sight of even half an eye, with my beak broken, my claws fallen off, not a feather left, all I ask is that which is impossible: I WANT TO DIE, and I CANNOT."

Conscious that the aim must be formulated in accordance with knowledge and not just desire, Alexander the Great stood up and hastened away.

From *Reflections*

Delights of a Visit to Hell

A MAN ONCE thought:

"How I wish I could be master of the option, to be dead or alive, so that I might know what it was like to be dead!"

This idea so dominated his mind that he sought out a dervish and enrolled himself as his pupil. When, after many months, he judged the moment suitable, he said to his teacher:

"Reverend Sir, I have for years desired one thing: to be able to be alive or dead, as I wished. This is because I find it difficult to visualize what it would be like to be in that condition. Would you make it possible for me to achieve it?"

The dervish said:

"It would not help you at all."

"I am sure that all experience is useful," said the man. And he continued to plague the dervish, until he agreed.

"Very well," said the dervish, "adopt these special exercises, and you will be able to enter the domain of death and return at your own desire."

The man performed his exercises until he had perfected them, and when he felt that he was ready, he threw himself into the condition which is generally considered to be death.

He found himself disembodied and waiting at the exit-door of life.

A subtle form in the shape of a man came up to him, and said: "What is your desire?"

"As I am now dead," said the man, "I would like to see Heaven and Hell, so that I may be able to understand the advantages and disadvantages of each."

"Certainly," said the angel, "and which would you like to visit first?"

"Heaven," said the man.

The angel took him to a place where people were walking about surrounded by every luxury and dressed in beautiful garments, eating precious fruits. They were all undoubtedly beings of the greatest purity and honesty, but the visitor felt that there was not enough variety in their life for him.

He said to his guide: "Please may I now see Hell?"

"By all means," answered the angel, and took him to another place.

Here he saw people reveling and romping, laughing and crying, making and breaking friendships, building houses and destroying them, and living a remarkably similar life to the one which we all know on Earth.

But Hell seemed to have distinct advantages. It was more interesting than Heaven, and there were opportunities for personal gain evident to the visitor, which had not yet been observed by the inhabitants, and which far exceeded those open to people on Earth.

He said to his guide: "As I am master of the option of living or dying, I think that I will now settle down in Hell. Can you arrange it for me?"

"Nothing easier," said the angel, "providing that you will change permanently from the status of a visitor to that of a resident."

The man affirmed that he indeed wished to remain in Hell for all time.

Then the angel knocked on a door, and two massive demons of frightful aspect appeared. "Take him away," said the angel, "for he has decided to join you."

The demons seized the man, and crushing him in gigantic talons, began to bear him off toward a furnace.

"Stop!" cried the man, and he appealed to the angel:

"If this is Hell, what was that place which you showed me saying that it was Hell, when it was not?"

"That," said the angel, "is not the Hell for the permanent residents. It is the one which is shown to visitors."

From *Reflections*

The Two Brothers

THERE WERE ONCE two brothers who jointly farmed a field, and always shared its yield.

One day one of them woke up in the night and thought:

"My brother is married and has children. Because of this he has anxieties and expenses which are not mine. So I will go and move some sacks from my share into his storeroom, which is only fair. I shall do this under cover of night, so that he may not, from his generosity, dispute with me about it."

He moved the sacks, and went back to bed.

Soon afterward the other brother woke up and thought to himself:

"It is not fair that I should have half of all the corn in our field. My brother, who is unmarried, lacks my pleasures in having a family, and I shall therefore try to compensate a little by moving some of my corn into his storeroom."

So saying, he did so.

The next morning, each was amazed that he still had the same number of sacks in his storeroom, and afterward neither could understand why, year after year, the number of sacks remained the same even when each of them shifted some by stealth.

From *Caravan of Dreams*

The Bear

A MAN ONCE saved the life of a bear, which became attached to him and grateful for what he had done.

The man, being tired, lay down to sleep, with the bear beside him.

Another man passing by told him to be careful, saying that the friendship of a fool was worse than opposition.

But the first man only thought that the second was jealous of him, and took no notice of these words. He even thought that the other man was trying to deprive him of the security of a faithful companion.

When, however, he lay down to sleep and dozed off, the bear, seeing flies approach, tried to strike them with a stone, and in so doing, killed the man who had saved him.

From *The Hundred Tales of Wisdom*

The King's Hawk and the Owls

THERE WAS ONCE a noble hawk, which belonged to a king. Flying one day, the hawk became tired and settled on a ruined building to rest. The ruin was, however, the home of a colony of owls, who resented his presence.

The owls attacked this noble creature, who told them that he meant no harm, and that he was only passing through their domain.

But the owls cried:

"Do not listen to him! How could he have anything to do with a king? He is lying, in order to deprive us of our home by guile!"

From *The Hundred Tales of Wisdom*

The Turkish Maiden

IT IS RELATED that Hiri was once asked to look after a Turkish maiden by a Persian merchant who was going on a journey. Hiri became infatuated with this girl and decided that he must seek out his teacher, Abu-Hafs the Blacksmith. Abu-Hafs told him to travel to Raiyy, there to obtain the advice of the great Sufi, Yusuf al-Razi.

When he arrived in Raiyy and asked people there where the sage's dwelling was, they told him to avoid such a heretic and freethinker, and so he went back to Nishapur. Reporting to Abu-Hafs, he was told to ignore the people's opinions of al-Razi, and seek him out again.

In spite of the almost unanimous urgings of the people of Raiyy, he made his way to where al-Razi sat. There he found the ancient, accompanied by a beautiful youth who was giving him a wine-cup.

Scandalized, Hiri demanded an explanation of how such a reverend contemplative could behave in such a manner.

But al-Razi explained that the youth was his son and the wine-cup contained only water, and had been abandoned by someone else. This was the reality of his state, which everyone imagined to be a life of dissolution.

But Hiri now wanted to know why the Sufi behaved in such a manner that people interpreted it as heretical.

Al-Razi said: "I do these things so that people may not burden me with Turkish maidens."

From *Learning How to Learn*

The Limbless Fox

IN THE *BOSTAN* of Saadi, there is the tale of the man who once saw a limbless fox and wondered how it managed to be so well-fed. Deciding to watch it, he found that it had positioned itself where a lion brought its kill. After eating, the lion would go away, and the fox would eat its leavings. So the man decided to allow fate to serve him in the same way. Sitting down in a street and waiting, all that happened was that he became more and more weak and hungry, for nobody and nothing took any interest in him.

Eventually a voice spoke and said: "Why should you behave like a lamed fox? Why should you not be a lion, so that others might benefit from your leavings?"

This story is itself an interesting test. One sometimes finds that it encourages people with a desire to teach to set themselves up as teachers, and enables others, who are more humble, to rearrange their ideas, so that they can learn first, no matter what they readily imagine about being able to teach and benefit others before getting their own focus right.

Everything man needs is in the world. How does he use it? Think of the Eastern proverb: "God provides the food, men provide the cooks."

From *Learning How to Learn*

Nature

A CERTAIN SCORPION, wanting to cross a river, was scuttling about on the bank, looking for a means of getting to the other side. Seeing his problem, a tortoise offered to carry him across.

The scorpion thanked the tortoise, and climbed on his back. As soon as the tortoise had finished his swim and unloaded the scorpion, the scorpion gave him a really powerful sting.

"How can you do such a thing to me?" cried the tortoise. "My nature is to be helpful, and I have used it to help you. Now I get stung!"

"My friend," said the scorpion, "your nature is to be helpful, and you were. Mine is to sting, and I have. Why, therefore, do you seek to transform your nature into virtue and mine into villainy?"

From *The Commanding Self*

The Pay and the Work

A HORSE ONCE met a frog. The horse said: "Take this message to a snake for me, and you can have all the flies which surround me."

The frog answered: "I like the pay, but I cannot say that I can complete the work."

From *The Way of the Sufi*

The Beloved
ONE WENT TO the door of the Beloved and knocked. A voice asked: "Who is there?"

He answered: "It is I."

The voice said: "There is no room here for me and thee." The door was shut.

After a year of solitude and deprivation this man returned to the door of the Beloved. He knocked.

A voice from within asked: "Who is there?"

The man said: "It is Thou."

The door was opened for him.

From *The Way of the Sufi*

The Tattooed Lion
ONCE THERE WAS a man who wanted to have a lion tattooed on his back.

He went to a tattoo artist and told him what he wanted.

But as soon as he felt the first few pricks, this man began to moan and groan: "You are killing me. What part of the lion are you marking?"

"I am just doing the tail now," said the artist.

"Then let us leave out the tail," howled the other.

So the artist started again. And again the client could not stand the pricks. "What part of the lion is it this time?" he cried, "For I cannot stand the pain."

"This time," said the tattooist, "it is the lion's ear."

"Let us have a lion without an ear," gasped his patient.

So the tattooist tried again. No sooner had the needle entered his skin than the victim squirmed again: "Which part of the lion is it this time?"

"This is the lion's stomach," wearily answered the artist.

"I don't want a lion with a stomach," said the other man.

Exasperated and distraught, the tattoo artist stood awhile. Then he threw his needle down and cried: "A lion without a head, with no tail, without a stomach? Who could draw such a thing? Even God did not!"

– Rumi
From *The Way of the Sufi*

The Mad King's Idol

THERE WAS ONCE a violent, ignorant and idolatrous king. One day he swore that if his personal idol accorded him a certain advantage in life, he would capture the first three people who passed by his castle, and force them to dedicate themselves to idol-worship.

Sure enough, the king's wish was fulfilled, and he immediately sent soldiers on to the highway to bring in the first three people whom they could find.

These three were, as it happened, a scholar, a Sayed (descendant of Muhammad the Prophet) and a prostitute.

Having them thrown down before his idol, the unbalanced king told them of his vow, and ordered them all to bow down in front of the image.

The scholar said:

"This situation undoubtedly comes within the doctrine of 'force majeure.' There are numerous precedents allowing anyone to appear to conform with custom if compelled, without real legal or moral culpability being in any way involved."

So he made a deep obeisance to the idol.

The Sayed, when it was his turn, said:

"As a specially protected person, having in my veins the blood of the Holy Prophet, my actions themselves purify anything which is done, and therefore there is no bar to my acting as this man demands."

And he bowed down before the idol.

The prostitute said:

"Alas, I have neither intellectual training nor special prerogatives, and so I am afraid that, whatever you do to me, I cannot worship this idol, even in appearance."

The mad king's malady was immediately banished by this remark. As if by magic he saw the deceit of the two worshipers of the image. He at once had the scholar and the Sayed decapitated, and set the prostitute free.

From *Wisdom of the Idiots*

Generosity

THE GREAT TEACHER Sahl of Tustar relates that God told Moses that real self-sacrifice for the sake of others is the basis of the greatest capacity for perception of the divine: the extreme self-sacrifice which was given to Muhammad and his followers.

Imam Ghazzali relates, in the Third Book of his *Revival of Religious Sciences*, how a man who was famed as generous learned what generosity really was:

The Black Slave and the Dog

ABDULLAH IBN JA'FAR owned an orchard and went one day to visit it. He passed through a vineyard, where he saw a black slave sitting, with some bread in front of him and a dog nearby.

As Abdullah watched, the slave took a piece of the bread and threw it to the dog, which ate it. Then he gave it another piece, and another.

Abdullah asked:

"How much bread are you given every day?"

The slave answered:

"That quantity which you have just seen eaten by the dog."

"Why," Abdullah asked, "do you give it to a dog, instead of attending first to your own need?"

"There are no dogs hereabouts," said the black man, "and this one has come from a great distance and is hungry. Because of this I did not desire to eat my bread."

"But how will you manage for food today?" asked the generous Abdullah.

"I shall endure the hunger!" said the black man.

Abdullah thought, "I am the one who has the reputation for generosity, and yet this slave is more philanthropic."

He bought the vineyard and gave it to the slave, also buying his freedom and releasing him.

From *Seeker After Truth*

Imam Baqir

IMAM MUHAMMED BAQIR is said to have related this illustrative fable:

"Finding I could speak the language of ants, I approached one and inquired, 'What is God like? Does he resemble the ant?'

"He answered, 'God! No, indeed – we have only a single sting but God, He has *two*!'"

From *Thinkers of the East*

The Design

A SUFI OF the Order of the Naqshbandis was asked:

"Your Order's name means, literally, 'The Designers.' What do you design, and what use is it?"

He said:

"We do a great deal of designing, and it is most useful. Here is a parable of one such form.

"Unjustly imprisoned, a tinsmith was allowed to receive a rug woven by his wife. He prostrated himself upon the rug day after day to say his prayers, and after some time he said to his jailers:

"'I am poor and without hope, and you are wretchedly paid. But I am a tinsmith. Bring me tin and tools and I shall make small artifacts which you can sell in the market, and we will both benefit.'

"The guards agreed to this, and presently the tinsmith and they were both making a profit, from which they bought food and comforts for themselves.

"Then, one day, when the guards went to the cell, the door was open, and he was gone.

"Many years later, when this man's innocence had been established, the man who had imprisoned him asked him how he had escaped, what magic he had used. He said:

"'It is a matter of design, and design within design. My wife is a weaver. She found the man who had made the locks of the cell door, and got the design from him. This she wove into the carpet, at the spot where my head touched in prayer five times a day. I am a metal-worker, and this design looked to me like the inside of a lock. I designed the plan of the artifacts to obtain the materials to make the key – and I escaped.'

"That," said the Naqshbandi Sufi, "is one of the ways in which man may make his escape from the tyranny of his captivity."

From *Thinkers of the East*

Vine Thought

ONCE THERE WAS a vine which realized that people came every year and took its grapes.

It observed that nobody ever showed any gratitude.

One day a wise man came along and sat down nearby.

"This," thought the vine, "is my opportunity to have the mystery solved."

It said:

"Wise man, as you may have observed, I am a vine. Whenever my fruit is ripe, people come and take the grapes away. None shows any sign of gratitude. Can you explain this conduct to me?"

The wise man thought for a time. Then he said:

"The reason, in all probability, is that all those people are under the impression that you cannot help producing grapes."

From *Thinkers of the East*

Pitcher Love

HAVE YOU HEARD about the tragedy of the little pitcher?

He heard a thirsty man calling for water from his sickbed in a corner of a room.

The pitcher was so full of compassion for the man that by a supreme effort of will he actually managed to roll to within an inch of the sufferer's hand.

When the man opened his eyes and saw a pitcher beside him, he was full of wonderment and relief. He managed to pick up the jug and held it to his lips. Then he realized that it was empty.

With almost the last remains of his strength, the invalid threw the pitcher against a wall, where it smashed into useless pieces of clay.

From *Thinkers of the East*

Scientific Advance

A MOTH WAS fluttering outside a window, having seen a light in a room beyond it.

A spider said to it:

"When will you moths learn that flames are hot and destructive? You are annoyed at the presence of the glass. But it is the glass which saves you from destruction."

The moth laughed. "Granddad," it said, "there are two answers to you. First, you are an insect-eater and your advice to insects, however true, can never be accepted by them.

"Second, we moths of the present generation know more than you think. I happen to know that the delicious light in that room is cold light. There have been scientific developments since your time, you know.

"I shall enter through this chink and snuggle up to the light."

So saying, the moth struggled into the room.

There was nobody there to stop him. No spider had made a web which might be a hazard.

The moth fluttered around the cold light in an ecstatic dance.

But scientific advances had indeed taken place.

The light was protected by a film of DDT.

From *The Magic Monastery*

Tiger

A DEER, IN flight before a hunting tiger, paused long enough to call out to a mouse whom he saw sitting quietly beside his hole:

"The Lord of the Jungle approaches, the Tiger is in a killing mood, flee for your life!"

The mouse nibbled a piece of grass and said:

"If you had news of a marauding *cat*, that would be something which might interest *me!*"

From *The Magic Monastery*

The Young Sufi

AN OLD MAN visited a young Sufi, sitting among a group of friends. The other visitors were scornful when he said:

"All my life I have hoarded money, and I have spent no time in reflecting upon man and his inner reality."

The Sufi said:

"Each man does, with what he has, what he can."

"Yes," said the ancient miser, "and, since I do not know any other way to honor you, whom I now recognize, I give you this. It is a gem which I bought at the goldsmith's. I paid for it every penny which I have saved these past sixty years. It is the best thing he had in his shop. *I* am too old to change, but each man speaks in his own language."

The young Sufi stood up and started to rend his clothes. He said to the assembled company:

"You are thinking that this man is materialistic, and lacks knowledge. But he is parting with the most precious thing he has, because of *his* nobility of spirit, not mine! From this day on, this man is your teacher, and I shall go into seclusion."

From *The Magic Monastery*

4

Poetry

HERE WE ARE, all of us: in a dream-caravan.
A caravan, but a dream – a dream, but a caravan.
And we know which are the dreams.
Therein lies the hope.

Bahaudin, El Shah
From *Caravan of Dreams*

PERSIAN LITERATURE IS *extraordinary because almost all the major poetic classics have been written by Sufis. School children read Saadi's* Gulistan, The Rose Garden, *a collection of poems and stories, which Sufis contend contains further depths of meaning beyond the overt morals. The grand master of Persian literature – Jalaludin Rumi – whose* Masnavi i Ma'anavi *is often called by the dazzling sobriquet "the Quran in Persian" is a major Sufi figure.*

In his discussions on Sufi poetry, Idries Shah warns against too literal an approach. Much of Omar Khayyam's poetry, for instance, he says is intended to make the reader think clearly through reducing life to absurdity and should not be taken in the superficial sense that Khayyam was a "pessimist."

Sufis use poetry in many ways and one of them is to afford a glimpse at the "other" – the realm beyond our own world, which they claim is merely an illusion. The following selection gives a flavor.

Editor's note

Thou Art There

THE FLITTING OF a light in desert dusk – thou art there.

The weary duty of the Magian's forced ritual – thou art there.

The movement in response to another movement – thou art there.

Not in the book of the scribe, but in the smile at it – thou art there.

The Grace of the graceful, not the mind of the graceful – thou art there.

The question and answer: between them, not in them – thou art there.

Between the lumbering paces of the elephant – thou art there.

In harmony, in love, in being itself, in truth, in absoluteness – thou art there.

The pearl rejected by the oyster-fancier – thou art there.

The inexplicability of non-rhythm, of seeming change – thou art there.

The interchange, pulsation, sweetness, silence, rest:

In congruity and in incongruity – thou art there.

In the glow, the spark, the leaping flame, the warmth and the burning; in the relaxation and the agitation: Thou art there!

– Haykali
From *The Way of the Sufi*

Follow the Path

Do not speak of your heartache – for He is speaking.
    Do not seek Him – for He is seeking.
    He feels even the touch of an ant's foot;
    If a stone moves under water – He knows it.
    If there is a worm in a rock
    He knows its body, smaller than an atom.
    The sound of its praise, and its hidden perception,
    He knows by His divine knowledge.
    He has given the worm its sustenance;
    He has shown you the Path of the Teaching.

– Hakim Sanai
From *The Way of the Sufi*

Man Asleep

While mankind remains mere baggage in the world
    It will be swept along, as in a boat, asleep.
    What can they see in sleep?

What real merit or punishment can there be?

– Hakim Sanai
From *The Way of the Sufi*

Impressions
TIME BROUGHT A thousand impressions.
Not one of them had I seen in the mirror of the imagination.

– *Anwar-i-Suhaili*
From *The Dermis Probe*

Seeds Like These
IN CELL AND cloister, in monastery and synagogue:
Some fear hell and others dream of Paradise.
But no man who really knows the secrets of his God
Has planted seeds like this within his heart.

– Omar Khayyam
From *The Way of the Sufi*

Since the lot of man in this bitter land
Is nothing but suffering and sadness
Happy is he who quickly leaves
And he who never came at all.

– Omar Khayyam
(*orally quoted by Idries Shah*)

I Am

THEY SAY THAT I am a wine-worshiper – I am
  They say that I am an adept – I am;
  Do not look so much at my exterior
  For in my interior I am, I am.

– Omar Khayyam
From *Caravan of Dreams*

The Enemy of Faith

I DRINK WINE, and opponents from right and left say:
  "Drink no drink for it is against faith."
  Since I know that wine is against faith,
  By God let me drink – the blood of the enemy is
lawful to me.

– Omar Khayyam
From *The Way of the Sufi*

The Atom

CRACK THE HEART of any atom: from its midst you
will see a sun shining.

  If you give all you have to Love, I'll be called
a Pagan if you suffer a molecule of loss. The soul
passed through the fire of Love will let you see the
soul transmuted.

  If you escape the narrowness of dimensions, and
will see the "time of what is placeless," you will hear

what has never been heard, and you will see what has never been seen;

Until they deliver you to a place where you will see "a world" and "worlds" as one.

You shall love Unity with heart and soul; until, with the true eye, you will see Unity...

– Sayed Ahmad Hatif
From *The Way of the Sufi*

On Entering, Living in – and Leaving – the World

MAN, YOU ENTER the world reluctantly, crying, as a forlorn babe;

Man, you leave this life, deprived again, crying again, with regret.

Therefore live this life in such a way that none of it is really wasted.

You have to become accustomed to it after not having been accustomed to it.

When you have become accustomed to it, you will have to become used to being without it. Meditate upon this contention.

Die, therefore, "before you die," in the words of the Purified One.

Complete the circle before it is completed for you.

Until you do, unless you have – then expect bitterness at the end as there was in the beginning; in the middle as there will be at the end.

You did not see the pattern as you entered; and when you entered – you saw another pattern.

When you saw this apparent pattern, you were prevented from seeing the threads of the coming pattern.

Until you see both, you will be without contentment – *Whom* do you blame? And *why* do you blame?

– Hashim the Sidqi, on Rumi
From *The Way of the Sufi*

If to be a lover is to be a poet, I am a poet;

If to be a poet is to be a magician, I am a magician;

If to be a magician is to be thought evil, I can be thought evil;

If to be thought evil is to be disliked by worldlings, I am content to be such.

Disliked by wordlings is to be a lover of the true reality, more often than not.

I affirm that I am a Lover!

– Anwari
From *The Sufis*

The Pearl

A RAINDROP, DRIPPING from a cloud,
  Was ashamed when it saw the sea.
  "Who am I where there is a sea?" it said.

When it saw itself with the eye of humility,
A shell nurtured it in its embrace.

– Sheikh Saadi of Shiraz
From *The Way of the Sufi*

I am the Life of my Beloved

WHAT CAN I do, Muslims? I do not know myself.

I am no Christian, no Jew, no Magian, no Musulman.

Not of the East, not of the West. Not of the land, not of the sea.

Not of the Mine of Nature, not of the circling heavens,

Not of earth, not of water, not of air, not of fire;

Not of the throne, not of the ground, of existence, of being;

Not of India, China, Bulgaria, Saqseen;

Not of the kingdom of the Iraqs, or of Khorasan;

Not of this world or the next: of heaven or hell;

Not of Adam, Eve, the gardens of Paradise or Eden;

My place placeless, my trace traceless.

Neither body nor soul; all is the life of my Beloved...

– Jalaludin Rumi
From *The Way of the Sufi*

Two insects eat from the same place
But from one a sting and the other honey.
Both kinds of deer have the same grazing and
water –
From one dung and the other musk.
Each of two canes feeds from one thing:
This one is empty, the other is full of sugar.

– Jalaluddin Rumi
From *Neglected Aspects of Sufi Study*

One went to the door of the Beloved and knocked.
A voice asked: "Who is there?"
He answered, "It is I."
The voice said, "There is no room for Me and
Thee."
The door was shut.
After a year of solitude and deprivation he
returned and knocked.
A voice from within asked, "Who is there?"
The man said: "It is Thee."
The door was opened for him.

– Jalaluddin Rumi
From *The Sufis*

He Was in No Other Place

CROSS AND CHRISTIANS, end to end, I examined.
He was not on the Cross.
I went to the Hindu temple, to the ancient pagoda.

In none of them was there any sign.
To the uplands of Herat I went, and to Kandahar.
He was not on the heights or in the lowlands.
Resolutely, I went to the summit of the [fabulous] mountain of Kaf.
There only was the dwelling of the [legendary] Anqa bird.
I went to the Kaaba of Mecca.
He was not there.
I asked about him from Avicenna the philosopher.
He was beyond the range of Avicenna...
I looked into my own heart.
In that, his place, I saw him. He was in no other place.

– Jalaludin Rumi
From *The Way of the Sufi*

Thou and I

JOYFUL THE MOMENT when we sat in the bower, Thou and I;
In two forms and with two faces – with one soul, Thou and I. The color of the garden and the song of the birds give the elixir of immortality
The instant we come into the orchard, Thou and I.
The stars of Heaven come out to look upon us –
We shall show the Moon herself to them, Thou and I.
Thou and I, with no "Thou" or "I," shall become one through our tasting;

Happy, safe from idle talking, Thou and I.
The gay parrots of heaven will envy us –
When we shall laugh in such a way, Thou and I.
This is stranger, that Thou and I, in this corner
here...
Are both in one breath in Iraq, and in Khorasan –
Thou and I.

– Jalaludin Rumi
From *The Way of the Sufi*

What Shall I Be

I HAVE AGAIN and again grown like grass;
   I have experienced seven hundred and seventy
molds.
   I died from minerality and became vegetable;
   And from vegetativeness I died and became animal.
   I died from animality and became man.
   Then why fear disappearance through death?
   Next time I shall die
   Bringing forth wings and feathers like angels:
   After that soaring higher than angels –
   What you cannot imagine. I shall be that.

– Jalaludin Rumi
From *The Way of the Sufi*

The Man of God

   The Man of God is drunken without wine:
   The Man of God is sated without meat.

The Man of God is rapturous, amazed:
The Man of God has neither food nor sleep.

The Man of God is a king beneath a humble cloak:
The Man of God is a treasure in a ruin.

The Man of God is not of wind and earth:
The Man of God is not of fire and water.

The Man of God is a sea without a shore:
The Man of God rains pearls without a cloud.

The Man of God has a hundred moons and skies:
The Man of God has a hundred sunshines.

The Man of God is wise through Truth:
The Man of God is not a scholar from a book.

The Man of God is beyond faith and disbelief
alike:
For the Man of God what "sin" or "merit" is
there?

The Man of God rode away from Non-being:
The Man of God has come, sublimely riding.

The Man of God Is, Concealed, O Shamsudin!
Search for, and find – The Man of God.

> – Jalaludin Rumi
> From *The Way of the Sufi*

5

Proverbs and Aphorisms

Go higher – Behold the Human Spirit.

– Jalaludin Rumi
From *The Way of the Sufi*

IDRIES SHAH ARGUED *that wisdom has been
encapsulated by our ancestors in many forms and still
lurks, underrated, in our culture. Proverbs – which
are easily remembered and transmitted from person
to person, from age to age – are one of those forms.*

*As well as being an enthusiastic collector of
proverbs and aphorisms from both East and West,
he coined a number of his own sayings, many of
them published in his compilation* Reflections.

*Sufism, he said, is recognizable from the wishy-
washy emotionalism often mistaken for spirituality
because of its "bite."*

*Even the shortest saying can force the mind to think
in a different way, to provide insights. This moment
of intuitive recognition is known as an impact and it
is said to be a form of minor enlightenment in itself.*

Editor's note

Virtue

IF YOUR OWN vice happens to be the search for virtue, recognize that it is so.

From *Reflections*

Tasting

HE WHO TASTES, knows.
But he who only thinks he tastes – will not leave anyone alone.

From *Reflections*

Belief and Knowledge

KNOWLEDGE IS SOMETHING which you can use.
Belief is something which uses you.

From *Reflections*

Shade

HAVE YOU NOTICED how many people who walk in the shade curse the Sun?

From *Reflections*

Optimist and Pessimist
SOMETIMES A PESSIMIST is only an optimist with extra information.

From *Reflections*

What did you Learn?
PLEASE, NOT AGAIN what you studied, how long you spent at it, how many books you wrote, what people thought of you – but: *what did you learn?*

From *Reflections*

Against God
HOW CURIOUS THAT people should be more interested in the charge that I am "against God," than in the question whether God is against *me*.

From *Reflections*

Voice in the Night
A VOICE WHISPERED to me last night:
    "There is no such thing as a voice whispering in the night!"

– Haidar Ansari
From *Wisdom of the Idiots*

Three Things

THREE THINGS CANNOT be retrieved:
    The arrow once sped from the bow
    The word spoken in haste
    The missed opportunity.

(Ali the Lion, Caliph of Islam,
son-in-law of Muhammad the Prophet)
From *Caravan of Dreams*

Dwelling Place

MAKE MANKIND YOUR dwelling-place.

(Hariri)
From *The Dermis Probe*

The Bird and the Water

A BIRD WHICH has not heard of fresh water
    Dips his beak in salt water year after year.

– Anwar-i-Suhaili
From *The Dermis Probe*

Rights

THE RIGHTS THAT others have over you – remember them.

The rights that you have over others – forget them.

> – Sayedna Ali
> From *Thinkers of the East*

Worship

O LORD!

If I worship you from fear of hell, cast me into hell.

If I worship you from desire for paradise, deny me paradise.

> – Rabia el-Adawia
> From *The Way of the Sufi*

Good and Evil

"BEING" IS ABSOLUTELY good.

It if contains any evil, it is not Being.

> – Shabistari
> From *The Way of the Sufi*

The World

THE WORLD HAS no being except as an appearance;
From end to end its state is a sport and a play.

> – Shabistari, *Gulshan-i-Raz*
> From *The Way of the Sufi*

Remedy

YOUR MEDICINE IS in you, and you do not observe it.
Your ailment is from yourself, and you do not register it.

> – Hazrat Ali
> From *The Way of the Sufi*

Riches

AIM FOR KNOWLEDGE. If you become poor it will be wealth for you: if you become rich it will adorn you.

> – El-Zubeir son of Abu-Bakr
> From *The Way of the Sufi*

Destructive

THREE THINGS IN this life are destructive:
Anger, Greed, Self-esteem.

> – The Prophet
> From *The Way of the Sufi*

Detach from fixed ideas and preconceptions. And face what is to be your lot.

– Sheikh Abu-Said Ibn Abi Khair
From *The Sufis*

The donkey which brought you to this door must be dismounted before you can get through it.

From *Neglected Aspects of Sufi Study*

Do not regret the past and do not worry about the future.

– Dhun-Nun
From *The Way of the Sufi*

Proverbs

THE DOG MAY bark, but the caravan moves on.

From *Caravan of Dreams*

If you regret kissing me – take back your kiss.

From *Caravan of Dreams*

He who has made a door and a lock, has also made a key.

From *Caravan of Dreams*

Learn to behave from those who cannot.

From *Caravan of Dreams*

May your shadow never grow less.

From *Caravan of Dreams*

The answer to a fool is silence.

From *Caravan of Dreams*

Every round thing is not a cake.

From *Neglected Aspects of Sufi study*

Whoever has not first dug a well, should not steal a minaret.

From *The Dermis Probe*

When tomorrow comes, think tomorrow's thoughts.

From *The Dermis Probe*

If you are penniless you will have a thousand dreams.
Get even a single piece of money, however, and you will have only twenty options.

From *The Dermis Probe*

One lie will keep out forty truths.

From *The Dermis Probe*

The repentance of the wolf is – death.

From *The Dermis Probe*

A solved problem is as useful to a man's mind as a broken sword on a battlefield.

From *The Dermis Probe*

It's a good life, if you don't weaken.

From *Darkest England*

6

Teaching-Stories

SOMEONE SAID TO Bahaudin Naqshband:
"You relate stories, but you do not tell us how to understand them."

He said:

"How would you like it if the man from whom you bought fruit consumed it before your eyes, leaving you only the skin?"

From *Thinkers of the East*

TEACHING-STORIES ARE TOLD in public and form part of the outer activity of dervishes. They are intended to lay a basis of knowledge about Sufism and its characteristic methods of thought. They are seldom employed for didactic purposes.

The "inner dimensions" of teaching stories, however, are held to make them capable of revealing, according to the stage of development of the student, more and more planes of significance.

It is the theory that "one may work on different layers of the same material" which is unfamiliar to many people, who tend to prefer being told that a story has one message or one use only.

From The Way of the Sufi

The Magic Horse

THIS TALE IS *of great importance because it belongs to an instructional corpus of mystical materials with inner content but – beyond entertainment value – without immediate external significance.*

The teaching-story was brought to perfection as a communication instrument many thousands of years ago. The fact that it has not developed greatly since then has caused people obsessed by some theories of our current civilizations to regard it as the product of a less enlightened time. They feel that it must surely be little more than a literary curiosity, something fit for children, the projection, perhaps, of infantile desires, a means of enacting a wish fulfillment.

Hardly anything could be further from the truth of such pseudo-philosophical, certainly unscientific, imaginings. Many teaching-stories are entertaining to children and to naïve peasants. Many of them in the forms in which they are viewed by conditioned theorists have been so processed by unregenerate amateurs that their effective content is distorted. Some apply only to certain communities, depending upon special circumstances for their correct unfolding: circumstances whose absence effectively prevents the action of which they are capable.

So little is known to the academics, the scholars and the intellectuals of this world about these materials, that there is no word in modern languages which has been set aside to describe them.

But the teaching-story exists, nevertheless. It is a part of the most priceless heritage of mankind.

Real teaching-stories are not to be confused with parables; which are adequate enough in their intention, but still on a lower level of material, generally confined to the inculcation of moralistic principles, not the assistance of interior movement of the human mind. What we often take on the lower level of parable, however, can sometimes be seen by real specialists as teaching-stories; especially when experienced under the correct conditions.

Unlike the parable, the meaning of the teaching-story cannot be unraveled by ordinary intellectual methods alone. Its action is direct and certain, upon the innermost part of the human being, an action incapable of manifestation by means of the emotional or intellectual apparatus.

The closest that we can come to describing its effect is to say that it connects with a part of the individual which cannot be reached by any other convention, and that it establishes in him or in her a means of communication with a non-verbalized truth beyond the customary limitations of our familiar dimensions.

Some teaching-stories cannot now be reclaimed because of the literary and traditionalistic, even ideological, processing to which they have been subjected. The worst of such processes is the historicizing one, where a community comes to believe that one of their former teaching-stories represents literal historical truth.

This tale is given here in a form which is innocent of this and other kinds of maltreatment.

ONCE UPON A time – not so very long ago – there was a realm in which the people were exceedingly prosperous. All kinds of discoveries had been made by them, in the growing of plants, in harvesting and preserving fruits, and in making objects for sale to other countries, and in many other practical arts.

Their ruler was unusually enlightened, and he encouraged new discoveries and activities, because he knew of their advantages for his people.

He had a son named Hoshyar, who was expert in using strange contrivances, and another – called Tambal – a dreamer, who seemed interested only in things which were of little value in the eyes of the citizens.

From time to time the king, who was named King Mumkin, circulated announcements to this effect:

"Let all those who have notable devices and useful artifacts present them to the palace for examination, so that they may be appropriately rewarded."

Now there were two men of that country – an ironsmith and a woodworker – who were great rivals in most things, and each delighted in making strange contraptions. When they heard this announcement one day, they agreed to compete for an award, so that their relative merits could be decided once and for all, by their sovereign, and publicly recognized.

Accordingly, the smith worked day and night on a mighty engine, employing a multitude of talented specialists, and surrounding his workshop with high walls so that his devices and methods should not become known.

At the same time the woodworker took his simple tools and went into a forest where, after long and solitary reflection, he prepared his own masterpiece.

News of the rivalry spread, and people thought that the smith must easily win, for his cunning works had been seen before, and while the woodworker's products were generally admired, they were only of occasional and undramatic use.

When both were ready, the king received them in open court.

The smith produced an immense metallic fish which could, he said, swim in and under the water. It could carry large quantities of freight over the land. It could burrow into the earth; and it could even fly slowly through the air. At first the court found it hard to believe that there could be such a wonder made by man; but when the smith and his assistants demonstrated it, the king was overjoyed and declared the smith among the most honored in the land, with a special rank and the title of "Benefactor of the Community."

Prince Hoshyar was placed in charge of the making of the wondrous fishes, and the services of this new device became available to all mankind.

Everyone blessed the smith and Hoshyar, as well as the benign and sagacious monarch whom they loved so much.

In the excitement, the self-effacing carpenter had been all but forgotten. Then, one day, someone said: "But what about the contest? Where is the entry of the woodworker? We all know him to be an ingenious man. Perhaps he has produced something useful."

"How could anything possibly be as useful as the wondrous fishes?" asked Hoshyar. And many of the courtiers and the people agreed with him.

But one day the king was bored. He had become accustomed to the novelty of the fishes and the reports of the wonders which they so regularly performed. He said: "Call the woodcarver, for I would now like to see what he has made."

The simple woodcarver came into the throne-room, carrying a parcel, wrapped in coarse cloth. As the whole court craned forward to see what he had, he took off the covering to reveal – a wooden horse. It was well enough carved, and it had some intricate patterning chiseled into it, as well as being decorated with colored paints but it was only... "A mere plaything!" snapped the king.

"But, Father," said Prince Tambal, "let us ask the man what it is for..."

"Very well," said the king, "what is it for?"

"Your majesty," stammered the woodcarver, "it is a magic horse. It does not look impressive, but it has, as it were, its own inner senses. Unlike the fish, which has to be directed, this horse can interpret the desires of the rider, and carry him wherever he needs to go."

"Such a stupidity is fit only for Tambal," murmured the chief minister at the king's elbow; "it cannot have any real advantage when measured against the wondrous fish."

The woodcarver was preparing sadly to depart when Tambal said: "Father, let me have the wooden horse."

"All right," said the king, "give it to him. Take the woodcarver away and tie him on a tree somewhere, so that he will realize that our time is valuable. Let him contemplate the prosperity which the wondrous fish has brought us, and perhaps after some time we shall let him go free, to practice whatever he may have learned of real industriousness, through true reflection."

The woodcarver was taken away, and Prince Tambal left the court carrying the magic horse.

Tambal took the horse to his quarters, where he discovered that it had several knobs, cunningly concealed in the carved designs.

When these were turned in a certain manner, the horse – together with anyone mounted on it – rose into the air and sped to whatever place was in the mind of the person who moved the knobs.

In this way, day after day, Tambal flew to places which he had never visited before. By this process he came to know a great many things. He took the horse everywhere with him.

One day he met Hoshyar, who said to him: "Carrying a wooden horse is a fit occupation for such as you. As for me, I am working for the good of all, toward my heart's desire!"

Tambal thought: "I wish I knew what was the good of all. And I wish I could know what my heart's desire is."

When he was next in his room, he sat upon the horse and thought: "I would like to find my heart's desire." At the same time he moved some of the knobs on the horse's neck.

Swifter than light the horse rose into the air and carried the prince a thousand days' ordinary journey away, to a far kingdom, ruled by a magician-king.

The king, whose name was Kahana, had a beautiful daughter called Precious Pearl, Durri-Karima. In order to protect her, he had imprisoned her in a circling palace, which wheeled in the sky, higher than any mortal could reach. As he was approaching the magic land, Tambal saw the glittering palace in the heavens, and alighted there.

The princess and the young horseman met and fell in love.

"My father will never allow us to marry," she said, "for he has ordained that I become the wife of the son of another magician-king who lives across the cold desert to the east of our homeland. He has vowed that when I am old enough, I shall cement the unity of the two kingdoms by this marriage. His will has never been successfully opposed."

"I will go and try to reason with him," answered Tambal, as he mounted the magic horse again.

But when he descended into the magic land, there were so many new and exciting things to see that he did not hurry to the palace. When at length he approached it, the drum at the gate, indicating the absence of the king, was already beating.

"He has gone to visit his daughter in the Whirling Palace," said a passer-by when Tambal asked him when the king might be back; "and he usually spends several hours at a time with her."

Tambal went to a quiet place where he willed the horse to carry him to the king's own apartment. "I will approach him at his own home," he thought to himself, "for if I go to the Whirling Palace without his permission, he may be angry."

He hid behind some curtains in the palace when he got there, and lay down to sleep.

Meanwhile, unable to keep her secret, the Princess Precious Pearl had confessed to her father that she had been visited by a man on a flying horse, and that he wanted to marry her. Kahana was furious.

He placed sentries around the Whirling Palace, and returned to his own apartment to think things over. As soon as he entered his bedchamber, one of the tongueless magic servants guarding it pointed to the wooden horse lying in a corner. "Aha!" exclaimed the magician-king. "Now I have him. Let us look at this horse and see what manner of thing it may be."

As he and his servants were examining the horse, the prince managed to slip away and conceal himself in another part of the palace.

After twisting the knobs, tapping the horse and generally trying to understand how it worked, the king was baffled. "Take that thing away. It has no virtue now, even if it ever had any," he said. "It is just a trifle, fit for children."

The horse was put into a store-cupboard.

Now King Kahana thought that he should make arrangements for his daughter's wedding without delay, in case the fugitive might have other powers or devices with which to try to win her. So he called her to his own palace and sent a message to the other magician-king, asking that the prince who was to marry her be sent to claim his bride.

Meanwhile, Prince Tambal, escaping from the palace by night when some guards were asleep, decided that he must try to return to his own country. His quest for his heart's desire now seemed almost hopeless. "If it takes me the rest of my life," he said to himself, "I shall come back here, bringing troops to take this kingdom by force. I can only do that by convincing my father that I must have his help to attain my heart's desire."

So saying, he set off. Never was a man worse equipped for such a journey. An alien, traveling on foot, without any kind of provisions, facing pitiless heat and freezing nights interspersed with sandstorms, he soon became hopelessly lost in the desert.

Now, in his delirium, Tambal started to blame himself, his father, the magician-king, the woodcarver, even the princess and the magic horse itself. Sometimes he thought he saw water ahead of him, sometimes fair cities, sometimes he felt elated, sometimes incomparably sad. Sometimes he even thought that he had companions in his difficulties, but when he shook himself he saw that he was quite alone.

He seemed to have been traveling for an eternity. Suddenly, when he had given up and started again several times, he saw something directly in front of him. It looked like a mirage: a garden, full of delicious fruits, sparkling and almost, as it were, beckoning him toward them.

Tambal did not at first take much notice of this, but soon, as he walked, he saw that he was indeed passing through such a garden. He gathered some of the fruits and tasted them cautiously. They were delicious. They took away his fear as well as his hunger and thirst. When he was full, he lay down in the shade of a huge and welcoming tree and fell asleep.

When he woke up he felt well enough, but something seemed to be wrong. Running to a nearby pool, he looked at his reflection in the water. Staring up at him was a horrible apparition. It had a long beard, curved horns, ears a foot long. He looked down at his hands. They were covered with fur.

Was it a nightmare? He tried to wake himself, but all the pinching and pummeling had no effect. Now, almost bereft of his senses, beside himself with fear and horror, thrown into transports of screaming, racked with sobs, he threw himself on the ground. "Whether I live or die," he thought, "these accursed fruits have finally ruined me. Even with the greatest army of all time, conquest will not help me. Nobody would marry me now, much less the Princess Precious Pearl. And I cannot imagine the beast who would not be terrified at the sight of me – let alone my heart's desire!" And he lost consciousness.

When he woke again, it was dark and a light was approaching through the groves of silent trees. Fear and hope struggled in him. As it came closer, he saw that the light was from a lamp enclosed in a brilliant star-like shape, and it was carried by a bearded man, who walked in the pool of brightness which it cast around.

The man saw him. "My son," he said, "you have been affected by the influences of this place. If I had not come past, you would have remained just another beast of this enchanted grove, for there are many more like you. But I can help you."

Tambal wondered whether this man was a fiend in disguise, perhaps the very owner of the evil trees. But, as his sense came back, he realized that he had nothing to lose.

"Help me, father," he said to the sage.

"If you really want your heart's desire," said the other man, "you have only to fix this desire firmly in your mind, not thinking of the fruit. You then have to take up some of the dried fruits, not the fresh, delicious ones, lying at the foot of all these trees, and eat them. Then follow your destiny."

So saying, he walked away.

While the sage's light disappeared into the darkness, Tambal saw that the moon was rising, and in its rays he could see that there were indeed piles of dried fruits under every tree.

He gathered some and ate them as quickly as he could.

Slowly, as he watched, the fur disappeared from his hands and arms. The horns first shrank, then vanished. The beard fell away. He was himself again. By now it was first light, and in the dawn he heard the tinkling of camel bells. A procession was coming through the enchanted forest.

It was undoubtedly the cavalcade of some important personage, on a long journey. As Tambal stood there, two outriders detached themselves from the glittering escort and galloped up to him.

"In the name of the Prince, our lord, we demand some of your fruit. His celestial Highness is thirsty and has indicated a desire for some of these strange apricots," said an officer.

Still Tambal did not move, such was his numbed condition after his recent experiences. Now the Prince himself came down from his palanquin and said:

"I am Jadugarzada, son of the magician-king of the East. Here is a bag of gold, oaf. I am having some of your fruit, because I am desirous of it. I am in a hurry, hastening to claim my bride, Princess Precious Pearl, daughter of Kahana, magician-king of the West."

At these words Tambal's heart turned over. But, realizing that this must be his destiny which the sage had told him to follow, he offered the Prince as much of the fruit as he could eat.

When he had eaten, the Prince began to fall asleep. As he did so, horns, fur and huge ears started to grow out of him. The soldiers shook him, and the Prince began to behave in a strange way. He claimed that *he* was normal, and that *they* were deformed.

The councilors who accompanied the party restrained the prince and held a hurried debate. Tambal claimed that all would have been well if the prince had not fallen asleep. Eventually it was decided to put Tambal in the palanquin to play the part of the prince. The horned Jadugarzada was tied to a horse with a veil thrown over his face, disguised as a servingwoman.

"He may recover his wits eventually," said the councilors, "and in any case he is still our Prince. Tambal shall marry the girl. Then, as soon as possible, we shall carry them all back to our own country for our king to unravel the problem."

Tambal, biding his time and following his destiny, agreed to his own part in the masquerade.

When the party arrived at the capital of the West, the king himself came out to meet them. Tambal was taken to the princess as her bridegroom, and she was so astonished that she nearly fainted. But Tambal managed to whisper to her rapidly what had happened, and they were duly married, amid great jubilations.

In the meantime, the horned prince had half recovered his wits, but not his human form, and his escort still kept him under cover. As soon as the feasting was over, the chief of the horned prince's party (who had been keeping Tambal and the princess under a very close watch) presented himself to the court. He said: "O just and glorious monarch, fountain of wisdom, the time has now come, according to the pronouncements of our astrologers and soothsayers, to conduct the bridal pair back to our own land, so that they may be established in their new home under the most felicitous circumstances and influences."

The princess turned to Tambal in alarm, for she knew that Jadugarzada would claim her as soon as they were on the open road, and make an end of Tambal into the bargain.

Tambal whispered to her, "Fear nothing. We must act as best we can, following our destiny. Agree to go, making only the condition that you will not travel without the wooden horse."

At first, the magician-king was annoyed at this foible of his daughter's. He realized that she wanted the horse because it was connected with her first suitor. But the chief minister of the horned prince said: "Majesty, I cannot see that this is anything worse than a whim for a toy, such as any young girl might have. I hope that you will allow her to have her plaything, so that we may make haste homeward."

So the magician-king agreed, and soon the cavalcade was resplendently on its way. After the king's escort had withdrawn, and before the time of the first night-halt, the hideous Jadugarzada threw off his veil and cried out to Tambal:

"Miserable author of my misfortunes! I now intend to bind you hand and foot, to take you captive back to my own land. If, when we arrive there, you do not tell me how to remove this enchantment, I will have you flayed alive, inch by inch. Now, give me the Princess Precious Pearl."

Tambal ran to the princess and, in front of the astonished party, rose into the sky on the wooden horse with Precious Pearl mounted behind him.

Within a matter of minutes the couple alighted at the palace of King Mumkin. They related everything that had happened to them, and the king was almost overcome with delight at their safe return. He at once gave orders for the hapless woodcarver to be released, recompensed and applauded by the entire populace.

When the king was gathered to his fathers, Princess Precious Pearl and Prince Tambal succeeded him. Prince Hoshyar was quite pleased, too, because he was still entranced by the wondrous fish.

"I am glad for your own sakes, if you are happy," he used to say to them, "but, for my own part, nothing is more rewarding than concerning myself with the wondrous fish."

And this history is the origin of a strange saying current among the people of that land, yet whose beginnings have now been forgotten. The saying is: "Those who want fish can achieve much through fish, and those who do not know their heart's desire may first have to hear the story of the wooden horse."

From *Caravan of Dreams*

Mushkil Gusha

WHEN A NUMBER *of people come together, and if these people are harmonized in a certain way, excluding some who make for disharmony – we have what we call an event. This is by no means what is generally understood in contemporary cultures as an event. For them, something which takes place and which impresses people by means of subjective impacts – is called an event. This is what some term a "lesser event," because it takes place in the lesser world, that of human relationships easily produced, synthesized, commemorated.*

The real event, of which the lesser event is a useful similitude (no more and no less), is that which belongs to the higher realm.

We cannot accurately render a higher event in stilted terrestrial representation and retain accuracy. Something of surpassing importance in a higher realm could not entirely be put in terms of literature, science, or drama, without loss of essential value. But certain tales, providing that they contain elements from the high-event area which may seem absurd, unlikely, improbable or even defective, can (together with the presence of certain people) communicate to the necessary area of the mind the higher event.

Why should it be valuable to do so? Because familiarity with the "high event," however produced, enables the individual's mind to operate in the high realm.

The tale of Mushkil Gusha is an example. The very "lack of completeness" in the events, the "untidiness" of the theme, the absence of certain factors which we have come to expect in a story: these in this case are indications of the greater parallel.

The Story of Mushkil Gusha

ONCE UPON A time, not a thousand miles from here, there lived a poor old woodcutter, who was a widower, and his little daughter. He used to go every day into the mountains to cut firewood which he brought home and tied into bundles. Then he used to have breakfast and walk into the nearest town, where he would sell his wood and rest for a time before returning home.

One day, when he got home very late, the girl said to him, "Father, I sometimes wish that we could have some nicer food, and more and different kinds of things to eat."

"Very well, my child," said the old man; "tomorrow I shall get up much earlier than I usually do. I shall go further into the mountains where there is more wood, and I shall bring back a much larger quantity than usual. I will get home earlier and I will be able to bundle the wood sooner, and I will go into town and sell it so that we can have more money, and I shall bring you back all kinds of nice things to eat."

The next morning, the woodcutter rose before dawn and went into the mountains. He worked very hard cutting wood and trimming it and made it into a huge bundle which he carried on his back to his little house.

When he got home, it was still very early. He put his load of wood down, and knocked on the door, saying, "Daughter, Daughter, open the door, for I am hungry and thirsty and I need a meal before I go to market."

But the door was locked. The woodcutter was so tired that he lay down and was soon fast asleep beside his bundle. The little girl, having forgotten all about their conversation the night before, was fast asleep in bed. When he woke up a few hours later, the sun was high. The woodcutter knocked on the door again and said, "Daughter, Daughter, come quickly; I must have a little food and go to market to sell the wood; for it is already much later than my usual time of starting."

But, having forgotten all about the conversation the night before, the little girl had meanwhile got up, tidied the house, and gone out for a walk. She had locked the door, assuming in her forgetfulness that her father was still in the town.

So the woodcutter thought to himself, "It is now rather late to go into the town. I will therefore return to the mountains and cut another bundle of wood, which I will bring home, and tomorrow I will take a double load to market."

All that day the old man toiled in the mountains cutting wood and shaping the branches. When he got home with the wood on his shoulders, it was evening.

He put down his burden behind the house, knocked on the door and said, "Daughter, Daughter, open the door for I am tired and I have eaten nothing all day. I have a double bundle of wood which I hope to take to market tomorrow. Tonight I must sleep well so that I will be strong."

But there was no answer, for the little girl when she came home had felt very sleepy, and had made a meal for herself, and gone to bed. She had been rather worried at first that her father was not at home, but she decided that he must have arranged to stay in the town overnight.

Once again the woodcutter, finding that he could not get into the house, tired, hungry and thirsty, lay down by his bundles of wood and fell asleep. He could not keep awake, although he was fearful for what might have happened to the little girl.

Now the woodcutter, because he was so cold and hungry and tired, woke very, very early the next morning, before it was even light.

He sat up, and looked around, but he could not see anything. And then a strange thing happened. The woodcutter thought he heard a voice saying: "Hurry, hurry! Leave your wood and come this way. If you need enough, and you *want* little enough, you shall have delicious food."

The woodcutter stood up and walked in the direction of the voice. And he walked and he walked; but he found nothing.

By now he was colder and hungrier and more tired than ever, and he was lost. He had been full of hope, but that did not seem to have helped him. Now he felt sad, and he wanted to cry. But he realized that crying would not help him either, so he lay down and fell asleep.

Quite soon he woke up again. It was too cold, and he was too hungry, to sleep. So he decided to tell himself, as if in a story, everything that had happened to him since his little daughter had first said that she wanted a different kind of food.

As soon as he had finished his story, he thought he heard another voice, saying, somewhere above him, out of the dawn, "Old man, what are you doing sitting there?"

"I am telling myself my own story," said the woodcutter.

"And what is that?" said the voice.

The old man repeated his tale. "Very well," said the voice. And then the voice told the old woodcutter to close his eyes and to mount, as it were, a step. "But I do not see any step," said the old man. "Never mind, but do as I say," said the voice.

The old man did as he was told. As soon as he had closed his eyes, he found that he was standing up and as he raised his right foot, he felt that there was something like a step under it. He started to ascend what seemed to be a staircase. Suddenly the whole flight of steps started to move, very fast, and the voice said, "Do not open your eyes until I tell you to do so."

In a very short time, the voice told the old man to open his eyes. When he did, he found that he was in a place which looked rather like a desert, with the sun beating down on him. He was surrounded by masses and masses of pebbles; pebbles of all colors: red, green, blue and white. But he seemed to be alone. He looked all around him, and could not see anyone, but the voice started to speak again.

"Take up as many of these stones as you can," said the voice. "Then close your eyes, and walk down the steps once more."

The woodcutter did as he was told, and he found himself, when he opened his eyes again at the voice's bidding, standing before the door of his own house.

He knocked at the door and his little daughter answered it. She asked him where he had been, and he told her, although she could hardly understand what he was saying, it all sounded so confusing.

They went into the house, and the little girl and her father shared the last food which they had, which was a handful of dried dates. When they had finished, the old man thought that he heard a voice speaking to him again, a voice just like the other one which had told him to climb the stairs.

The voice said, "Although you may not know it yet, you have been saved by Mushkil Gusha. Remember that Mushkil Gusha is always here. Make sure that every Thursday night you eat some dates and give some to any needy person, and tell the story of Mushkil Gusha. Or give a gift in the name of Mushkil Gusha to someone who will help the needy. Make sure that the story of Mushkil Gusha is never, never forgotten. If you do this, and if this is done by those to whom you tell the story, the people who are in real need will always find their way."

The woodcutter put all the stones which he had brought back from the desert in a corner of his little house. They looked very much like ordinary stones, and he did not know what to do with them.

The next day, he took his two enormous bundles of wood to the market, and sold them easily for a high price. When he got home he took his daughter all sorts of delicious kinds of food, which she had never tasted before. And when they had eaten it, the old woodcutter said, "Now I am going to tell you the whole story of Mushkil Gusha. Mushkil Gusha is 'the remover of all difficulties.' Our difficulties have been removed through Mushkil Gusha and we must always remember it."

For nearly a week after that the old man carried on as usual. He went into the mountains, brought back wood, had a meal, took the wood to market and sold it. He always found a buyer without difficulty.

Now the next Thursday came, and, as is the way of men, the woodcutter forgot to repeat the tale of Mushkil Gusha.

Late that evening, in the house of the woodcutter's neighbors, the fire had gone out. The neighbors had nothing with which to relight the fire, and they went to the house of the woodcutter. They said, "Neighbor, neighbor, please give us a light from those wonderful lamps of yours which we see shining through the window."

"What lamps?" said the woodcutter.

"Come outside," said the neighbor, "and see what we mean."

So the woodcutter went outside and then he saw, sure enough, all kinds of brilliant lights shining through a window from the inside.

He went back to the house, and saw that the light was streaming from the pile of pebbles which he had put in the corner. But the rays of light were cold, and it was not possible to use them to light a fire. So he went out to the neighbors and said, "Neighbors, I am sorry, I have no fire." And he banged the door in their faces. They were annoyed and confused, and went back to their house, muttering. They leave our story here.

The woodcutter and his daughter quickly covered up the brilliant lights with every piece of cloth they could find, for fear that anyone would see what a treasure they had. The next morning, when they uncovered the stones, they discovered that they were precious, luminous gems.

They took the jewels, one by one, to neighboring towns, where they sold them for a huge price. Now the woodcutter decided to build for himself and for his daughter a wonderful palace. They chose a site just opposite the castle of the king of their country. In a very short time, a marvelous building had come into being.

Now that particular king had a beautiful daughter, and one day when she got up in the morning, she saw a sort of fairytale castle just opposite her father's and she was amazed. She asked her servants, "Who has built this castle? What right have these people to do such a thing so near to our home?"

The servants went away and made inquiries and they came back and told the story, as far as they could collect it, to the princess.

The princess called for the little daughter of the woodcutter, for she was very angry with her, but when the two girls met and talked, they soon became fast friends. They started to meet every day and went to swim and play in the stream which had been made for the princess by her father. A few days after they first met, the princess took off a beautiful and valuable necklace and hung it up on a tree just beside the stream. She forgot to take it down when they came out of the water, and when she got home, she thought it must have been lost.

The princess thought a little and then decided that the daughter of the woodcutter had stolen her necklace. So she told her father, and he had the woodcutter arrested; he confiscated the castle and declared forfeit everything that the woodcutter had. The old man was thrown into prison, and the daughter was put into an orphanage.

As was the custom in that country, after a period of time, the woodcutter was taken from the dungeon and put in the public square, chained to a post, with a sign around his neck. On the sign was written "This is what happens to those who steal from Kings."

At first people gathered around him, and jeered and threw things at him. He was most unhappy.

But quite soon, as is the way of men, everyone became used to the sight of the old man sitting there by his post, and took very little notice of him. Sometimes people threw him scraps of food, sometimes they did not.

One day he overheard somebody saying that it was Thursday afternoon. Suddenly, the thought came into his mind that it would soon be the evening of Mushkil Gusha, the remover of all difficulties, and that he had forgotten to commemorate him for so many days. No sooner had this thought come into his head, than a charitable man, passing by, threw him a tiny coin. The woodcutter called out: "Generous friend, you have given me money, which is of no use to me. If, however, your kindness could extend to buying one or two dates and coming and sitting and eating them with me, I would be eternally grateful to you."

The other man went and bought a few dates. And they sat and ate them together. When they had finished, the woodcutter told the other man the story of Mushkil Gusha. "I think you must be mad," said the generous man. But he was a kindly person who himself had many difficulties. When he arrived home after this incident, he found that all his problems had disappeared. And that made him start to think a great deal about Mushkil Gusha. But he leaves our story here.

The very next morning, the princess went back to her bathing-place. As she was about to go into the water, she saw what looked like her necklace down at the bottom of the stream. As she was going to dive in to try to get it back, she happened to sneeze. Her head went up, and she saw that what she had thought was the necklace was only its reflection in the water. It was hanging on the bough of the tree where she had left it such a long time before. Taking the necklace down, the princess ran excitedly to her father and told him what had happened. The King gave orders for the woodcutter to be released and given a public apology. The little girl was brought back from the orphanage, and everyone lived happily ever after.

These are some of the incidents in the story of Mushkil Gusha. It is a very long tale and it is never ended. It has many forms. Some of them are not even called the story of Mushkil Gusha at all, so people do not recognize it. But it is because of Mushkil Gusha that his story, in whatever form, is remembered by somebody, somewhere in the world, day and night, wherever there are people. As his story had always been recited, so it will always continue to be told.

Will *you* repeat the story of Mushkil Gusha on Thursday nights, and help the work of Mushkil Gusha?

From *Caravan of Dreams*

The Food of Paradise

ONLY A VERY *few Sufi tales, according to Halqavi (who is the author of "The Food of Paradise"), can be read by anyone at any time and still affect the "Inner consciousness" constructively.*

"Almost all others," he says, "depend upon where, when and how they are studied. Thus most people will find in them only what they expect to find: entertainment, puzzlement, allegory."

Yunus, son of Adam, was a Syrian, and died in 1670. He had remarkable healing powers and was an inventor.

YUNUS, THE SON of Adam, decided one day not only to cast his life in the balance of fate, but to seek the means and reason of the provision of goods for man.

"I am," he said to himself, "a man. As such I get a portion of the world's goods, every day. This portion comes to me by my own efforts, coupled with the efforts of others. By simplifying this process, I shall find the means whereby sustenance comes to mankind, and learn something about how and why. I shall therefore adopt the religious way, which exhorts man to rely upon almighty God for his sustenance.

Rather than live in the world of confusion, where food and other things come apparently through society, I shall throw myself upon the direct support of the Power which rules over all. The beggar depends upon intermediaries: charitable men and women, who are subject to secondary impulses. They give goods or money because they have been trained to do so. I shall accept no such indirect contributions."

So saying, he walked into the countryside, throwing himself upon the support of invisible forces with the same resolution with which he had accepted the support of visible ones, when he had been a teacher in a school.

He fell asleep, certain that Allah would take complete care of his interests, just as the birds and beasts were catered for in their own realm.

At dawn the bird chorus awakened him, and the son of Adam lay still at first, waiting for his sustenance to appear. In spite of his reliance upon the invisible force and his confidence that he would be able to understand it when it started its operations in the field into which he had thrown himself, he soon realized that speculative thinking alone would not greatly help him in this unusual field.

He was lying at the riverside, and spent the whole day observing nature, peering at the fish in the waters, saying his prayers. From time to time rich and powerful men passed by, accompanied by glitteringly accoutred outriders on the finest horses, harness-bells jingling imperiously to signal their absolute right of way, who merely shouted a salutation at the sight of his venerable turban. Parties of pilgrims paused and chewed dry bread and dried cheese, serving only to sharpen his appetite for the humblest food.

"It is but a test, and all will soon be well," thought Yunus, as he said his fifth prayer of the day and wrapped himself in contemplation after the manner taught him by a dervish of great perceptive attainments.

Another night passed.

As Yunus sat staring at the sun's broken lights reflected in the mighty Tigris, five hours after dawn on the second day, something bobbing in the reeds caught his eye. This was a packet, enclosed in leaves and bound around with palm-fiber. Yunus, the son of Adam, waded into the river and possessed himself of the unfamiliar cargo.

It weighed about three-quarters of a pound. As he unwound the fiber, a delicious smell assailed his nostrils. He was the owner of a quantity of the *halwa* of Baghdad. This halwa, composed of almond paste, rosewater, honey and nuts and other precious elements, was both prized for its taste and esteemed as a health-giving food. Harem beauties nibbled it because of its flavor; warriors carried it on campaigns because of its sustaining power. It was used to treat a hundred ailments.

"My belief is vindicated!" exclaimed Yunus. "And now for the test. If a similar quantity of halwa, or the equivalent, comes to me upon the waters daily or at other intervals, I shall know the means ordained by providence for my sustenance, and will then only have to use my intelligence to seek the source."

For the next three days, at exactly the same hour, a packet of halwa floated into Yunus' hands.

This, he decided, was a discovery of the first magnitude. Simplify your circumstances and Nature continued to operate in a roughly similar way. This alone was a discovery which he almost felt impelled to share with the world. For has it not been said: "When you know, you must teach?" But then he realized that he did not know; he only experienced. The obvious next step was to follow the halwa's course upstream until he arrived at the source. He would then understand not only its origin, but the means whereby it was set aside for his explicit use.

For many days Yunus followed the course of the stream. Each day with the same regularity but at a time correspondingly earlier, the halwa appeared, and he ate it.

Eventually Yunus saw that the river, instead of narrowing as one might expect at the upper part, had widened considerably. In the middle of a broad expanse of water there was a fertile island. On this island stood a mighty and beautiful castle. It was from here, he determined, that the food of paradise originated.

As he was considering his next step, Yunus saw that a tall and unkempt dervish, with the matted hair of a hermit and a cloak of multicolored patches, stood before him.

"Peace, Baba, Father," he said.

"Ishq, Hoo!" shouted the hermit. "And what is your business here?"

"I am following a sacred quest," explained the son of Adam, "and must in my search reach yonder castle. Have you perhaps an idea how this might be accomplished?"

"As you seem to know nothing about the castle, in spite of having a special interest in it," answered the hermit, "I will tell you about it.

"Firstly, the daughter of a king lives there, imprisoned and in exile, attended by numerous beautiful servitors, it is true, but constrained nevertheless. She is unable to escape because the man who captured her and placed her there, because she would not marry him, has erected formidable and inexplicable barriers, invisible to the ordinary eye. You would have to overcome them to enter the castle and find your goal."

"How can you help me?"

"I am on the point of starting on a special journey of dedication. Here, however, is a word and exercise, the *Wazifa*, which will, if you are worthy, help to summon the invisible powers of the benevolent Jinns, the creatures of fire, who alone can combat the magical forces which hold the castle locked. Upon you peace." And he wandered away, after repeating strange sounds and moving with a dexterity and agility truly wonderful in a man of his venerable appearance.

Yunus sat for days practicing his Wazifa and watching for the appearance of the halwa. Then, one evening as he looked at the setting sun shining upon a turret of the castle, he saw a strange sight. There, shimmering with unearthly beauty, stood a maiden, who must of course be the princess. She stood for an instant looking into the sun, and then dropped into the waves which lapped far beneath her on to the castle rocks a packet of halwa. Here, then, was the immediate source of his bounty.

"The source of the Food of Paradise!" cried Yunus. Now he was almost on the very threshold of truth. Sooner or later the Commander of the Jinns, whom through his dervish Wazifa he was calling, must come, and would enable him to reach the castle, the princess, and the truth.

No sooner had these thoughts passed through his mind than he found himself carried away through the skies to what seemed to be an ethereal realm, filled with houses of breathtaking beauty. He entered one, and there stood a creature like a man, who was not a man: young in appearance, yet wise and in some way ageless. "I," said this vision, "am the Commander of the Jinns, and I have had thee carried here in answer to thy pleading and the use of those Great Names which were supplied to thee by the Great Dervish. What can I do for thee?"

"O mighty Commander of all the Jinns," trembled Yunus, "I am a Seeker of the Truth, and the answer to it is only to be found by me in the enchanted castle near which I was standing when you called me here. Give me, I pray, the power to enter this castle and talk to the imprisoned princess."

"So shall it be!" exclaimed the Commander. "But be warned, first of all, that a man gets an answer to his questions in accordance with his fitness to understand and his own preparation."

"Truth is truth," said Yunus, "and I will have it, no matter what it may be. Grant me this boon."

Soon he was speeding back in a decorporealized form (by the magic of the Jinn), accompanied by a small band of Jinni servitors, charged by their Commander to use their special skills to aid this human being in his quest. In his hand Yunus grasped a special mirror-stone which the Jinn chief had instructed him to turn toward the castle to be able to see the hidden defenses.

Through this stone the son of Adam soon found that the castle was protected from assault by a row of giants, invisible but terrible, who smote anyone who approached. Those of the Jinns who were proficient at this task cleared them away. Next he found that there was something like an invisible web or net which hung all around the castle. This, too, was destroyed by the Jinns who flew and who had the special cunning needed to break the net. Finally there was an invisible mass as of stone, which, without making an impression, filled the space between the castle and the river bank. This was overthrown by the skills of the Jinns, who made their salutations and flew fast as light, to their abode.

Yunus looked and saw that a bridge, by its own power, had emerged from the riverbed, and he was able to walk dry shod into the very castle. A soldier at the gate took him immediately to the princess, who was more beautiful even than she had appeared at first.

"We are grateful to you for your services in destroying the defenses which made this prison secure," said the lady. "And I may now return to my father and want only to reward thee for thy sufferings. Speak, name it, and it shall be given to thee."

"Incomparable pearl," said Yunus, "there is only one thing which I seek, and that is truth. As it is the duty of all who have truth to give it to those who can benefit from it, I adjure you, Highness, to give me the truth which is my need."

"Speak, and such truth as it is possible to give will freely be thine."

"Very well, your Highness. How, and by what order, is the Food of Paradise, the wonderful halwa which you throw down every day for me, ordained to be deposited thus?"

"Yunus, son of Adam," exclaimed the princess, "the halwa, as you call it, I throw down each day because it is in fact the residue of the cosmetic materials with which I rub myself every day after my bath of asses' milk."

"I have at last learned," said Yunus, "that the understanding of a man is conditional upon his capacity to understand. For you, the remains of your daily toilet. For me, the Food of Paradise."

From *Tales of the Dervishes*

Paradise of Song

AHANGAR WAS A mighty swordsmith who lived in one of Afghanistan's remote eastern valleys. In time of peace he made steel plows, shod horses and, above all, he sang.

The songs of Ahangar, who is known by different names in various parts of Central Asia, were eagerly listened to by the people of the valleys. They came from the forests of giant walnut trees, from the snow-capped Hindu-Kush, from Qataghan and Badakhshan, from Khanabad and Kunar, from Herat and Paghman, to hear his songs.

Above all, the people came to hear the song of all songs, which was Ahangar's Song of the Valley of Paradise.

This song had a haunting quality, and a strange lilt, and most of all, it had a story which was so strange that people felt they knew the remote Valley of Paradise of which the smith sang. Often they asked him to sing it when he was not in the mood to do so, and he would refuse. Sometimes people asked him whether the Valley was truly real, and Ahangar could only say:

"The Valley of the Song is as real as real can be."

"But how do you know?" the people would ask. "Have you ever been there?"

"Not in any ordinary way," said Ahangar.

To Ahangar, and to nearly all the people who heard him, the Valley of the Song was, however, real, real as real can be.

Aisha, a local maiden whom he loved, doubted whether there was such a place. So, too, did Hasan, a braggart and fearsome swordsman who swore to marry Aisha, and who lost no opportunity to laugh at the smith.

One day, when the villagers were sitting around silently after Ahangar had been telling his tale to them, Hasan spoke:

"If you believe that this valley is so real, and that it is, as you say, in those mountains of Sangan yonder, where the blue haze rises, why do you not try to find it?"

"It would not be right, I know that," said Ahangar.

"You know what it is convenient to know, and do not know what you do not want to know!" shouted Hasan. "Now, my friend, I propose a test. You love Aisha, but she does not trust you. She has no faith in this absurd Valley of yours. You could never marry her, because when there is no confidence between man and wife, they are not happy and all manner of evils result."

"Do you expect me to go to the valley, then?" asked Ahangar.

"Yes," said Hasan and all the audience together.

"If I go and return safely, will Aisha consent to marry me?" asked Ahangar.

"Yes," murmured Aisha.

So Ahangar, collecting some dried mulberries and a scrap of bread, set off for the distant mountains.

He climbed and climbed, until he came to a wall which encircled the entire range. When he had ascended its sheer sides, there was another wall, even more precipitous than the first. After that there was a third, then a fourth, and finally a fifth wall.

Descending on the other side, Ahangar found that he was in a valley, strikingly similar to his own.

People came out to welcome him, and as he saw them, Ahangar realized that something very strange was happening.

Months later, Ahangar the Smith, walking like an old man, limped into his native village, and made for his humble hut. As word of his return spread throughout the countryside, people gathered in front of his home to hear what his adventures had been.

Hasan the swordsman spoke for them all, and called Ahangar to his window.

There was a gasp as everyone saw how old he had become.

"Well, Master Ahangar, and did you reach the Valley of Paradise?"

"I did."

"And what was it like?"

Ahangar, fumbling for his words, looked at the assembled people with a weariness and hopelessness that he had never felt before. He said:

"I climbed and I climbed, and I climbed. When it seemed as though there could be no human habitation in such a desolate place, and after many trials and disappointments, I came upon a valley. This valley was exactly like the one in which we live. And then I saw the people. Those people are not only like us people: they are *the same people*. For every Hasan, every Aisha, every Ahangar, every anybody whom we have here, there is another one, exactly the same in that valley.

"These are likenesses and reflections to us, when we see such things. But it is we who are the likeness and reflection of them – we who are here, we are their twins..."

Everyone thought that Ahangar had gone mad through his privations, and Aisha married Hasan the swordsman. Ahangar rapidly grew old and died. And all the people, everyone who had heard this story from the lips of Ahangar, first lost heart in their lives, then grew old and died, for they felt that something was going to happen over which they had no control and from which they had no hope, and so they lost interest in life itself.

It is only once in a thousand years that this secret is seen by man. When he sees it, he is changed. When he tells its bare facts to others, they wither and die out.

People think that such an event is a catastrophe, and so they must not know about it, for they cannot understand (such is the nature of their ordinary life) that they have more selves than one, more hopes than one, more chances than one – up there, in the Paradise of the Song of Ahangar the mighty smith.

From *Wisdom of the Idiots*

The Pulse of the Princess

ALTHOUGH THIS TALE – or at least part of it – has been called "one of the first records of dervish psychological diagnosis and psychotherapy," and attributed to the Caliph Jafar Sadiq (died 765), teacher of Jabir and descendant of the Prophet, it appears in Rumi, and also in oral recital.

It must, however, have been well known in the Europe of the Middle Ages, because the skeleton of it appears in the chief monkish storybook, with a devout Christian moral: "baptism is emblemed by the wife." (Gesta Romanorum, *trans. C. Swan, 1829, Tale 40, p. 145 of Vol. I.)*

SULTAN SANJAR HAD returned from the shrine of the Master Bahaudin in Bokhara, and ever since that he had been sad. Some people connected the two as cause and effect, but others held that the sorrow of the king was due to the mysterious illness of his daughter.

Princess Banu was wilting. Day by day her strange ailment seemed to get a stronger grip upon her. All the physicians who had been called in to advise were baffled.

Then, one day, a stranger arrived at the capital city of their country. He wore a green robe, walked bent, and called himself Shadrach the Physician. He offered to cure the princess. The king allowed him to see her, but threatened him that if he did not heal his daughter, he would be beheaded.

Surrounded by an interested audience, the physician approached the couch where the princess, wan and weary, lay. Instead of making any examination, instead of trying any remedy such as was expected of him, the green-robed man began to tell the princess tales.

They were stories of far distant lands, of wars and heroes, of peace and of glory. And as he did so, his fingers stayed on her pulse.

At length his diagnosis was finished. The princess withdrew, and Shadrach addressed the king. "Your Majesty, I have determined by the reactions of her pulse that she is in love. And that she is in love with someone who lives in Bokhara. That that person lives in the street of the jewelers. And that of all the men who live in the street of the jewelers in Bokhara it is none other than Abul-Fazl, a young and handsome man whom I have described to her, and at the mention of whose name she fainted. I happen to know everyone in Bokhara – as well as in many other places; and by this art I have arrived at the cause of her disease."

Now the king wondered at the skill of this physician. He also was relieved that the cause of her illness had been discovered. And he was furiously angry because the lady was in love with such an ignoble wretch – for such Abul-Fazl was known to be.

The jeweler, however, was sent for. As soon as he arrived, the princess began to recover. Within a few days she was well again, the jeweler was lording it over almost everyone, and the Physician Shadrach, as a reward, had been made Grand Vizier.

The king and the doctor realized that this insufferable youth was not for the princess. They also knew that they could not send him away, or otherwise dispose of him, because that would certainly cause the princess's malaise to return.

Shadrach provided the answer. He caused to be administered to Abul-Fazl a medicine which prematurely aged him, making him become older each day as if he had aged by twenty years. In no time at all the princess was beginning to be repulsed by his bent back and his grey locks.

At the same time Shadrach administered to himself another medicine. And by its effect, at the same pace at which the jeweler was ageing, Shadrach became younger and younger.

Before very long the princess fell in love with the young physician. When Abul-Fazl was driven from the court, Princess Banu hardly noticed.

She and the physician and the Sultan lived happily ever after. Thus do things sometimes develop in a manner contrary to their first probability – according to what influences are brought to bear.

From *Caravan of Dreams*

The Man Whose Time was Wrong

ABDUL QADIR OF *Gilan is widely venerated as a saint and numerous hagiographies dealing with his life are current in the East. Hiyat-i-Hazrat ("Life of the Presence"), which is one such book, begins like this:*

"His appearance was formidable. One day, only one disciple dared to ask a question. This was: 'Can you not give us power to improve the earth and the lot of the people of the earth?' His brow darkened, and he said: 'I will do better: I will give this power

to your descendants, because as yet there is no hope of such improvement being made on a large enough scale. The devices do not yet exist. You shall be rewarded; and they shall have the reward of their efforts and of your aspiration.'"

A similar sense of chronology is displayed in "The Man whose Time was Wrong."

ONCE UPON A time, there was a rich merchant who lived in Baghdad. He had a substantial house, large and small properties and dhows which sailed to the Indies with rich cargoes. He had gained these things partly through inheritance, partly through his own efforts, exercised at the right time and place, partly through the benevolent advice and direction of the King of the West, as the Sultan of Cordoba was called at that time.

Then something went wrong. A cruel oppressor seized the land and houses. Ships which had gone to the Indies foundered in typhoons, disaster struck his house and his family. Even his close friends seemed to have lost their power to be in a true harmony with him, although both he and they wanted to have the right kind of social relationship.

The merchant decided to journey to Spain to see his former patron, and he set off across the Western Desert. On the way, one accident after another overtook him. His donkey died; he was captured by bandits and sold into slavery, from which he escaped only with the greatest difficulty; his face was tanned by the sun until it was like leather; rough villagers drove him away from their doors. Here and there a dervish gave him a morsel of food and a rag to cover himself. Sometimes he was able to scoop a little fresh water from a pool, but more often than not it was brackish.

Ultimately, he reached the entrance of the palace of the King of the West.

Even here he had the greatest difficulty in gaining entry. Soldiers pushed him away with the hafts of their spears, chamberlains refused to talk to him. He was put to work as a minor employee at the Court until he could earn enough to buy a dress suitable to wear when applying to the Master of Ceremonies for admission to the Royal Presence.

But he remembered that he was near to the presence of the king, and the recollection of the Sultan's kindness to him long ago was still in his mind. Because, however, he had been so long in his state of poverty and distress, his manners had suffered, and the Master of Ceremonies decided that he would have to take a course in behavior and self-discipline before he could allow him to be presented at Court.

All this the merchant endured until, three years after he quit Baghdad, he was shown into the audience hall.

The king recognized him at once, asked him how he was, and bade him sit in a place of honor beside him.

"Your Majesty," said the merchant, "I have suffered most terribly these past years. My lands were usurped, my patrimony expropriated, my ships were lost and with them all my capital. For three years I have battled against hunger, bandits, the desert, people whose language I did not understand. Here I am, to throw myself upon Your Majesty's mercy."

The king turned to the Chamberlain. "Give him a hundred sheep, make him a Royal Shepherd, send him up yonder mountain, and let him get on with his work."

Slightly subdued because the king's generosity seemed less than he had hoped for, the merchant withdrew, after the customary salutation.

No sooner had he reached the scanty pasturage with his sheep than a plague struck them, and they all died. He returned to the Court.

"How are your sheep?" asked the king.

"Your Majesty, they died as soon as I got them to their pasture."

The king made a sign and decreed: "Give this man fifty sheep, and let him tend them until further notice."

Feeling ashamed and distraught, the shepherd took the fifty animals to the mountainside. They started to nibble the grass well enough, but suddenly a couple of wild dogs appeared and chased them over a precipice and they were all killed.

The merchant, greatly sorrowing, returned to the king and told him his story.

"Very well," said the king, "you may now take twenty-five sheep and continue as before."

With almost no hope left in his heart, and feeling distraught beyond measure because he did not feel himself to be a shepherd in any sense of the word, the merchant took his sheep to their pasture. As soon as he got them there he found that the ewes all gave birth to twins, nearly doubling his flock. Then, again, twins were born. These new sheep were fat and well-fleeced and made excellent eating. The merchant found that, by selling some of the sheep and buying others, the ones which he bought, at first so skimpy and small, grew strong and healthy, and resembled the amazing new breed which he was rearing. After three years he was able to return to the Court, splendidly attired, with his report of the way in which the sheep had prospered during his stewardship. He was immediately admitted to the presence of the king.

"Are you now a successful shepherd?" the monarch asked. "Yes indeed, Your Majesty. In an incomprehensible way my luck turned and I can say that nothing has gone wrong – although I still have little taste for raising sheep."

"Very well," said the king. "Yonder is the kingdom of Seville, whose throne is in my gift. Go, and let it be known that I make you king of Seville." And he touched him on the shoulder with the ceremonial axe.

The merchant could not restrain himself and burst out: "But why did you not make me a king when I first came to you? Were you testing my patience, already stretched almost to breaking point? Or was this to teach me something?"

The king laughed. "Let us just say that, on that day when you took the hundred sheep up the mountain and lost them, had you taken control of the kingdom of Seville, there would not have been one stone standing on top of another there today."

From *Tales of the Dervishes*

The High Cost of Learning

LEARNING CANNOT BE *expressed accurately, of course, in money terms. But here is an example where money is used as an allegory:*

THERE WAS ONCE a sage who set up business in the marketplace as a seller of knowledge.

One of his customers was a young man, newly married, who wanted to test out this strange form of commerce.

"How much is your knowledge, if I buy it piece by piece?" he asked the wise man.

"It can cost as much or as little as you can offer, but the advice will be proportionate to the price in its usefulness," was the answer.

"Very well," said the young man, "I'll try a piece for one copper coin."

"The advice is," replied the sage, "Don't eat more than you have to, and get exercise – or you'll get fat!"

"Nothing cheap without reason," thought the customer to himself. Aloud he said:

"What can I have for five pieces of copper?"

"For five I can tell you that if you neglect your duty, you may lose eighteen years of your life!"

"I shall certainly try not to have that happen to me; but what will you tell me for one silver piece?"

"For that I can tell you that if you attempt to act without a proper basis and lack understanding, you will ruin your life."

Partly out of politeness to the older man, whom he now thought of as perhaps a little mad, or perhaps just a minor swindler, the youth thanked him and said to himself, "Perhaps what I have learned today is to follow my own good sense and not to try to buy advice when I should gain wisdom by experience."

He put the whole matter out of his mind.

Not long afterward, the young man was walking along a street when he saw a beggar, who said to him: "It is your duty to give alms, and I call upon you in the name of that duty, so that good shall befall you and so that evil shall be averted!"

Instead of giving the man anything, he started to walk faster, muttering, "May God give you something!"

It so happened that his increasing his speed brought him face to face with a military patrol whose task it was to capture strong young men for the army, for the king of his country was waging a war. He was seized and spent the next eighteen years in fighting and captivity.

This gave him a great deal of time to think, and the words about the eighteen years which would be taken from his life if he failed in his duty now bore strongly upon his mind.

Finally he was ransomed, and he found himself back in his native town, looking for the house where he had left his wife, such a very long time before. No sooner had he approached the building than he saw a woman, whom he recognized as his wife, going in through the front door with a young man, holding him by the hand.

The blood rushed to his head, and he put his hand to his sword, thinking, "I might as well die for murder, but I cannot stand the sight of this infidelity!"

Then he remembered the words of the sage: "If you attempt to act without a proper basis and lack understanding, you will ruin your life." At that moment he could not see that there was any lack of understanding, or that there was no proper basis for killing the miscreants. But somehow he restrained himself, just in case there was some better course of action.

All that day he walked about, tortured by the thought that his wife had played him false, or, at the least, had given him up for dead and had taken a new husband or a lover. When evening fell, he went back to the house and lurked by the lighted window, almost resolved to commit the double murder.

Inside the room he could see the couple sitting together on a sofa. Then he heard the words of his wife: "I have been told that another ship has arrived in port, from foreign parts. Tomorrow morning you should go, my son, and inquire from the sailors, as we have done for almost twenty years, if there is any news of your father."

Thus it was that five pieces of copper were shown to be the price of eighteen years of suffering; while one silver piece was the value of three lives, although, without an understanding of how life works, nobody would have suspected it.

From *The Commanding Self*

The Happiest Man in the World

A MAN WHO was living in comfortable enough circumstances went one day to see a certain sage, reputed to have all knowledge. He said to him:

"Great Sage, I have no material problems, and yet I am always unsettled. For years I have tried to be happy, to find an answer to my inner thoughts, to come to terms with the world. Please advise me as to how I can be cured of this malaise."

The sage answered:

"My friend, what is hidden to some is apparent to others. Again, what is apparent to some is hidden to others. I have the answer to your ailment, though it is no ordinary medication. You must set out on your travels, seeking the happiest man in the world. As soon as you find him, you must ask him for his shirt, and put it on."

This seeker thereupon restlessly started looking for happy men. One after another he found them and questioned them. Again and again they said: "Yes, I am happy, but there is one happier than me."

After traveling through one country after another for many, many days, he found the wood in which everyone said lived the happiest man in the world.

He heard the sound of laughter coming from among the trees, and quickened his step until he came upon a man sitting in a glade.

"Are you the happiest man in the world, as people say?" he asked.

"Certainly I am," said the other man.

"My name is so-and-so, my condition is such-and-such, and my remedy, ordered by the greatest sage, is to wear your shirt. Please give it to me; I will give you anything I have in exchange."

The happiest man looked at him closely, and he laughed. He laughed and he laughed and he laughed. When he had quietened down a little, the restless man, rather annoyed at this reaction, said:

"Are you unhinged, that you laugh at such a serious request?"

"Perhaps," said the happiest man, "but if you had only taken the trouble to look, you would have seen that I do not possess a shirt."

"What, then, am I to do now?"

"You will now be cured. Striving for something unattainable provides the exercise to achieve that which is needed: as when a man gathers all his strength to jump across a stream as if it were far wider than it is. He gets across the stream."

The happiest man in the world then took off the turban whose end had concealed his face. The restless man saw that he was none other than the great sage who had originally advised him.

"But why did you not tell me all this years ago, when I came to see you?" the restless man asked in puzzlement.

"Because you were not ready then to understand. You needed certain experiences, and they had to be given to you in a manner which would ensure that you went through them."

From *The Way of the Sufi*

The Book of the Secrets of the Ancients

SIKANDAR OF BALKH was the owner of huge tracts of land and master of a hundred castles. He had herds of *karakul* sheep and forests of walnuts, as well as the possession of a book of the secrets of the ancients, which had been given him by his father. "My child," said his father, "this is the most precious thing which you have. It will enable you to do things which in these times no ordinary man can do."

Sikandar Khan had remarried in his middle years a beautiful, inquisitive and self-willed woman named Gulbadan (Rose-bodied) Begum.

As the years passed, Sikandar started to age. He thought to himself: "If I could find some formula from the book of the secrets of the ancients which would enable me to become young again, this would undoubtedly be a suitable usage and a great advantage to me."

He read carefully through the book, and found that there were many things in it, including a means of rejuvenating oneself. The writing was so difficult, and the symbols and words used were so old, that he had to go on frequent journeys to what few ancient sages remained, in order to complete his understanding of the whole process.

Sikandar erected a small pavilion in one of his gardens for the working of the magical process, and spent many days there in repeating formulae, in all manner of exercises prescribed by the book, and mixing the ingredients for the magical drink which was to give him new youth.

All this time his wife, Gulbadan, was becoming more and more curious about what he was doing. According to the ancient science's laws, however, Sikandar could not tell her the purpose of his actions, on pain of failure. He kept the pavilion securely locked, and allowed nobody to go near it.

Sikandar followed the instruction of the book to the letter. He imported all sorts of rare and interesting playthings and luxuries for Gulbadan, so that her curiosity might be diverted and in the hope that she would become less anxious about his activities.

In order to maintain his own tranquility, as the book suggested, he engaged himself upon his business and tribal affairs most thoroughly, in addition to attending to the needs of the ancient wisdom.

When the time came that he had completed the processes all but one, Sikandar followed the book's command to go on a pilgrimage to a very distant place in order to hear what was to be said to him by whatever adept happened to be in residence there.

Sikandar made Gulbadan promise not to approach, nor let anyone enter, the pavilion of secrets.

When he arrived at the shrine, he said to the sage who was presiding over it:

"Master, I am so-and-so, and my affair is such-and-such, and my problem is that I cannot carry out the last part of the process, for the book of the ancient wisdom tells me to do something which is against the behavior of dervishes and which is not consistent with chivalry, and which is forbidden by the Holy Law."

The sage said:

"My child. The wisdom of the ancients is in arranging and not in commanding. The passage in your book does not recommend you to do anything. It tells you to come on this pilgrimage, and it tells you that a certain ingredient will be needed. It does not say that you have to obtain the ingredient, any more than it tells you to pray at this shrine. The prayer is your invention, and the procuring is your own assumption.

"Each process must go step by step. I advise you to return to your home, now that you have fulfilled the recommendation of the book."

These words confused Sikandar. If an ingredient was needed, who was to obtain it other than himself? If he was to visit a shrine, what was he to do other than pray there?

But he still retained his determination and his respect, so he kissed the hand of the sage and made his difficult way homeward.

Meanwhile, Gulbadan had told her maid about the locked pavilion. She had not said what she thought it was for, but thought: "I must tell someone something about this, otherwise I shall burst."

The maid told a servant whom she met in the bazaar, and this woman told her son, who was a locksmith:

"Some Sikandar Khan, who is on a pilgrimage, has a vast treasure or something else of priceless worth locked in a garden pavilion."

The locksmith, whose name was Qulfsaz, thought:

"I shall go and see what I can find out about this matter. With my skills I can open and afterward shut the door so that nobody will know what I have done. Therefore there will be no damage. This does not mean theft, it means information."

So he went to the pavilion at the dead of night.

As soon as he touched the lock of the door, however, something seized him, and he fell to the ground, writhing and howling in agony.

When the lady of the house walked into the garden the following morning, she found the dead body of the locksmith stretched before the pavilion's door.

The matter was reported to the superintendent of police, who decided that the man had died naturally during an attempted burglary.

Now, a few days later, Sikandar Khan arrived home. He went straight to the pavilion before entering the house, took the substances which were the results of his efforts and set fire to them.

He said to himself:

"The wisdom of the ancients is indeed profound! It teaches how man may attain certain desired ends. But it also shows how impossible it is for him to reach them, because he is not able to do the things which are stipulated."

Then he went to see his wife, and after he had given her the presents which he had brought, and seen his children, and ordered bonfires, sword-dancing and feasting in thanksgiving for his safe return, he sat alone and at ease with her. Sikandar Khan told his wife:

"Since I have abandoned my foolish project in the pavilion, I may now assuage the pain of your curiosity. I was trying to produce, from the book of wisdom of the ancients, something to become young again.

"The final ingredient was something which I could not bring myself to add. I carried out the process as far as I could, in the hope that this ingredient had some alternative, inner, meaning. I hoped that during my pilgrimage to the Great Shrine the sage there would help me. But he only said, 'You do not have to procure the ingredient.'"

"So I have returned here and destroyed the whole working of the process."

Gulbadan said:

"You say that you want to relieve my curiosity, yet you have now produced a greater mystery than before! Whatever can this impossible ingredient be?"

161

"The ingredient," said Sikandar Khan, "is that during the last stages of the experiment – a locksmith should be sacrificed."

From *A Veiled Gazelle*

The King Without a Trade

THERE WAS ONCE a king who had forgotten the ancient advice of the sages that those who are born into comfort and ease have greater need for proper effort than anyone else. He was a just king, however, and a popular one.

Journeying to visit one of his distant possessions, a storm blew up and separated his ship from its escort. The tempest subsided after seven furious days, the ship sank, and the only survivors of the catastrophe were the king and his small daughter, who had somehow managed to climb upon a raft.

After many hours, the raft was washed upon the shore of a country which was completely unknown to the travelers. They were at first taken in by fishermen, who looked after them for a time, then said:

"We are only poor people, and cannot afford to keep you. Make your way inland, and perhaps you may find some means of earning a livelihood."

Thanking the fisherfolk, and sad at heart that he was not able to enlist himself among them, the king started to wander through the land. He and the princess went from village to village, from town to town, seeking food and shelter. They were, of course, no better than beggars, and people treated them as such. Sometimes they had a few scraps of bread, sometimes dry straw in which to sleep.

Every time the king tried to improve his condition by asking for employment, people would say: "What work can you do?" And he always found that he was completely unskilled in whatever task he was required to perform, and had to take to the road again.

In that entire country there were hardly any opportunities for manual work, since there were plenty of unskilled laborers. As they moved from place to place, the king realized more and more strongly that being a king without a country was a useless state. He reflected more and more often on the proverb in which the ancients have laid down:

"That only may be regarded as your property which will survive a shipwreck."

After years of this miserable and futureless existence, the pair found themselves, for the first time, at a farm where the owner was looking for someone to tend his sheep.

He saw the king and the princess and said: "Are you penniless?"

They said that they were.

"Do you know how to herd sheep?" asked the farmer.

"No," said the king.

"At least you are honest," said the farmer, "and so I will give you a chance to earn a living."

He sent them out with some sheep, and they soon learned that all they had to do was to protect them against wolves and keep them from straying.

The king and the princess were given a cottage, and as the years passed the king regained some of his dignity, though not his happiness, and the princess blossomed into a young woman of fairylike beauty. As they only earned enough to keep themselves alive, the two were unable even to plan to return to their own country.

It so happened that one day, the Sultan of that country was out hunting when he saw the maiden and fell in love with her. He sent his representative to ask her father whether he would give her in marriage to the Sultan.

"Ho, peasant," said the courtier who had been sent to see him, "the Sultan, my lord and master, asks for the hand of your daughter in marriage."

"What is his skill, and what is his work, and how can he earn a living?" asked the former king.

"Dolt! You peasants are all alike," shouted the grandee. "Do you not understand that a king does not need to have work, that his skill is in managing kingdoms, that you have been singled out for an honor such as is ordinarily beyond any possible expectation of commoners?"

"All I know," said the shepherd-king, "is that unless your master, Sultan or no Sultan, can earn his living, he is no husband for my daughter. And I know a thing or two about the value of skills."

The courtier went back to his royal master and told him what the stupid peasant had said, adding:

"We must not be hard on these people, Sire, for they know nothing of the occupations of kings..."

The sultan, however, when he had recovered from his surprise, said:

"I am desperately in love with this shepherd's daughter, and I therefore am prepared to do whatever her father may direct in order to win her."

So he left the empire in the hands of a regent, and apprenticed himself to a carpet-weaver. After a year or so, he had mastered the art of simple carpet-making. Taking some of his own handiwork to the shepherd-king's hut, he presented it to him and said:

"I am the sultan of this country, desirous of marrying your daughter, if she will have me. Having received your message that you require a future son-in-law to possess useful skills, I have studied weaving, and these are examples of my work."

"How long did it take you to make this rug?" asked the shepherd-king.

"Three weeks," said the sultan.

"And when sold, how long could you live on its profit?" asked the shepherd-king.

"Three months," answered the sultan.

"You may marry my daughter, if she will accept you," said the father.

The sultan was overjoyed, and his happiness was complete when the princess agreed to marry him. "Your father, though he may be only a peasant, is a wise and shrewd man," he told her.

"A peasant may be as clever as a sultan," said the princess, "but a king, if he has had the necessary experiences, may be as wise as the shrewdest peasant."

The sultan and the princess were duly married, and the king, borrowing some money from his new son-in-law, was able to return to his own country, where he became known for evermore as the benign and sagacious monarch who never tired of encouraging each and every one of his subjects to learn a useful trade.

From *Reflections*

Minai's Journey

MOHSIN MINAI WAS unsatisfied with his conventional life as an enameler's assistant, and set off to make his fortune.

He wandered out of his native town, looking for opportunities. He had just passed the main gate when someone whom he knew slightly, called out, "Mohsin, if you want a job as an enameler, I know someone who has a vacancy."

Minai said, "No thank you. I have abandoned that kind of life. I am in search of better things."

If, however, he had taken the offer, he would soon have become a famous enameler, and a revered artist; for such was the end of the opportunity whose beginning he declined to accept.

This encounter made him all the more anxious to follow his destiny. He said to himself, "If I had not started on my journey, and had only sat in that enameler's booth in the bazaar, I would not have been given that chance to become a fully fledged

enameler for several years. So I see that in travel
there is opportunity."

He continued on his way. Presently he met a
stranger who asked him, "What is your occupation?"

"I am a master enameler," said Mohsin, thinking
to himself, "well, I would have been such by now if
I had stayed in my own town. Why, then, should I
represent myself as only an assistant?"

The stranger said, "My sister is getting married
and I would like to give her some unique enamel
article. Would you care to make it for me, if I were
to give you all the materials and facilities?"

"Certainly," said Mohsin.

So he settled down in the nearby village and made
a magnificent enameled bracelet for the wedding.

Minai said to himself:

"Here I am, making money and earning credit and
admiration, by assuming a stature which I did not
have before in men's eyes, but which I am manifestly
able to sustain."

He had bought a shop from the proceeds of his
first large independent commission, and thought
that he would spend some time in that particular
town.

But, not long afterward, someone came into the
shop and said:

"I am an enameler, seeking somewhere to settle
down. I would like to buy your business." And he
offered Mohsin such a very large sum of money
for his shop and its goodwill that the transaction
was soon completed, and Minai was on the road
again.

After a day or two on his journey, Minai was attacked by brigands, who took all his money and left him stripped, beaten and helpless, by the road.

Minai did not realize that if he had stayed where he was, he would have been very much worse off, because on that very day, the shop which he had sold was swallowed by an earthquake, and his successor was killed.

Minai lay there, bemoaning his fate and his lack of ability to stick to one thing, regretting his selling the shop because of greed.

Presently a charitable man passing that way approached the luckless enameler.

"Come to my house," he said, "and I will help you."

Minai went to his new friend's house and stayed there while his wounds healed. The man gave him a job in his garden, and Minai spent three years there, afraid to travel again in case he was unlucky and something unfortunate should happen to him. He congratulated himself, at the same time, upon his own humility in being able to suspend his ambitions and upon his capacity to fill such a humble post as gardener when he was really a craftsman. He regarded himself as specially virtuous in repaying his debt to his rescuer by serving him in exchange for such instant compassion as had been shown to a penniless wanderer.

What Minai did not know, however, was that if he had stayed there by the wayside, something completely different would have happened.

The brigands had soon quarreled, when ill luck struck them several times in succession. The leader was killed by his second-in-command, who brought back all Minai's money, and more as well, and threw it down on the spot where Minai had been lying, to get rid of the "curse."

When he had worked for a thousand days in his patron's garden, Minai begged permission to leave, and he made for the nearest town. He got himself a job as an enameler's assistant, and in due course worked his way up to the position of head enameler with a goldsmith.

"Now," he said to himself, "I am really back on the track again, because this is where I would have been if I had never had such ideas of greatness and had not started on my journey at all."

But what he did not know was that his imaginings about his own humility, and his vain belief that all the events in his life formed some sort of coherent whole, were the barriers to his real progress.

When, through a misunderstanding, Minai was arrested and convicted for embezzlement, he started to rearrange his thoughts like this:

"If I had only stayed where I was I would have been better off. But such misfortunes as the present one are only trials, and I must be patient."

What he did not realize, and never understood throughout his entire life, was that various events are part of different cause-and-effect threads in a life. Anyone who tries to put them together into one whole story flattering to himself by postulating a single destiny will meet the kind of result which is no "test" of humility and patience at all, but a payment for his own stupidity. People who always imagine that they are under test when they are being requited, are suffering from vanity which prevents them even from imagining that at some time or other they may be reaping the harvest of something sown by them.

From *The Dermis Probe*

The Man who Went in Search of his Fate

THERE WAS ONCE a man – and there have been many like him both before and since – who decided that he should make a change in his life. "What is the point," he asked himself, "of trying to do things, or letting things happen to me, if I do not know my Fate?"

If he worked against his Fate, he reasoned, he would suffer; and in the end the fate would be the same. If, on the other hand, he did nothing, his destiny would be a minor and uninteresting one, like that of the thousands of ordinary people all over the world, who had uneventful lives.

He had to start somewhere, so he sold his few possessions and began to walk along the highway which passed through his hometown.

He had not been walking for very long when he came to a teahouse, where he saw a dervish sitting, talking to a number of people. The traveler – whose name was Akram – waited until the audience had gone, and then approached the man of wisdom.

"Reverend Man of the Path!" he said, "I am in search of my Fate, and wonder whether you can suggest how I might start on this important endeavor."

"This is easier believed possible than it is achieved," replied the dervish; "and it would be better to ask how to *recognize* your Fate than to assume that you can do so without preparation."

"But I am sure that I can recognize my Fate!" cried Akram, "because it is well known that one's Fate is a reflection of oneself: and surely I can tell if I meet someone who looks like me."

"Looking like you externally is not the same thing as being a reflection of you," said the dervish, "especially when, like everyone else, you have so many sides that you find it hard to see your own reflection in all its forms. The mirror of perception is as fleeting and as miscellaneous as the wavelets of the sea, each briefly shining forth with the borrowed light of the sun, as it breaks upon the seashore..."

The dervish continued in this vein for some time, and Akram, who had met dervishes before, stopped listening to him. He came to the conclusion that there would be nothing that he could profit from here. Still, he thought, it would be nice to have company on the journey. When the dervish had stopped talking, Akram said: "Mystical analogies are, of course, too deep for me to understand. But if you are traveling, might I accompany you, at least for part of the way? For I am unversed in the experiences and practices of journeying."

The dervish agreed, and they set off along the road.

Presently they saw a tree by the roadside, and from it was clearly to be heard a strong buzzing sound. The dervish said: "Put your ear to the trunk of the tree, and see what you can hear."

Akram followed his advice and realized that the tree was hollow. Inside there was a very large number of bees.

The dervish said: "The bees are trapped. If you can manage to break off that branch, they will be released and will be able to escape. It might be a kindly act – and who knows where it might lead?"

Akram answered: "Old man, you are not of this world! Has it not been said that one should not be distracted from one's objective by minor matters? Now, supposing that someone were to offer me some money for breaking the branch, I would accept, for I have no money for my journey. But to do it for nothing is absurd!"

"As you will," said the dervish, and they continued on their way.

When it was dark they lay down to sleep. In the morning they were woken by a man going past with two large jars strapped to the sides of his donkey. He stopped to pass the time of day.

"Where are you going?" asked the dervish.

"To market to sell this honey. It should fetch at least three pieces of gold. Yesterday I heard some bees in a hollow tree, and they seemed to want to get out. So I broke a dead branch and they swarmed. I found this huge amount of honey, and, from being a pauper, I am on the way to supporting myself!" And he went on his way.

Akram said to the dervish: "I should, perhaps, have got to the honey first, as you suggested. But, on the other hand, it may not have been the same tree,

and in that case I would probably have been stung –
and that is not the Fate I am looking for!"

The dervish said nothing.

Further along the road they came to a bridge over
a river, and stopped to admire the view. Suddenly
a fish poked its head out of the water and looked
at them, its mouth opening and shutting in a quite
pathetic way.

"What do you think that means?" Akram asked.

The dervish said: "Cup your hands with interlaced
fingers, and see whether you can understand the
speech of the fish."

When Akram did as the dervish suggested, he
found that he could indeed understand the fish, who
was saying:

"Help me, help me!"

The dervish called out:

"What help do you seek?"

The fish answered:

"I have swallowed a sharp stone. There is a certain
herb, growing in profusion on the riverbank. If you
would kindly pluck some and throw it to me, I could
bring up the stone and find some relief."

"A talking fish, indeed!" said Akram. "I think that
this is some sort of a trick of magic or ventriloquism.
I refuse to make myself ridiculous. In any case, I am in
search of my Fate. Dervish, if this strange happening
is anything to do with you, perhaps you might care
to help yonder fish yourself!"

The dervish only said, "No, I shall not do anything.
Let us be on our way."

Soon afterward they entered a town and sat down in the marketplace to rest. Presently a man came galloping into the square on a fine horse, obviously very excited. Dismounting, he shouted to the townspeople:

"A miracle, a miracle!"

As everyone gathered around the horseman, he said:

"I was crossing a bridge, when, believe it or not, a fish spoke to me. It asked me to throw it some herbs. I did so, and after eating them, it threw up a flawless diamond as big as both my fists!"

Akram called out: "How do you know that it is a real diamond?"

"I am a jeweler," said the man.

"How typical of life," said Akram, "that a man of wealth should get even more, while I, unable to succor the fish because I was on important business, am forced to beg my bread in the company of a most uninteresting dervish!"

The dervish said, "Oh well, perhaps it was not the same fish; perhaps, indeed, that man is lying. Let us look forward and not back!"

"That is all rather like a philosopher," said Akram, "but much the same thoughts were in my own mind."

They continued on their way.

The next event in their journey was when they stopped to eat beside a rock, embedded in the ground. A low humming seemed to be coming from the rock, and Akram put his ear to it. He found that the sound came from under the rock, and as he listened he could understand what it meant. It was a number of ants, and they were saying:

"If only we could move this rock, or get through it somehow, we would be able to extend our kingdom and find room for all our people. If only something could come to our aid! This hard material down here is too difficult to get through. If only someone or something would take it away!"

Akram looked at the dervish, and said:

"The ants want the rock moved, so that they can extend their kingdom. What have I to do with ants, rocks or kingdoms? First I must find my Fate!"

The dervish said nothing, and they continued on their way.

The following day, when they were rising from their miserable bivouac under a hedge, they heard the sound of many people coming their way, singing and shouting with glee. Presently they saw that a large band of rustics was on the road, dancing and playing fiddles and pipes, leaping and somersaulting with delight. As they passed, Akram asked one of them what had happened. The man said:

"A goatherd, believe it or not, heard some ants murmuring under a rock, in great distress. He moved it so that they could extend their nest. What do you think he found underneath? Why, a huge treasure of gold pieces! He took it and shared it with all his neighbors, and we are the lucky villagers who benefited!"

They went on their way, still delirious with delight.

The dervish said to Akram:

"You are a fool, for you have thrice failed to do even the simplest thing that might have brought you the fortune which you desired! You are a fool, because you are even less prepared to follow your fate than all those people who just did a kind action and were not obsessed by their Fate and their personal desires! You are a fool, for you have, instead of following your fate, distanced yourself from it, by your behavior and your failure to look at what is beneath your nose. Above all, you are a fool because you did not attend to what I am and what I have said, not said and indicated."

Akram, like many another before and since, became enraged. He shouted at the dervish:

"Self-satisfied and domineering know-all! Anyone can be wise, after the event! I noticed that you, a miserable and underfed wanderer on the face of the earth, did not take any advantage of the great things which you are now such an expert upon! Perhaps you can tell me why *that* is?"

"I can indeed," replied the dervish. "I could not benefit myself because I had other things to do. You see, I *am* your Fate!"

Then the dervish disappeared, and he has never been seen again; except, of course, by all the Akrams who have lived since that time, many, many years ago.

From *Seeker after Truth*

THE FOLLOWING EXCERPT is from a lecture by Idries Shah about the Sufi use of stories. It is a good example of how he used stories in context, in this case to explain something of the role of stories themselves.

Editor's note

The Teaching Story
PEOPLE WHO SPEAK little need only half a brain.

– Italian proverb

I CAN THINK of no better way of beginning a consideration of stories than with a very short, true story. It describes the intricacies of dealing with stories and also with the talking and hearing process itself.

I was giving a lecture recently on the difficulty that people have in taking things in, and was considering how a story might become a person's possession, so that it could be recalled to mind and looked at from various points of view.

"It has been noticed," I continued, "that much information is *not* absorbed because many people cannot really absorb something when they have heard it only once..."

Immediately a hand went up, and someone sitting in the front row asked me: "Would you mind saying that again?"

This time-lag, between the presentation of materials and their integration into the thinking and repertoire of action of the individual, has itself to be taught.

We find it easy to observe and to test in the story-telling and story-hearing atmosphere. The holistic mode of the brain will obtain certain parts, and the more literal mode others. Neither will perceive many dimensions until a skill has been developed.

This short Sufi tale is employed for the educational purpose of establishing in the mind the contention at least that one may need this time-lapse for this purpose, and it is not intended to make fun of any of the fictional figures appearing in it:

Time and Pomegranates

A DISCIPLE WENT to the house of a Sufi physician and asked to become an apprentice in the art of medicine.

"You are impatient," said the doctor, "and so you will fail to observe things which you will need to learn."

But the young man pleaded, and the Sufi agreed to accept him.

After some years, the youth felt that he could exercise some of the skills which he had learned. One day, a man was walking toward the house and the doctor – looking at him from a distance – said: "That man is ill. He needs pomegranates."

"You have made the diagnosis – let *me* prescribe for him, and I will have done half the work," said the student.

"Very well," said the teacher, "providing that you remember that action should also be looked at as illustration."

As soon as the patient arrived at the doorstep, the student brought him in and said: "You are ill. Take pomegranates."

"Pomegranates!" shouted the patient, "pomegranates to you – nonsense!" And he went away.

The young man asked his master what the meaning of the interchange had been.

"I will illustrate it the next time we get a similar case," said the Sufi.

Shortly afterward, the two were sitting outside the house when the master looked up briefly and saw a man approaching.

"Here is an illustration for you – a man who needs pomegranates," he said.

The patient was brought in, and the doctor said to him:

"You are a difficult and intricate case, I can see that. Let me see... yes, you need a special diet. This must be composed of something round, with small sacs inside it, naturally occurring. An orange... that would be of the wrong color... lemons are too acid... I have it: pomegranates!"

The patient went away, delighted and grateful.

"But Master," said the student, "why did you not say 'pomegranates' straight away?"

"Because," said the Sufi, "he needed *time* as well as pomegranates."

ON ONE LEVEL, the tales are *structures*, which make possible the holding of certain concepts in a particular relationship. They can sometimes help people to understand ranges of ideas which are not ordinarily linked in any other way.

Several Sufi tales in my *Tales of the Dervishes* which have no obvious "point" or which are susceptible to more than one interpretation, have been observed to work by bringing into greater action the right-hemisphere functions of the brain and the attenuation of the left.

This, too, may well be the reason for such disjointed injunctions as "Think of the sound of no sound." The holistic overall mode cannot of course compete in sequential activity, and seems to take over when the logical one is jammed.

One of the specialities of the Sufis is to approach the needs of the student from many different directions, so that by what we call "scatter" (a constellation of impacts), the picture ultimately comes together and he understands.

The following story might make this versatility of approach clearer:

There was once a Sufi teacher who dressed his disciples in robes of wool, had them carry begging bowls made of sea-coconuts, taught them to whirl in a mystic dance, and intone passages from certain classics.

A philosopher asked him: "What would you do, as a Sufi teacher, if you went to a country where there were no sheep for the wool, where sea-coconuts were unknown, where dancing was considered immoral, and where you were not allowed to teach classics?"

He immediately answered: "I would find, in such a place, quite a different kind of disciple."

Sufis contend that all secondary ideas and things exist only to be dispensed with when a higher level is reached. This holds out the possibility of becoming quite a different type of disciple, learner or teacher.

STORIES MAY HAVE a testing function. The chief feature of this testing, however, is to illustrate to the person himself what some of his major characteristics of thought are. This may allow him to modify them or detach from them, instead of being their slave.

One such story – The Tale of the Sands – sometimes shows people their own dependency situation. In this tale the river, aware of its existence, runs toward the sea, but arrives at a stretch of sand, and starts to run away into nothingness, to become at best, a marsh. Terrified of losing its identity, but with no real alternative, the river allows itself to be lifted up by the wind – though only after much debate and soul-searching. The wind carries it out of danger and allows it to fall, as water, safely as it precipitates against a mountain, at the other side.

Some people love this story. For others it has all the awful quality of reminding them that they must die or that they may be being asked to choose someone or something, of whom or of which they know next to nothing, of a different kind from themselves, to submit to this and to be carried away to somewhere or something of which they have no knowledge or guarantee. Do these two reactions describe the story or the people who are commenting on it?

People exposed to this story can learn a lot about themselves just by testing its effect upon their feelings.

When I did a documentary program for British television, I told a group of children a tale which is familiar in Central Asia, and which we used in England as part of the teaching in the children's school at our house.

The Lion who Saw his Face in the Water

THERE WAS ONCE a lion who lived in a desert which was very windy; and because of this, the water in the holes from which he usually drank was never still, for the wind riffled the surface and never reflected anything.

One day this lion wandered into a forest, where he hunted and played, until he felt rather tired and thirsty. Looking for water, he came across a pool of the coolest, most tempting, and most placid water that you could possibly imagine. Lions, like other wild animals, can smell water, and the scent of this water was like ambrosia to him.

So the lion approached the pool, and extended his neck to have a good drink. Suddenly, though, he saw his reflection – and imagined that it must be another lion.

"Oh dear," he thought to himself, "this must be water belonging to another lion – I had better be careful."

He retreated, but then thirst drove him back again, and again he saw the head of a fearsome lion looking back at him from the surface of the pool.

This time our lion hoped that he might be able to frighten the "other lion" away; and so he opened his mouth and gave a terrible roar. But no sooner had he bared his teeth than, of course, the mouth of the "other" lion opened as well, and this seemed to our lion to be an awful and dangerous sight.

Again and again the lion retreated and then returned to the pool. Again and again he had the same experience.

After a long time, however, he was so thirsty and desperate that he decided to himself: "Lion or no lion, I am going to drink from that pool!"

And, lo and behold, no sooner had he plunged his face into the water than the "other lion" disappeared!

THERE WAS NO special intention of spreading this story as a psychological support or therapeutic tool for parents with fearful children. But I got a good many letters after the TV film was shown, saying how parents had been able to use the story to reassure various youngsters who had fears of the unknown or of unfamiliar situations. It is true that these tales are told to children in the East, instead of the more gruesome ones which are often found in Hans Andersen and the Brothers Grimm; and no doubt there is a gap which could be filled here. They would be useful to children, and certainly entertain them, as we have found for many years.

The stories have become something of a rage in schools and partly through BBC educational broadcasting, laying down a stratum of interest which results in constant inquiries and callers from all over the place.

But there is no instant application of the stories as a sort of magic wand, or even as some kind of band-aid dressing.

The stories, as a body, and correctly used, offer a remarkable way into another way of thinking and of being. If they are considered only as individual items to add to a repertoire, for therapy or for any other instantly obvious purpose, they lose much of their usefulness.

I have made the whole, holistic body of material available. I would ask you not to be satisfied with imitations. These are characterized by crypticism on the one hand and telling you what you want to hear on the other. No form of education I know about does that, but cults do.

I can do no better than to quote at this point Rumi, one of our greatest masters: "You may have a magic ring – but you must be a Solomon, master of invisible powers, to make it work."

NO ACCOUNT OF teaching-stories can be really useful without a recital of some of these tales without any explanation at all. This is because some of the effect can be prevented by an interpretation; and the difference between an exposition and a teaching-event is precisely that in the latter nobody knows what his or her reaction is supposed to be (from any doctrinal standpoint) so that there can be a private reaction and a personal absorption of the materials.

The Sufi practice is to take a number of tales and ask a group of people to look at them. They then have to note down the points which interested them in the stories. Instead of magnetizing themselves upon those points, they have to set them aside, and look at the points that did *not* catch their attention, and ask themselves *why they missed these*. What censorship or lack of understanding was operating? People first make their notes separately, then study them in unison, so that everyone taking part is possessed of all the reactions of the others. In this way a mosaic is built up, people all contribute, one to the other's understanding. Now a Sufi teacher goes through the results and indicates the points which nobody has noticed, which are then fed back into the minds of the group, which is able to add to its individual and collective knowledge the material which it could not provide from among its own members. When this process has been completed, one may expect a dramatic improvement in the understanding-capacity of all the people involved.

This is what we regard as proper teaching and learning. First you do what you can. Then you profit from what others are doing, and they from you. Finally you get the additional element which was absent from your own knowledge stock, provided by your teacher.

My published collections of tales in themselves constitute teaching-frames which make it possible to deal with some of these barriers oneself, but the existence of a teacher is central to the whole enterprise. There are limits beyond which the familiarization and feedback system ordinarily employed in study cannot operate without the active assistance of an instructor who is a real, not a self-appointed, one.

Sufis do not insist on the primacy of the teaching function because they want to, but because they must. It is, indeed, the Sufi's objective to render the need for a teacher obsolete. But first he or she must make available the information and the methods which are not to be found yet, for practical purposes, among the generality of the people who want to learn.

The Sufi enterprise, in which the stories can play an essential part, is to operate in areas which have been neglected. This is the Sufi contribution toward the vision of a better world.

Abridged from *A Perfumed Scorpion*

7

Teachings of the Classics

I ASKED A child, walking with a candle,
  "From where comes that light?"
  Instantly he blew it out. "Tell me where
  it is gone – then I will tell you where it
  came from."

> – Hasan of Basra
> From *The Sufis*

IDRIES SHAH MADE *the almost heretical claim that Sufi
works of literature were written for a specific people
at a specific time.*

*Rumi, for instance, he said, had instituted dervish
dancing because the people he found in thirteenth
century Konya were too lethargic and needed a
corrective. At other times, classical writers were
obliged to disguise their writings with heavily
religious overlay in order to gain acceptance from
oppressively theological authorities.*

*Shah dared to stress the need for selection and
adaptation, pointing out that, if one were to follow
the Sufi classics doggedly, one might turn oneself
into a perfect twelfth-century man. He spent much
of his working life stripping such materials of their*

religious and cultural overlay and presenting the sections which he said were suitable for the people of the West, at their particular time.

This, of course, made him unpopular with academics and religious traditionalists alike. He insisted, however, that he was working from neither an academic nor an emotionalist point of view, but was trying to reclaim their instrumental Sufic function.

He often drew attention to Sufi methodology at work in these books, calling, for instance, Rumi's masterpiece, the Masnavi, *"a phenomenal example of the method of scatter, whereby a picture is built up of multiple impacts to infuse into the mind the Sufi message" (*The Sufis*).*

For this reason, he said, Sufi literature, containing as it does many layers of thought, can only be adequately translated by a Sufi.

Editor's note

El-Ghazali

Twelfth-century philosopher and Sufi El-Ghazali quotes in his *Book of Knowledge* this line from El-Mutanabbi: "To the sick man, sweet water tastes bitter in the mouth."

This could very well be taken as Ghazali's motto. Eight hundred years before Pavlov, he pointed out and hammered home (often in engaging parables, sometimes in startlingly "modern" words) the problem of conditioning.

In spite of Pavlov and the dozens of books and reports of clinical studies into human behavior made since the Korean war, the ordinary student of things of the mind is unaware of the power of indoctrination.[2] Indoctrination, in totalitarian societies, is something which is desirable providing that it furthers the beliefs of such societies. In other groupings its presence is scarcely even suspected. This is what makes almost anyone vulnerable to it.

Ghazali's work not only predates, but also exceeds, the contemporary knowledge of these matters. At the time of writing, informed opinion is split between whether indoctrination (whether overt or covert) is desirable or otherwise, whether, too, it is inescapable or not.

Ghazali not only points out that what people call belief may be a state of obsession, he states clearly, in accordance with Sufi principles, that it is not inescapable, but insists that it is essential for people to be able to identify it.

His books were burned by Mediterranean bigots from Spain to Syria. Nowadays they are not put into the flames, but their effect, except among Sufis, is perhaps less; they are not read very much.

---

2 One of the most striking peculiarities of contemporary man is that, while he now has abundant scientific evidence to the contrary, he finds it intensely difficult to understand that his beliefs are by no means always linked with either his intelligence, his culture or his values. He is therefore almost unreasonably prone to indoctrination.

He regarded the distinction between opinion and knowledge as something which can easily be lost. When this happens, it is incumbent upon those who know the difference to make it plain as far as they are able.

Ghazali's scientific, psychological, discoveries, though widely appreciated by academics of all kinds, have not been given the attention they deserve because he specifically disclaims the scientific or logical method as their origin. He arrived at his knowledge through his upbringing in Sufism, among Sufis, and through a form of direct perception of the truth which has nothing to do with mechanical intellection. This, of course, at once puts him outside the pale for scientists. What is rather curious, however, is that his discoveries are so astonishing that one would have thought that investigators would have liked to find out how he made them.

"Mysticism" having been given a bad name like the dog in the proverb, if it cannot be hanged, can at least be ignored. This is a measure of scholastic psychology: accept the man's discoveries if you cannot deny them, but ignore his method if it does not follow your beliefs about method.

If Ghazali had produced no worthwhile results, he would naturally have been regarded as only a mystic, and a proof that mysticism is educationally or socially unproductive.

The influence of Ghazali on Western thought is admitted on all hands to be enormous. But this influence itself shows the working of conditioning; the philosophers of medieval Christendom who adopted many of his ideas did so selectively, completely ignoring the parts which were embarrassing to their own indoctrination activities.

Ghazali's way of thought attempted to bring to a wider audience than the comparatively small Sufi one a final distinction between belief and obsession. He stressed the role of upbringing in the inculcation of religious beliefs, and invited his readers to observe the mechanism involved. He insisted upon pointing out that those who are learned may be, and often are, stupid as well, and can be bigoted, obsessed. He affirms that, in addition to having information and being able to reproduce it, there is such a thing as knowledge, which happens to be a higher form of human thought.

The habit of confusing opinion with knowledge, a habit which is to be met with every day at the current time, Ghazali regards as an epidemic disease.

In saying all these things, with a wealth of illustration and in an atmosphere which was most unconducive to scientific attitudes, Ghazali was not merely playing the part of a diagnostician. He had acquired his own knowledge in a Sufic manner, and he realized that higher understanding – being a Sufi, in fact – was only possible to people who could see and avoid the phenomena which he was describing.

Ghazali produced numerous books and published many teachings. His contribution to human thought and the relevance of his ideas hundreds of years later are unquestioned. Let us partly repair the omission of our predecessors by seeing what he has to say about method. What was the Way of El-Ghazali?

What does man have to do in order to be like him – he who was admittedly one of the world's giants of philosophy and psychology?

Ghazali on the Path
A HUMAN BEING is not a human being while his tendencies include self-indulgence, covetousness, temper and attacking other people.

A student must reduce to the minimum the fixing of his attention upon customary things like his people and his environment, for attention-capacity is limited.

The pupil must regard his teacher like a doctor who knows the cure of the patient. He will serve his teacher. Sufis teach in unexpected ways. An experienced physician prescribes certain treatments correctly. Yet the outside observer might be quite amazed at what he is saying and doing; he will fail to see the necessity or the relevance of the procedure being followed.

This is why it is unlikely that the pupil will be able to ask the right questions at the right time. But the teacher knows what and when a person can understand.

The Difference Between Social and Initiatory Activity
GHAZALI INSISTS UPON the connection and also the difference between the social or diversionary contact of people, and the higher contact.

What prevents the progress of an individual and a group of people, from praiseworthy beginnings, is their stabilizing themselves upon repetition and what is a disguised social basis.

If a child, he says, asks us to explain to him the pleasures which are contained in wielding sovereignty, we may say that it is like the pleasure which he feels in sport; though, in reality, the two have nothing in common except that they both belong to the category of pleasure.

Parable of the People with a Higher Aim
IMAM EL-GHAZALI RELATES a tradition from the life of Isa, ibn Maryam: Jesus, Son of Mary.

Isa one day saw some people sitting miserably on a wall, by the roadside. He asked: "What is your affliction?" They said: "We have become like this through our fear of Hell."

He went on his way, and saw a number of people grouped disconsolately in various postures by the wayside. He said: "What is your affliction?" They said: "Desire for Paradise has made us like this."

He went on his way, until he came to a third group of people. They looked like people who had endured much, but their faces shone with joy.

Isa asked them: "What has made you like this?" and they answered: "The Spirit of Truth. We have seen Reality, and this has made us oblivious of lesser goals."

Isa said: "These are the people who attain. On the Day of Accounting these are they who will be in the Presence of God."

The Three Functions of the Perfected Man

THE PERFECTED MAN of the Sufis has three forms of relationship with people. These vary with the condition of the people.

The three manners are exercised in accordance with

(1) The form of belief which surrounds the Sufi;
(2) The capacity of students, who are taught in accordance with their ability to understand;
(3) A special circle of people who will share an understanding of the knowledge which is derived from direct inner experience.

Attraction of Celebrities

A MAN WHO is being delivered from the danger of a fierce lion does not object, whether this service is performed by an unknown or an illustrious individual. Why, therefore, do people seek knowledge from celebrities?

Love and Self-Interest

IF ONE LOVES someone because it gives pleasure, one should not be regarded as loving that person at all. The love is, in reality, though this is not perceived, directed toward the pleasure. The source of the pleasure is the secondary object of attention, and it is perceived only because the perception of the pleasure is not well enough developed for the real feeling to be identified and described.

You Must Be Prepared

YOU MUST PREPARE yourself for the transition in which there will be none of the things to which you have accustomed yourself, says Ghazali. After death, your identity will have to respond to stimuli of which you have a chance to get a foretaste here. If you remain attached to the few things with which you are familiar, it will only make you miserable.

Ignorance

PEOPLE OPPOSE THINGS because they are ignorant of them.

Ceremonies of Music and Movement

SUCH MEETINGS MUST be held in accordance with the requirements of time and place. Onlookers whose motives are not worthy shall be excluded. The participants in audition must sit silently and not look at each other. They seek what may appear from their own "hearts."

The Dance

A DISCIPLE HAD asked permission to take part in the "dance" of the Sufis.

The Sheikh said: "Fast completely for three days. Then have luscious dishes cooked. If you then prefer the 'dance,' you may take part in it."

Man Was Made for Learning

A CAMEL IS stronger than a man; an elephant is larger; a lion has greater valor; cattle can eat more than man; birds are more virile. Man was made for the purpose of learning.

Possessions
YOU POSSESS ONLY whatever will not be lost in a shipwreck.

From *The Way of the Sufi*

ALMOST A THOUSAND years have passed since Ghazali wrote his monumental work *Restoration of Religious Sciences.*

In it he shows that the element which the Sufis call "knowledge" is employed as a technical term, and that its functions for the human being go far beyond what one would ordinarily regard as knowledge. It could be called the very force which maintains humanity.

Knowledge, he says – the goal of the Sufi – supports life to such an extent that if its transmission were to be interrupted for three days, the kernel of the individual dies, just as someone would die if he were deprived of food, or as a patient dies when deprived of certain medicines. Sufi knowledge, therefore, is something which continually pours into man. It is the perception and employment of this knowledge which is the aim of mystics.

Wisdom is sometimes used as "understanding the special knowledge." Sometimes this causes people to depart from ordinary habits. Naturally, such conduct is opposed by the ordinary.

Ordinary people are those who are blind to the

urgent need for knowledge. This blindness Ghazali likens to a disease. It causes arrogance. When there is arrogance, knowledge cannot operate.

The problem of men in seeking true knowledge is great because they do not know where to look for it or how to do so. This is because they have been deceived into mistaking rules and discipline, or scholasticism, or argument, for instance, as the search for knowledge.

What is this special knowledge which maintains man? It is so much more advanced a thing than, say, belief (what people call faith) that "those who really know are seven hundred degrees in rank above those who only believe."

"The purpose of the exercise of the science of knowledge, or Sufism as it is known," says al-Ghazali, "is to gain an eternally durable existence."

From *Thinkers of the East*

Omar Khayyam

OMAR KHAYYAM WAS an important philosopher, scientist and practical instructor in Sufism. His name is well known in European literature mainly because of Edward Fitzgerald, who in Victorian times published a few of Omar's quatrains in English. Fitzgerald – like, it must be noted, many Eastern scholastics – imagined that because Khayyam was at times talking about widely conflicting points of view, he himself was a victim to some sort of alternation of mind. This attitude, while characteristic of many academicians, is just about as profound as that of a man who thinks that if someone shows you something he must believe it; and that if he shows you several things, he must be subject to identification with these things.

Fitzgerald was guilty of far more, however, than poor thinking capacity. His interpolation of anti-Sufi propaganda into his rendering of Khayyam cannot be excused even by his most ardent supporters. As a result, they tend to ignore this amazing dishonesty, and shout about other subjects instead.

Omar Khayyam's teaching-poems, and those of other members of his school which have become an accepted part of this material, are based upon the special terminology and allegory of Sufism. A full investigation and translation was made by Swami Govinda Tirtha in 1941, published under the title *The Nectar of Grace.*

This book is virtually the last word on the question of the meaning (so far as it can be transposed into English) of the materials. It is interesting to note that few Western scholars have made use of this essential work in their expositions of Khayyam.

The result is that Khayyam effectively remains all but unknown.

Under the Earth
YOU ARE NOT gold, ignorantly heedless one:
    That, once put in the earth, anyone
    Will bring you out again.

Man
Do you know what a man of earth may be, Khayyam
A lantern of imaginings, and inside a lamp.

Do Not Go Empty-Handed...
Take some substance from Here to There –
You will make no profit if you go with empty
hand.

I Am
Every clique has a theory about me –
I am mine; what I am, I am.

From *The Way of the Sufi*

Attar of Nishapur

Although Attar is one of the greatest of Sufi
classical literary masters, and an inspirer of Rumi,
his *Memorials of the Saints*, tales and teachings
of Sufi sages, had to wait nearly seven and a half
centuries for an English translation. In spite of the
accelerating Western interest in Sufism, it was the
Hindu hermit Dr Bankey Behari who published
sixty-two selections from this book in 1961.

Attar wrote in all about one hundred and fourteen
books, among which the most famous are the Sufic
Divine Book, the *Parliament of the Birds*, and the
Book of Counsel.

His teachings were carried on by means of
illustrative biography, fables, maxims and apologues,

which contain not only moral teaching but allegories describing specific stages in human development. In the *Parliament of the Birds*, for instance, he sketches individual phases in human consciousness, though these are represented as happening to different individuals or to a whole community.

Attar used the theme of a "journey" or "quest" as an analogy of the successive stages of the human soul in search of perfection.

Refusing to accept honors from the hands of the Mongol invaders of Central Asia, he is reported to have died at the hands of the soldiers of Genghis Khan, after having dismissed his disciples – sending them to places of safety – when he predicted the Mongol invasion of the thirteenth century.

The traditions of Sufism assert that Attar's work is important because, read as a whole, it helps to maintain the social fabric and ethical standards of Islam; while special selections from it contain initiatory material which is concealed by the heavily theological parts.

An Answer of Jesus

SOME ISRAELITES REVILED Jesus one day as he was walking through their part of town.

But he answered by repeating prayers in their name.

Someone said to him:

"You prayed for these men, did you not feel incensed against them?"

He answered:

"I could spend only of what I had in my purse."

The Heart
SOMEONE WENT UP to a madman who was weeping in the bitterest possible way.

He said:

"Why do you cry?"

The madman answered:

"I am crying to attract the pity of His Heart."

The other told him:

"Your words are nonsense, for He has no physical heart."

The madman answered:

"It is you who are wrong, for He is the owner of all the hearts which exist. Through the heart you can make your connection with God."

The Tale of Fazl-Rabbi
ONE DAY A penurious old man went to see Fazl-Rabbi to discuss some matter or other.

Because of weakness and nervousness, this ancient stuck the iron point of his walking-stick to wound Fazl-Rabbi's foot.

Listening courteously to what the old man had to say, Fazl-Rabbi said no word, although he went pale and then flushed, from the pain of the wound and the iron, as it stayed lodged in his foot.

Then, when the other had finished his business, he took a paper from him and put his signature to it.

When the old man had gone, delighted that he had been successful in his application, Fazl-Rabbi allowed himself to collapse.

One of the attendant nobles said:

"My lord, you sat there with blood pouring from your foot, with that old man in his dotage piercing it with his iron-tipped staff, and you said nothing, nothing at all."

Fazl-Rabbi answered:

"I made no sign of pain because I feared that the old man's distress might cause him to withdraw in confusion, and that he might abandon his application for my help. Poor as he was, how could I add to his troubles in that manner?"

Be a real man; learn nobility of thought and action, like that of Fazl-Rabbi.

The Slave Without a Master

WANDERING IN A patchwork robe, his face blackened by the sun, a certain dervish arrived at Kufa, where he was seen by a merchant.

The merchant spoke to him, and decided that he must be a lost slave.

"Because of your mild manner, I will call you 'Khair' [good]," he said. "Are you not a slave?"

"That I am," said Khair.

"I will take you home, and you can work for me until I find your master."

"I would like that," said Khair, "for I have been seeking my master for such a long time."

He worked for many years with this man, who taught him to be a weaver; hence his second name: "Nassaj" ("weaver").

After his long services, feeling guilty of his exploitation, the merchant said to him: "I do not know who you are, but you are now free to go."

Khair Nassaj, the great Master of the Way, traveled onward to Mecca, without regrets, for he had discovered how to continue his development in spite of having no name and being treated like a slave.

He was the teacher of Shibli, Ibrahim Khawwas and many more of the great Teachers of the Sufis. He died over a thousand years ago, at the age of one hundred and twenty.

The Moon
THE MOON WAS asked:
"What is your strongest desire?"
It answered:
"That the Sun should vanish, and should remain veiled for ever in clouds."

The Five Hundred Gold Pieces
ONE OF JUNAID's followers came to him with a purse containing five hundred gold pieces.
"Have you any more money than this?" asked the Sufi.
"Yes, I have."
"Do you desire more?"
"Yes, I do."
"Then you must keep it, for you are more in need than I; for I have nothing and desire nothing. You have a great deal and still want more."

The Religious Framework
ONE DAY WHEN the Companion Omar was looking through a Jewish holy book, the Prophet Muhammad said to him:

"You are too casual with that book. If you want to gain any value from it, you will have to become a Jew. To be a perfect Jew is better than to be an incomplete Muslim; and dallying with the Jewish book is half-hearted and will give you no benefit one way or the other.

"Your mistake is that you are neither one thing nor another in behaving in this manner. You do not believe, neither do you disbelieve. What, then, is your condition, how can it be described?"

– Kitab-Ilahi

A Story of Moses

ONCE MOSES WAS asking God to show him one of God's friends, and a voice answered:

"Go to a certain valley and there you will find one who loves me, one of the chosen, who treads the Path."

Moses went and found this man, dressed in rags, plagued by every kind of insect and crawling thing.

He said: "Can I do anything for you?"

The man answered: "Emissary of God, bring me a cup of water, for I am thirsty."

When Moses returned with the water he found the man lying dead. He went away to look for a piece of cloth for a winding-sheet. When he came back he found that the body had been all but devoured by a desert lion.

Moses was distressed beyond measure, and cried out:

"All-Powerful and All-Knowing One, you convert mud into human beings. Some are carried to paradise, others driven through tortures; one is happy, another in misery. This is the paradox which none can understand."

Then an inner voice spoke to Moses, saying:

"This man had relied upon Us for drink and then turned back from that trust. He relied upon Moses for his sustenance, trusting in an intermediary. His was the fault in asking for help from another after having been content with Us..."

Your heart attaches itself again and again to objects. You have to know how to keep the connection with your origins...

– Ilahi-Nama

Souls Before the Creation of the Body
KNOW ABOUT THE time when there were souls and no bodies.

This was a time of a few years, but each of those years was one of our millennia.

The souls were all arrayed in line. The world was presented to their sight. Nine out of ten of the souls ran toward it.

Then paradise was presented to the remaining souls. Out of these, nine out of ten ran toward it.

Then hell was shown to the remaining souls. Nine out of ten of them ran away from it in horror.

Then there were only a few souls, those who were affected by nothing at all. They had not been attracted by the earth or by paradise, nor had they feared hell.

The Celestial Voice spoke to these survivors, saying:

"Idiot souls, what is it that you want?"

The souls answered in unison:

"You who know all know that it is You whom we desire, and that we do not desire to leave Your Presence."

The voice said to them:

"Desire of Us is perilous, causes hardship and innumerable perils."

The souls answered him:

"We will gladly experience anything for the sake of being with You, and lose everything in order that we may gain everything."

– Ilahi-Nama

The Tree Unaware of its State

A MAN CUT down a tree one day.

A Sufi who saw this taking place said:

"Look at this fresh branch which is full of sap, happy because it does not yet know that it has been cut off.

"Ignorant of the damage which it has suffered it may be – but it will know in due time.

"Meanwhile, you cannot reason with it."

This severance, this ignorance, these are the state of man.

King Mahmud and the Beans

THE MIGHTY KING Mahmud of Ghazna, out hunting one day, was separated from his party. He came upon the smoke of a small fire and rode to the spot, where he found an old woman with a pot.

Mahmud said:

"You have as guest today the monarch. What are you cooking on your fire?"

The crone said:

"This is a bean stew."

The emperor asked her:

"Old lady, will you not give me some?"

"I will not," she said, "for this is only for me. Your kingdom is not worth what these beans are worth. You may want my beans, but I don't want anything you have. My beans are worth a hundred times more than all you have. Look at your enemies, who challenge your possessions in every particular. I am free, and I have my own beans."

The mighty Mahmud looked at the undisputed owner of the beans, thought of his disputed domains, and wept.

The Two Rings

A MAN LOVED two women equally. They asked him to tell them which one was his favorite.

He asked them to wait for a time until his decision should be known.

Then he had two rings made, each exactly resembling the other.

To each of the women, separately, he gave one ring.

Then he called them together and said:
"The one whom I love best is she who has the ring."

This, Too, Will Pass

A POWERFUL KING, ruler of many domains, was in a position of such magnificence that wise men were his mere employees. And yet one day, he felt himself confused and called the sages to him.

He said:

"I do not know the cause, but something impels me to seek a certain ring, one that will enable me to stabilize my state.

"I must have such a ring. And this ring must be one which, when I am unhappy, will make me joyful. At the same time, if I am happy and look upon it, I must be made sad."

The wise men consulted one another, and threw themselves into deep contemplation, and finally they came to a decision as to the character of this ring which would suit their king.

The ring which they devised was one upon which was inscribed the legend:

THIS, TOO, WILL PASS

The King Who Divined his Future

A KING WHO was also an astrologer read in his stars that on a certain day and at a particular hour, a calamity would overtake him.

He therefore built a house of solid rock and posted numerous guardians outside.

One day, when he was within, he realized that he could still see daylight. He found an opening which he filled up, to prevent misfortune entering. In blocking this door he made himself a prisoner with his own hands.

And because of this the king died.

From *The Way of the Sufi*

Ibn El-Arabi

MOHIUDIN IBN EL-ARABI is one of the great Sufis of the Middle Ages whose life and writings are shown nowadays to have deeply penetrated the thought of East and West alike. He was known to the Arabs as Sheikh el-Akbar, "the Greatest Sheikh," and to the Christian West by a direct translation of this title: "Doctor Maximus." He died in the thirteenth century.

Whence Came the Title?

JAFAR THE SON of Yahya of Lisbon determined to find the Sufi "Teacher of the Age," and he traveled to Mecca as a young man to seek him. There he met a mysterious stranger, a man in a green robe, who said to him before any word had been spoken:

"You seek the Greatest Sheikh, Teacher of the Age. But you seek him in the East, when he is in the West. And there is another thing which is incorrect in your seeking."

He sent Jafar back to Andalusia, to find the man he named – Mohiudin, son of el-Arabi, of the tribe of Hatim-Tai. "He is the Greatest Sheikh."

Telling nobody why he sought him, Jafar found
the Tai family in Murcia and inquired for their son.
He found that he had actually been in Lisbon when
Jafar set off on his travels. Finally he traced him to
Seville.

"There," said a cleric, "is Mohiudin." He pointed
to a mere schoolboy, carrying a book on the Traditions, who was at that moment hurrying from a lecture-hall.

Jafar was confused, but stopped the boy and said:
"Who is the Greatest Teacher?"

"I need time to answer that question," said the
other.

"Art thou the *only* Mohiudin, son of el-Arabi, of
the Tribe of Tai?" asked Jafar.

"I am he."

"Then I have no need of thee."

Thirty years later in Aleppo, he found himself
entering the lecture-hall of the Greatest Sheikh,
Mohiudin ibn el-Arabi, of the tribe of Tai. Mohiudin
saw him as he entered, and spoke:

"Now that I am ready to answer the question you
put to me, there is no need to put it at all. Thirty years
ago, Jafar, thou hadst no need of me. Hast thou still
no need of me? The Green One spoke of something
wrong in thy seeking. It was time and place."

Jafar son of Yahya became one of the foremost
disciples of el-Arabi.

The Three Forms of Knowledge
Ibn el-Arabi of Spain instructed his followers in
this most ancient dictum:

There are three forms of knowledge. The first is intellectual knowledge, which is in fact only information and the collection of facts, and the use of these to arrive at further intellectual concepts. This is intellectualism.

Second comes the knowledge of states, which includes both emotional feeling and strange states of being in which man thinks that he has perceived something supreme but cannot avail himself of it. This is emotionalism.

Third comes real knowledge, which is called the Knowledge of Reality. In this form, man can perceive what is right, what is true, beyond the boundaries of thought and sense. Scholastics and scientists concentrate upon the first form of knowledge. Emotionalists and experimentalists use the second form. Others use the two combined, or either one alternately.

But the people who attain to truth are those who know how to connect themselves with the reality which lies beyond both these forms of knowledge. These are the real Sufis, the Dervishes who have Attained.

Truth
SHE HAS CONFUSED all the learned of Islam,
  Everyone who has studied the Psalms,
  Every Jewish Rabbi,
  Every Christian priest.

A Higher Love
THE ORDINARY LOVER adores a secondary phenomenon.

I love the Real.

Attainments of a Teacher

PEOPLE THINK THAT a Sheikh should show miracles and manifest illumination. The requirement in a teacher, however, is only that he should possess all that the disciple needs.

My Heart can take on any Appearance

MY HEART CAN take on any appearance. The heart varies in accordance with variations of the innermost consciousness. It may appear in form as a gazelle meadow, a monkish cloister, an idol-temple, a pilgrim Kaaba, the tablets of the Torah for certain sciences, the bequest of the leaves of the Qur'an.

My duty is the debt of Love. I accept freely and willingly whatever burden is placed upon me. Love is as the love of lovers, except that instead of loving the phenomenon, I love the Essential. That religion, that duty, is mine, and is my faith. A purpose of human love is to demonstrate ultimate, real love. This is the love which is conscious. The other is that which makes man unconscious of himself.

Straying from the Path

WHOEVER STRAYS FROM the Sufi Code will in no way attain to anything worthwhile; even though he acquires a public reputation which resounds to the heavens.

From *The Way of the Sufi*

Saadi of Shiraz

IT IS HARD to find words to approach a description of the achievement of the thirteenth-century classical author Saadi. Western critics are amazed that Saadi could write *The Orchard* (*Bostan*) and *The Rose Garden* (*Gulistan*), the two great classics, in the space of two or three years. These major works, known to every Persian and regarded as supreme accomplishments, contain a richness of material and beauty of poetry which are almost unparalleled. Saadi was a man of no resources, and spent most of his time as a wanderer on the face of the earth. He was instructed by the Sufi masters Gilani and Suhrawardi.

In the case of *The Rose Garden*, Saadi has accomplished the feat (still not attained in any Western language) of writing a book which is so simple in vocabulary and structure that it is used as a first textbook for students of Persian, and appears to contain only moralistic aphorisms and stories, while at the same time it is recognized by the most eminent Sufis as concealing the whole range of the deepest Sufi knowledge which can be committed to writing.

The sense of wonderment at this achievement, when one sees the different levels of material interlocked in this manner, cannot be expressed.

These two books are not only mines of quotations, proverbs and practical wisdom and texts of states of mind, they are written in such a way as to be accepted by the most blinkered of religious bigots.

In this way did Saadi receive, shape and transmit the Sufi lore. His choice of the format of classical literature ensured for all time the preservation and communication of his message; for nobody could ever cut Saadi out of Persian literature, and hence Sufism is protected in this manner.

The following extracts are translated literally, to show how the texts look to the ordinary reader.

Jewels and Dust
IF A GEM falls into mud, it is still valuable.
    If dust ascends to heaven, it remains valueless.

Dominion
DOMINION OF THE world from end to end
    Is worth less than a drip of blood upon the earth.

The Thief and the Blanket
A THIEF ENTERED the house of a Sufi, and found nothing there. As he was leaving, the dervish perceived his disappointment and threw him the blanket in which he was sleeping, so that he should not go away empty-handed.

Learning
NONE LEARNED THE art of archery from me
    Who did not make me, in the end, the target.

The Unshaped One
FOR ONE UNSHAPED one in the community
    The hearts of the Wise will suffer pain –

As if a pool had been filled with rose-water,
And a dog fell in, polluting it.

The Scorpion
A SCORPION WAS asked:
    "Why do you not come out in winter?"
    It said:
    "What treatment do I get in summer, that I should
go out in winter as well?"

    Green wood can be bent;
    When it is dry, it is only straightened by fire.

The Ark
WHEN NOAH IS the captain, what is there to fear?

The Destiny of a Wolf-Cub
THE DESTINY OF a wolf-cub is to become a wolf,
even if it is reared among the sons of men.

The Barren Tree
NO ONE THROWS a stone at a barren tree.

Conceit
HE WHO HAS self-conceit in his head –
    Do not imagine that he will ever hear the truth.

The Straight Path
I HAVE NEVER seen a man lost who was on a straight
path.

Doing Good to the Evil
MERELY DOING GOOD to the evil may be equivalent
to doing evil to the good.

Reward
CHILD, LOOK FOR no reward from A,
   If you are working in the house of B.

The Alternatives
THE SANCTUARY IS in front of you and the thief is
behind you. If you go on, you will win; if you sleep,
you die.

   That building without a firm base: do not build
it high;
   Or, if you do – be afraid.

Asleep and Awake
WHEN A MAN'S sleep is better than his waking –
   It is better that he should die.

The Harvest
YOU WILL KNOW at the harvest
   That laziness is not planting.

The Elephant-Keeper
MAKE NO FRIENDSHIP with an elephant-keeper
   If you have no room to entertain an elephant.

Safety and Riches
DEEP IN THE sea are riches beyond compare.
   But if you seek safety, it is on the shore.

The Fox and the Camels

A FOX WAS seen running away in terror. Someone asked what was troubling it. The fox answered: "They are taking camels for forced labor."

"Fool!" he was told, "the fate of camels has nothing to do with you, who do not even look like one."

"Silence!" said the fox, "for if an intriguer were to state that I was a camel, *who* would work for my release?"

Horse and Camel

THE ARAB HORSE speeds fast. The camel plods slowly, but it goes by day and night.

The Foundation of Tyranny

THE FOUNDATION OF tyranny in the world was trifling at first. Everyone added to it until it attained its present magnitude. For the half-egg that the Sultan considers right to take by force, his troops will put a thousand fowls on the spit.

If you Cannot Stand a Sting

IF YOU CANNOT stand a sting, do not put your finger in a scorpion's nest.

Ambition

TEN DERVISHES CAN sleep beneath one blanket; but two kings cannot reign in one land. A devoted man will eat half his bread, and give the other half to dervishes. A ruler may have a realm, but yet plot to overcome the world.

The Danger of Ecstasy
IF A DERVISH remained in a state of ecstasy,
   He would be fragmented in both worlds.

The Dervish and the Camel Rider
WHEN WE WERE heading for southern Arabia, a
barefooted and bareheaded dervish joined our
caravan at Kufa (in the north).

I saw that he was penniless, but he strode along
purposefully, reciting as he walked:

> Neither do I burden a camel
> Nor do I carry a camel's burden;
> Neither do I rule, nor am I ruled.
> Neither have I anxieties about the
> Past, the Present or the Future.
> Fully I breathe, fully I live life.

A certain merchant, mounted on a camel,
advised him to turn back. Otherwise, he said, the
dervish would certainly die of hardship and lack of
nourishment.

Ignoring this advice, the dervish marched on.

When we reached Beni Hamud oasis, the merchant
died. The dervish, standing by the bier, exclaimed:

> I did not die of my hardships;
> But you, on your camel, have died.

Fools burn lamps during the day. At night they
wonder why they have no light.

The Sick Man
THROUGHOUT THE LONG night a man wept
  At the bedside of a sick man.
  When day dawned the visitor was dead –
  And the patient was alive.

The Dervish in Hell
ONE NIGHT A king dreamed that he saw a king in paradise and a dervish in hell.

The dreamer exclaimed: "What is the meaning of this? I should have thought that the positions would be reversed."

A voice answered: "The king is in heaven because he respected dervishes. The dervish is in hell because he compromised with kings."

Heedless Man
WHOEVER GIVES ADVICE to a heedless man is himself in need of advice.

The Poor Man's Yoghurt
IF A POOR man brings you a gift of yoghurt, he will have bought it at such a price that it will be two parts water to one of real yoghurt.

The Road
I FEAR THAT you will not reach Mecca, O Nomad!

For the road which you are following leads to Turkestan!

Prayer of Saadi
DO TO ME what is worthy of Thee,
   And not what is worthy of me.

> – Saadi, *Gulistan*
> From *The Way of the Sufi*

Hakim Jami

JAMI (1414–92) WAS a genius and knew it, which made ecclesiastics and literary men of his time acutely uncomfortable, since the convention was that no man was great unless he appeared intensely humble. In his *Alexandrian Book of Wisdom*, Jami shows that the Sufi esoteric transmission link of the Asian Khajagan ("Masters") was the same as that used by Western mystical writers. He cites as teachers in the Sufi transmission such names as Plato, Hippocrates, Pythagoras and Hermes Trismegistos.

Jami was a disciple of Sadedin Kashgari, the chief of the Naqshbandis, whom he succeeded in the direction of the Herat area of Afghanistan. His higher allegiance was to Khaja Obaidullah Ahrar, General of the Order.

One of Jami's succinct sayings illustrates the problem of all Sufi teachers who refuse to accept students on their own valuation of themselves:

"Seekers there are in plenty: but they are almost all seekers of personal advantage. I can find so very few Seekers after Truth."

Nor was this his only concern. Certain religious enthusiasts in Baghdad, trying to discredit him, misquoted a passage from his *Chain of Gold*, and created a rumpus which was only stilled after a ridiculous and trivial debate in public. Most of all Jami lamented that such things could happen at all in the community called human.

Jami's writings and teachings in the end made him so celebrated that contemporary monarchs, from the Sultan of Turkey downward, were constantly irritating him with offers of enormous amounts of gold and other presents, and appeals to adorn their courts. His acclaim by the public annoyed him, too, to the mystification of the populace, who could not understand that he wanted them not to adopt him as a hero but to do something about themselves.

He never tired of pointing out that many people who tried to overcome pride were doing so because in this way they would be able to inflate themselves with such a victory.

Luxuriant Growth

IF THE SCISSORS are not used daily on the beard, it will not be long before the beard is, by its luxuriant growth, pretending to be the head.

Unity

LOVE BECOMES PERFECT only when it transcends itself –

Becoming One with its object;
Producing Unity of Being.

The Prayer and the Nose

I SAW A man prostrating himself in prayer, and exclaimed:

"You lay the burden of your nose upon the ground on the excuse that it is a requirement of prayer."

Love

ORDINARY HUMAN LOVE is capable of raising man to the experiences of real love.

The Beggar

A BEGGAR WENT to a door, asking for something to be given to him. The owner answered, and said: "I am sorry, but there is nobody in."

"I don't want anybody," said the beggar. "I want food."

Pride

DO NOT BOAST that you have no pride because it is less visible than an ant's foot on a black stone in a dark night.

And do not think that bringing it out from within is easy, for it is easier to extract a mountain from the earth with a needle.

What shall we Do?

THE ROSE HAS gone from the garden; what shall we do with the thorns?

The Shah is not in the city; what shall we do with his court?

The fair are cages, beauty and goodness the bird;

When the bird has flown, what shall we do with the cage?

The State
JUSTICE AND FAIRNESS, not religion or atheism,
Are needful for the protection of the State.

The Heaviest Wave
BEFORE NUSHIRVAN THE Just wise sages discussed the heaviest wave in this deep of sorrow.
One of them said that it was illness and suffering;
Another that it was old age and poverty;
A third that it was approaching death with lack of work.
And in the end this one was accepted.

From *The Way of the Sufi*

Hakim Sanai

THE MASTER SANAI lived during the eleventh and twelfth centuries, and is reckoned as the earliest Afghan teacher to use the love-motif in Sufism. Rumi acknowledged him as one of his inspirations.

Attempts were made by religious fanatics to brand him an apostate from Islam, but they did not succeed. Characteristically, his words have regularly been employed since then by the spiritual descendants of these narrow clerics to bolster their own pretensions. By a quite familiar process, when Sufi terminology and organization had been adopted by religious enthusiasts to the extent that the distinction between the Sufis and these superficialists had been blurred, the fanatics tried more than once to claim that Sanai was not a Sufi at all. The reason for this was that his thoughts could not be easily reconciled with narrow religiosity.

The Walled Garden of Truth, one of Sanai's most important works, is composed in such a manner as to give several readings for many passages. This effects a shift in the perceptions which is analogous to a change of focus on one and the same object. If one series of interpretation methods is used with this book, a most interesting framework of instructional material, almost a system, is revealed.

Sanai is also known for his *Parliament of the Birds*, which is on the surface an allegory of the human quest for higher enlightenment. His *Dervish Songs* represents the lyrical presentation of Sufi experience.

The Sealed Book
THE HUMAN'S PROGRESS is that of one who has been given a sealed book, written before he was born. He carries it inside himself until he "dies." While man is subject to the movement of Time, he does not know the contents of that sealed book.

Levels of Truth
WHAT APPEARS TO be truth is a worldly distortion of objective truth.

The Infant
MAN DOES NOT notice that he is like an infant in the hands of a nurse. Sometimes he is happy, sometimes sad, at what happens to him. The nurse sometimes chides the child, sometimes soothes him. At times she spanks him, at others shares his sorrow. The superficial person, the stranger passing by, may think that the nurse is unmindful of the child. How can he know that this is the way in which she must behave?

From *The Way of the Sufi*

Seeing Double
A FATHER SAID to his double-seeing son:
"Son, you see two instead of one."
"How can that be?" the boy replied. "If I were, there would seem to be *four* moons up there in place of two."

From *Caravan of Dreams*

Jalaludin Rumi
RUMI'S MAJOR WORK, generally considered to be one of the world's greatest books, is his *Mathnavi-i-Maanavi* (*Couplets of Inner Meaning*). His table-talk (*Fihi Ma Fihi*), letters (*Maktubat*), *Diwan* and the hagiography *Munaqib el-Arifin*, all contain important parts of his teachings.

The following selections, from all of these sources, are meditation-themes which can be taken as aphorisms and declarations of dogma, or as pieces of sage advice. Their Sufic usage, however, goes far beyond this. Rumi, like other Sufi authors, plants his teachings within a framework which as effectively screens its inner meaning as displays it. This technique fulfills the functions of preventing those who are incapable of using the material on a higher level from experimenting effectively with it; allowing those who want poetry to select poetry; giving entertainment to people who want stories; stimulating the intellect in those who prize such experiences.

One of the most revealing of his sentences is the title of his table-talk: "In it what is in it?" ("You get out of it what is in it for you").

Rumi had the uncomfortable Sufi habit of excelling in literary and poetic ability beyond all his contemporaries, while constantly affirming that such an attainment was a minor one compared with Sufihood.

How Far you have Come!

ORIGINALLY, YOU WERE clay. From being mineral, you became vegetable. From vegetable, you became animal, and from animal, man. During these periods man did not know where he was going, but he was being taken on a long journey nonetheless. And you have to go through a hundred different worlds yet.

The Way

THE WAY HAS been marked out.

If you depart from it, you will perish.

If you try to interfere with the signs on the road, you will be an evil-doer.

The Owls and the King's Hawk

A ROYAL HAWK alighted for a time on the wall of a ruin inhabited by owls. The owls feared him. He said: "This may seem a prosperous place to you, but my place is upon the wrist of a king."

Some of the owls shouted to the others: "Do not believe him! He is using guile to steal our home."

Another Dimension

THE HIDDEN WORLD has its clouds and rain, but of a different kind.

Its sky and sunshine are of a different kind.

This is made apparent only to the refined ones – those not deceived by the seeming completeness of the ordinary world.

Profiting by Experience

EXALTED TRUTH IMPOSES upon us
Heat and cold, grief and pain,
Terror and weakness of wealth and body
Together, so that the coin of our innermost being
Becomes evident.

Those Who Know, Cannot Tell

WHENEVER THE SECRETS of Perception are taught to anyone, His lips are sewn against speaking of the Consciousness.

Joha and Death
A BOY WAS crying and shouting before his father's coffin, saying:

"Father! They are taking you to a place where nothing covers the floors. There is no light, no food; no door nor helpful neighbor..."

Joha, alarmed since the description seemed to fit, called out to his own father:

"Respected Parent, by Allah, they are taking him to *our* house!"

Intelligence and Real Perception
INTELLIGENCE IS THE shadow of objective Truth.

How can the shadow vie with sunshine?

True Reality
OF THIS THERE is no academic proof in the world;
For it is hidden, and hidden, and hidden.

Detachment Brings Perception
O HEART! UNTIL, in this prison of deception, you can see the difference between This and That,

For an instant detach from this Well of Tyranny; stand outside.

Two Reeds
TWO REEDS DRINK from one stream. One is hollow, the other is sugarcane.

Truth
THE PROPHET SAID that Truth has declared:

"I am not hidden in what is high or low

Nor in the earth nor skies nor throne.
This is certainty, O beloved:
I am hidden in the heart of the faithful.
If you seek me, seek in these hearts."

Dust on the Mirror
LIFE/SOUL IS LIKE a clear mirror; the body is dust
on it.
Beauty in us is not perceived, for we are under
the dust.

How long shall we, in the Earth-world, like
children
Fill our laps with dust and stones and scraps?
Let us leave earth and fly to the heavens,
Let us leave babyhood and go to the assembly of
Man.

The House
IF TEN MEN want to enter a house, and only nine find
their way in, the tenth must not say: "This is what
God ordained."
He must find out what his own shortcoming was.

Owls
ONLY SWEET-VOICED BIRDS are imprisoned.
Owls are not kept in cages.

Efforts
TIE TWO BIRDS together.
They will not be able to fly, even though they now
have four wings.

This Task
YOU HAVE A duty to perform. Do anything else, do
any number of things, occupy your time fully, and
yet, if you do not do this task, all your time will have
been wasted.

The Community of Love
THE PEOPLE OF Love are hidden within the populace;
    Like a good man surrounded by the bad.

A Book
THE AIM OF a book may be to instruct,
    Yet you can also use it as a pillow;
    Although its object is to give knowledge, direction,
profit.

Epitaph of Jalaludin Rumi
WHEN WE ARE dead, seek not our tomb in the earth,
but find it in the hearts of men.

From *The Way of the Sufi*

NEW ORGANS OF perception come into being as a
result of necessity.
    Therefore, O man, increase your necessity, so that
you may increase your perception.

From *Tales of the Dervishes*

8

Methods of the Masters

IT MAY BE *said*: "They came in vain."
Let it not *be* that they came in vain.

We leave this, the bequest, to you:
We finished what we could, we left the rest to you.

Remember, this is work entrusted –
Remember, beloved, we shall meet again.

– Dervish Song
From *Wisdom of the Idiots*

IDRIES SHAH MAINTAINED *that, unlike other branches of study, Sufi learning may not be carried out anywhere, anytime... it needs the right combination of time, place and people.*

Moreover, he said, beyond a certain point, Sufi learning requires a teacher; somebody qualified and not a self-appointed one.

However, he believed that written materials had an invaluable role in familiarizing the student with the characteristics of Sufi thought. He delved into archives and oral histories to translate the practical methods and doings of Sufi teachers through history.

In the excerpts that follow, Sufis approach things in a way nobody else would. Yet, as if seeing by a light invisible to other eyes, they are generally vindicated by events. Apparent also are the humor and common sense of Sufi practitioners from whom, he said, Sufism, could be "caught" as well as taught.

Editor's note

The Plant

AT THE ENTRANCE to the house of Abdul-Qadir Gilani was one day to be seen a flower in a pot. Beside it was a notice: "Smell this and guess what it is."

Each person who entered was given writing materials, and was invited to write the answer, if he wished, to the conundrum.

At the end of the day, Abdul-Qadir handed a box containing the answers to a disciple. He said:

"Everyone who has answered 'A rose' may remain if he desires, to proceed with the teaching. Anyone who has written nothing, or anything other than 'A rose,' is dismissed."

Someone asked: "Is it necessary to resort to superficial methods to judge fitness for discipleship?"

The great teacher answered: "I know the answers, but I wish to demonstrate for all the others that superficial manifestations signal interior character." And he thereupon handed the company a list. This contained, although he had not seen the answers of the entrants, a list of the names of each one who had written "A rose."

This illustrates one meaning of the phrase: "The obvious is the link to the True." What Abdul-Qadir saw inwardly could be shown outwardly as well. In this way, and for this reason, is a certain kind of conduct expected of disciples.

From *The Way of the Sufi*

Muhammad Shah, Murshid of Turkestan

MUHAMMAD SHAH, MURSHID ("Guide") of Turkestan, was a nineteenth-century teacher who took his examples from the "juice" (real inner content) of ordinary actions and life. This is a typical account of his methods.

MUHAMMAD SHAH TOOK a group of his Halka ("circle") to see certain sights. One was a tall minaret set beside a river. "This was built by people who persevere," he said.

Then he took them to see a party of Brahmin pilgrims walking to the holy Jumna river. "These are people who persevere," he said. On another day, he took his people to watch a caravan which had come through the desert wastes of China. "These are people who persevere," he said. Finally, he bade them go to Tibet to watch pilgrims measuring their length along the ground, making a holy journey. "Those were people who persevere," he told them when they returned.

After some months, he made them watch magistrates trying cases, to observe the efforts of the magistrate, the energy of the witnesses, the aspirations of the plaintiffs, the efforts of the accused. "In all of these things you see men and women persevering," he said.

"Men everywhere persevere. The yield of this perseverance is what is of account. This they can harvest and use. If, on the other hand, during the perseverance, they become beguiled by the thing for which they persevere, they cannot make use of the training of the struggle of perseverance. All that happens to them is that they become trained in persevering after something."

From *The Way of the Sufi*

Stained

IT IS RELATED that a man went to the assembly of the master Baqi-Billah of Delhi and said:

"I have been reading the famous verse of the Master Hafiz, 'If your teacher bids you stain your prayer-carpet with wine, obey him,' but I have a difficulty."

Baqi-Billah said:

"Dwell apart from me for some time and I shall illustrate the matter for you."

After a considerable period of time, the disciple received a letter from the sage. It said: "Take all the money you have and give it to the gatekeeper of any brothel."

The disciple was shocked, and for a time thought that the master must be a fraud. After wrestling with himself for days, however, he went to the nearest house of ill-fame and presented the man at the door with all the money which he had.

"For such a sum of money," said the doorman, "I shall allot you the choicest gem of our collection, an untouched woman."

As soon as he entered the room, the woman there said:

"I have been tricked into being in this house, and am held here by force and threats. If your sense of justice is stronger than your reason for coming here, help me to escape."

Then the disciple knew the meaning of the poem of Hafiz, "If your teacher bids you stain your prayer-carpet with wine, obey him."

From *Wisdom of the Idiots*

Hariri The Good Man

HARIRI ALWAYS TRIED to behave in as exemplary a manner as possible. He acquired such a reputation for correct conduct that a certain merchant who had to go on a journey chose him as the obvious person with whom to entrust the welfare of his beautiful slave-girl.

But Hariri developed a passion for the girl. He went to Haddad, his Sufi preceptor, and asked for his advice. Haddad said:

"Go to Yusuf, son of Hussain."

When Hariri approached the place where Yusuf was to be found, people said:

"Do not go near the Son of Hussain, pious man, for he has a bad reputation, is a heretic and a wine-drinker."

Not believing this, Hariri arrived at Yusuf's door, where he saw, sure enough, Yusuf was sitting with a young boy and a flask of wine.

Hariri at once said to Yusuf:

"What is the meaning of this behavior?"

Yusuf said, reading his thoughts:

"I behave like this in appearance, because it prevents people entrusting their beautiful slaves to my keeping."

From *Thinkers of the East*

Choosing

"CHOOSING" (ISTIFA) is the emptying of the heart of all things other than the search for completion. This resembles a visualization that the body is empty, and that all thoughts have left it for a moment, during which time the true thoughts flood in.

– Hujwiri
From *The Way of the Sufi*

Iskandar of Balkh

HIS SON ASKED Iskandar of Balkh on his deathbed:

"What is the source of your power, your wealth and your miracles?"

His father murmured:

"If I were to tell you, it would cut you off from contact with this source, so I cannot tell you where it is, only what it is."

He continued:

"Our lifeline is the Sufi Way, and we are strangers as it were among savages on this earth, but now I go to join our own."

His son said:

"Why did you not tell everyone this during your life? For this example of yours, which will live a thousand years, would cause men to enter the Sufi Way in throngs, and would give them the blessings of the Elect."

Iskandar sighed and said:

"The greed to possess a secret would make most of them attracted, and the desire for more than others have got. My son, I taught abstemiousness all my life in the hope that it would still the covetousness which destroys man, even if he covets goodness."

"Then what shall I do?" asked his son.

"You shall desire Truth for its own sake, and nothing for your own sake."

"But how shall I know whether I am desiring something for myself and not for itself?"

"You shall become aware, through daily practice, that what you imagine to be yourself is concocted from beliefs put into you by others, and is not yourself at all. You shall seek the Teacher of the Age until you find him. And if you fail to recognize the Leader of the Epoch, it will be because you inwardly reject him, not because he is not evident as what he is."

This is the testimony of the great Sufi Suleiman Najami, the son of Iskandar of Balkh. Giving it to his own son, he said:

"In a long life, I cannot say that I have learned more than this, my father's bequest of wisdom to me. I do therefore offer it to you."

From *Thinkers of the East*

The Sanctuary of John the Baptist

SAADI, THE SUFI author of the Persian classic *The Rose Garden*, writes of a visit to the burial-place of John the Baptist, in Syria.

He arrived there one day, exhausted and footsore. But then, as he was feeling sorry for himself, he saw a man who was not only tired, but had no feet. Saadi gave thanks to God that he, at least, had feet.

This story, on the obvious level, means "be grateful for small mercies." Its teaching on that level is found in all cultures. It is useful to help one to find a greater perspective in his situation if he is suffering from disabling self-pity.

The employment of such tales for emotional purposes – to switch the mental attitude, even to make a person content with and perhaps momentarily grateful for, his lot – is characteristic of the conventional type of instruction.

Modern sophisticates say: "All that Saadi did was to inculcate so-called moral virtues – his work is outmoded." Traditional, crude sentimentalists may say: "How beautiful to dwell on the misery of others and one's own comparative good luck."

But Saadi, being a Sufi, included in his writings materials which had more than one possible function. This tale is one of them.

In Sufi schools the piece is treated for what it is – an exercise. The student may benefit from whatever "uplifting" moral may be the conventional interpretation. But, without introspection but with self-observation he should be able to say: "I realize that changes in my mood are dependent on emotional stimuli. Do I always have to be dependent upon 'seeing a man with no feet,' or reading about it, before I realize that 'I have feet'? How much of my life is being wasted while I wait for someone to tell me what to do, or something to happen which will change my condition and frame of mind?"

According to the Sufis, man has better, more reliable, inner sense and capacities for educating them than constant emotional stimulus.

The object of the Sufi interpretation of this lesson would be nullified if it caused people to start an orgy of self-questioning of an emotional kind.

The purpose of pointing out this Sufi usage of the narrative is for it to be registered in the mind, so that the student may in future notice a higher form of assessment of his situation, when it begins to operate in him.

From *Wisdom of the Idiots*

The People Who Attain

IMAM EL-GHAZALI RELATES a tradition from the life of Isa, ibn Maryam.

Isa one day saw some people sitting miserably on a wall, by the roadside.

He asked: "What is your affliction?"

They said: "We have become like this through our fear of hell."

He went on his way, and saw a number of people grouped disconsolately in various postures by the wayside. He said: "What is your affliction?" They said: "Desire for Paradise has made us like this."

He went on his way, until he came to a third group of people. They looked like people who had endured much, but their faces shone with joy.

Isa asked them: "What has made you like this?"

They answered: "The Spirit of Truth. We have seen Reality, and this has made us oblivious of lesser goals."

Isa said: "These are the people who attain. On the Day of Accounting, these are they who will be in the Presence of God."

From *Tales of the Dervishes*

Instrumental

Q: WHAT ARE *the roles of rituals and beliefs and studies for the Sufi?*

A: To be a Sufi and to study the Way is to have a certain attitude. This attitude is produced by the effect of Sufi teachers, who exercise the instrumental function in relation to the Seeker. Rituals and beliefs, and studies, can only have an instrumental effect suitable for Sufi progress when they are correctly used, and by people who are not affected by them in the customary manner.

This has all been very clearly laid down by Abul' Hasan Nuri, over a thousand years ago:

"A Sufi," he says, "is one who is not bound by anything nor does he bind anything." This means that he does what he does from free choice and not from compulsion or conditioning. Equally, he is not attached to things and does not bind others to him. Nuri continues: "Sufism is not a doctrine or worldly knowledge. If it were ceremonial, this would have to be practiced (regularly). If it were ordinary learning, it would have to be taught by formal methods. In fact, it is a matter of disposition."

This disposition is the "attitude" which I have mentioned, which is attained by the instrumental function, not by attachment or rituals.[3]

From *Seeker After Truth*

Money

UWAIS EL-QARNI WAS offered some money. He said:

"I do not need it, as I already have a coin."

The other said:

"How long will that last you – it is nothing."

---

3   Quoted by Fariduddin Attar in his *Memorials of the Saints*.

Uwais answered:

"Guarantee me that I shall live longer than this sum will suffice me, and I will accept your gift."

From *The Way of the Sufi*

Inner Senses

A CERTAIN SUFI was asked:

"Why is it that people have no inner senses?"

He said:

"O man of high promise! If they had *no* inner senses, they would not even appear to be people at all. When people lack inner sense, they behave in a completely destructive or totally passive manner. Being *aware* of an inner sense is another matter."

From *The Magic Monastery*

Ghulam Haidar of Kashmir

HEARING A DISCUSSION among his disciples about the importance of meticulous observance of the religious law as a means to illumination, Ghulam Haidar gave orders that, on any pretext, the following were to be collected and brought before him:

One Jew, one Christian, one Zoroastrian, one Hindu priest, one Sikh, one Buddhist, one Farangi ("Frank" or Christian), one Shiah, one Sunni, one pagan, and several others. The last included traders, workmen, farmers, clerics and clerks, a baker and various women of all types.

For three years his adherents worked to collect these people in one place at one time, not telling them that their presence was required by their master. In order to do this they spread rumors of treasure in Kashmir, became merchants, sent to distant places for tutors and servants. At last all were assembled. When he was informed that they were there, Ghulam Haidar instructed that they were all to be invited to a meal at his Hall of Teaching, the Zawiya.

When all had eaten, the Pir (Ghulam Haidar) addressed the company, of whom a very large proportion were those strangers who did not adhere to his doctrine. Also present were all the disciples, who had been told to take no part in the proceedings except to watch.

The Pir spoke in several languages, explaining the need for man to dedicate himself to effort, and to master the mysteries which were his birthright, regardless of his prejudices.

Without exception the strangers were desirous of following the Pir, and their mutual enmity vanished. It is from this company that sprang the teachers known as the "Loaves of Bread": those whose "dough had been fashioned by the Kashmiri Pir," regardless of their basic prejudices.

From *The Way of the Sufi*

Food and Pens

ONCE UPON A time – and this is a true story – there was a student. He used to go every day to sit at the feet of a Sufi teacher, to take down on paper what the master said.

Because he was so fully occupied with his studies, he was unable to follow any gainful occupation. One evening when he arrived home, his wife placed a bowl before him, covered with a napkin.

He took the cloth and put it around his neck, and then he saw that the dish was full of – pens and paper.

"Since this is what you do all day," she said, "just try to eat it."

The next morning, the student went, as usual, to learn from his teacher. Although his wife's words had distressed him, he continued to follow the accustomed pattern of his studies, and did not go out looking for a job.

After a few minutes' writing, he found that his pen was not working well. "Never mind," said the master, "go into that corner and bring the box you will find there and put it in front of you."

When he sat down with the box and opened its lid, he found that it was full of – food.

From *Wisdom of the Idiots*

The Time, the Place and the People

IN ANCIENT TIMES there was a king who called a dervish to him and said:

"The dervish Path, through a succession of masters reaching back in unbroken succession to the earliest days of man, has always provided the light which has been the motivating cause of the very values of which my kingship is no more than a wan reflection."

The dervish answered: "It is so."

"Now," said the king, "since I am so enlightened as to know the foregoing facts, eager and willing to learn the truths which you, in your superior wisdom, can make available – teach me!"

"Is that a command or a request?" asked the dervish.

"It is whatever you make of it," said the king, "for if it will work as a command, I shall learn. If it operates successfully as a request, I shall learn."

And he waited for the dervish to speak.

Many minutes passed, and at length the dervish lifted his head from the attitude of contemplation and said:

"You must await the 'moment of transmission.'"

This confused the king, for, after all, if he wanted to learn, he felt he had a right to be told, or shown, something or other.

The dervish left the court.

After that, day after day, the dervish continued to attend upon the king. Day in and day out, the affairs of state were transacted, the kingdom passed through times of joy and trial, the counselors of state gave their advice, the wheel of heaven revolved.

"The dervish comes here every day," thought the king, each time he caught sight of the figure in the patched cloak, "and yet he never refers to our conversation about learning. True, he takes part in many of the activities of the Court; he talks and he laughs, he eats and he, no doubt, sleeps. Is he waiting for a sign of some kind?" But, try as he might, the king was unable to plumb the depths of this mystery.

At length, when the appropriate wave of the unseen lapped upon the shore of possibility, a conversation was taking place at court. Someone was saying: "Daud of Sahil is the greatest singer in the world."

And the king, although ordinarily this sort of statement did not move him, conceived a powerful desire to hear this singer.

"Have him brought before me," he commanded.

The master of ceremonies was sent to the singer's house, but Daud, monarch among singers, merely replied: "This king of yours knows little of the requirements of singing. If he wants me just to look at my face, I will come. But if he wants to hear me sing, he will have to wait, like everyone else, until I am in the right mood to do so. It is knowing when to perform and when not which has made me, as it would make any ass which knew the secret, into a great singer."

When this message was taken to the king, he alternated between wrath and desire, and called out: "Is there nobody here who will force this man to sing for me? For, if he sings only when the mood takes him, I, for my part, want to hear him while I still want to hear him."

It was then that the dervish stepped forward and said:

"Peacock of the age, come with me to visit this singer."

The courtiers nudged one another. Some thought that the dervish had been playing a deep game, and was now gambling upon making the singer perform. If he succeeded, the king would surely reward him. But they remained silent, for they feared a possible challenge.

Without a word the king stood up and commanded a poor garment to be brought. Putting it on, he followed the dervish into the street.

The disguised king and his guide soon found themselves at the singer's house. When they knocked, Daud called down:

"I am not singing today, so go away and leave me in peace."

At this the dervish, seating himself upon the ground, began to sing. He sang Daud's favorite piece, and he sang it right through, from beginning to end.

The king, who was no great connoisseur, was very much moved by the song, and his attention was diverted to the sweetness of the dervish's voice. He did not know that the dervish had sung the song slightly off-key deliberately, in order to awaken a desire to correct it in the heart of the master-singer.

"Please, please, do sing it again," begged the king, "for I have never heard such a sweet melody."

But at that moment Daud himself began to sing. At the very first notes the dervish and the king were as men transfixed, and their attention was riveted to the notes as they flowed faultlessly from the throat of the nightingale of Sahil.

When the song was finished, the king sent a lavish present to Daud. To the dervish he said: "Man of Wisdom! I admire your skill in provoking the Nightingale to perform, and I would like to make you an adviser at the court."

But the dervish simply said: "Majesty, you can hear the song you wish only if there is a singer, if you are present, and if there is someone to form the channel for the performance of the song. As it is with master-singers and kings, so it is with dervishes and their students. The time, the place, the people and the skills."

From *Tales of the Dervishes*

The King and the Woodcutter

AHMAD SHAH WAS crowned King with a wreath by a certain dervish, respected by all. From that time on, he often wore the dervish mantle, and roamed among his subjects, seeking to improve the quality of his rule.

One day he visited, in this disguise, a woodcutter, living in a forest shack. "What would you do if you could not sell your wood?" he asked. "Respected Dervish," said the woodcutter, "I would trust in God and find something."

The next day the king had it proclaimed that no woodcutters were to be allowed into the city, and a day or two later visited the man again, in his disguise.

"How are you living, now that the King has taken such a strange attitude toward woodcutters?" he asked.

"Well, now I make leather belts and sell them to the shops. Trusting in God, I have enough to eat."

The king left him and sometime later issued an edict that no item of leather was to be sold in the shops.

When Ahmad Shah visited his poor woodcutter-leather-belt-maker again, he said: "How are you getting on, now that Fate seems to be pursuing you and has stopped your new career?"

"Sir," said the other man, "I trust in God and work as a market porter. All is well, and I have enough to eat."

Ahmad Shah now caused all market porters to be conscripted into the Palace Guard, without any pay, and not even to be given anywhere to sleep.

That night the king went in his dervish cloak to see his friend, and found him in his hut, eating some food and whittling wood.

"What are you doing?" asked the king. "I have been taken into the Royal Guard, but without food or anywhere to sleep," said the man; "so I have pawned the sword they issued me, bought the necessary food, and I am making a dummy sword until my future shall further be known."

The king went back to his palace.

The following morning, the Commander of the Guard called the woodcutter and ordered him to behead a prisoner. They walked together to the place of execution, where the king, as was the custom, was waiting. The woodcutter did not recognize the king in his crown and royal robes, but saying "Trusting in God," he drew his wooden sword and awaited the order to strike. The prisoner said: "In the Name of God, may this sword refuse to cut – for I am innocent!" The woodcutter dropped his sword on the ground. After an investigation the condemned man was found to be innocent after all. Ahmad Shah was so impressed that he made this man his Grand Vizier. From that time the Afghan kings always used before their names "Al Mutawakkil ala Allah" – he who trusts in God.

From *Learning How to Learn*

The King who Decided to be Generous

THERE WAS A king of Iran who said to a dervish: "Tell me a story."

The dervish said: "Your Majesty, I will tell you the tale of Hatim Tai, the Arabian King and the most generous man of all time; for if you could be like him, you would indeed be the greatest king alive."

"Speak on," said the king, "but if you do not please me, having cast aspersions upon my generosity, you will lose your head." He talked in this way because in Persia it is customary for those at Court to tell the monarch that he already has the most excellent qualities of anyone in the world – past, present or future.

"To continue," said the dervish, in the manner of dervishes (for they are not easily discountenanced), "Hatim Tai's generosity excelled, in letter and spirit, that of all other men." And this is the story which the dervish told.

Another Arabian king coveted the possessions, the villages and oases, the camels and the fighting-men of Hatim Tai. So this man declared war upon Hatim, sending him a messenger with the declaration of war: "Yield to me, otherwise I shall surely overrun you and your lands, and possess myself of your sovereignty."

When this message reached Hatim's court, his advisers at once suggested that he mobilize the warriors in defense of his realm saying: "There is surely not an able-bodied man or woman among your followers who will not gladly lay down his life in defense of our beloved king."

But Hatim, contrary to the expectation of the people, said:

"No, instead of your riding forth and shedding your blood for me, I shall flee. It would be far from the path of generosity if I were to become the cause of the sacrifice of a life of a single man or woman. If you yield peaceably, this king will content himself with taking only your services and rents, and you will have suffered no material loss. If, on the other hand, you resist, by the conventions of war he will be entitled to regard your possessions as booty, and if you lose the war you will be penniless."

So saying, Hatim took only a stout staff and went into the nearby mountains, where he found a cave and sank himself in contemplation.

Half of the people were deeply affected by this sacrifice of his wealth and position by Hatim Tai on their behalf. But others, especially those who sought to make a name for themselves on the field of valor, muttered: "How do we know that this man is not a simple coward?" And others, who had little courage, muttered against him saying: "He has, in a sense, saved himself; for he has abandoned us to a fate which is unknown to us. Perhaps we may become the slaves of this unknown king who is, after all, enough of a tyrant to declare war upon his neighbors."

Others again, uncertain as to what to believe, remained silent, until they should have some means of making up their minds.

And so it was that the tyrant king, accompanied by his glittering hosts, took possession of Hatim Tai's domain. He did not increase the taxes, he did not usurp for himself more than Hatim had taken from the people in exchange for being their protector and administrator of justice. But one thing disturbed him. It was the fact that he heard whispers that, although he had possessed himself of a new realm, yet it had been yielded up to him as an act of generosity by Hatim Tai. These were the words spoken by some of the people.

"I cannot be real master of this land," declared the tyrant, "until I have captured Hatim Tai himself. While he lives, there is still a loyalty toward him in the hearts of some of these people. This means that they are not completely my subjects, even though they behave outwardly as such."

So he published an edict that whoever should bring him Hatim Tai would be rewarded with five thousand pieces of gold. Hatim Tai knew nothing of this until one day, he was sitting outside his cave and he heard a conversation between a woodcutter and his wife.

The woodcutter said: "My dear wife, I am now old and you are much younger than I. We have small children, and in the natural order of events, I may be expected to die before you and while the children are youngsters. If we could only find and capture Hatim Tai, for whom there is a reward of five thousand pieces of gold from the new king, your future would be secure."

"Shame on you!" said his wife. "Better that you should die, and that I and our children should starve, than that our hands should be stained with the blood of the most generous man of all time, who sacrificed all for our sake."

"That is all very well," said the old man, "but a man has to think of his own interests. I have, after all, responsibilities. And, in any case, every day more and more people believe that Hatim is a coward. It will only be a matter of time before they have searched every possible piece of cover for him."

"The belief in Hatim's cowardice is fueled by love of gold. Much more of this kind of talk and Hatim will have lived in vain."

At that moment Hatim Tai stood up and revealed himself to the astonished pair. "I am Hatim Tai," he said. "Take me to the new king and claim your reward."

The old man was ashamed, and his eyes filled with tears. "No, great Hatim," he said, "I cannot bring myself to do it."

While they were arguing, a number of people, who had been searching for the fugitive king, gathered around.

"Unless you do so," said Hatim, "I will surrender myself to the king and tell him that you have been hiding me. In that case, you will be executed for treason."

Realizing that this was Hatim, the mob moved forward, seized their former king, and carried him to the tyrant, with the woodcutter following miserably behind.

When they got to the court, each claimed that he had himself captured Hatim. The former king, seeing irresolution on the face of his successor, asked to be allowed to speak: "Know, O King, that my evidence should also be heard. I was captured by this old woodcutter and not by yonder mob. Give him, therefore, his reward, and do what you will with me..."

At this the woodcutter stepped forward and told the king the truth about Hatim's having offered himself as a sacrifice for the future security of his family.

The new king was so overwhelmed by this story that he ordered his army to withdraw, placed Hatim Tai back on his throne, and retired to his own country.

When he had heard this story, the king of Iran, forgetting his threat against the dervish, said: "An excellent tale, O dervish, and one from which we can benefit. You, at any rate, cannot benefit, having abandoned already your expectations of this life and being possessed of nothing. But I, I am a king. And I am rich. Arab kings, people who live on boiled lizards, cannot match a Persian when it comes to real generosity. An idea strikes me! Let us to work!"

Taking the dervish with him, the king of Iran summoned his greatest architects to a large open space and ordered them to design and build an immense palace. It was to be composed of a central strongroom and forty windows.

When it was completed, the king caused every available means of transport to be assembled and the palace to be filled with pieces of gold. After months of this activity, a proclamation went forth:

"Lo, the King of Kings, Fountain of Generosity, has ordained that a palace with forty windows be constructed. He will personally, every day, dispense gold to all needy people, from these windows."

Not unnaturally, large crowds of necessitous ones collected and the king handed out one gold piece to every applicant, appearing at one window each day. Then he noticed that there was a certain dervish who presented himself every day at the window, took his piece of gold and went away. At first the king thought: "Perhaps he wants to carry the gold to someone who is in need." Then, when he saw the man again, he thought: "Perhaps he is applying the dervish rule of secret charity, and redistributes the gold." And every day when he saw the dervish, he excused him in his own mind, until the fortieth day when the king found that his patience could not endure further. Seizing the hand of the dervish, he said: "Ungrateful wretch! You neither say 'Thank you' nor do you show any esteem for me. You do not smile, you do not bow, you come back day after day. How long can this process continue? Are you saving up from my bounty to become rich, or are you lending out the gold on interest? Far indeed are you from the behavior of those with the honorable badge of the patched robe."

As soon as these words had been said, the dervish threw down the forty pieces of gold which he had received. He said to the king: "Know, O King of Iran, that generosity cannot exist without three things preceding it. The first is giving without the sentiment of generosity; the second is patience; the third is having no suspicions."

But the king never learned. To him, generosity was bound up with what people would think of him, and how he felt about being "generous."

From *Tales of the Dervishes*

The Water of Paradise

HARITH THE BEDOUIN and his wife Nafisa, moving from place to place, pitched their ragged tent wherever a few date palms, grazing scrub for their camel or a pool of brackish water were to be found.

This had been their way of life for many years, and Harith seldom varied his daily round: trapping desert rats for their skins, twisting ropes from palm fibers to sell to passing caravans.

One day, however, a new spring appeared in the sands, and Harith scooped a little of the water into his mouth. To him this seemed the very water of paradise, for it was far less foul than his usual drink. To us it would have seemed repulsively full of salt. "This," he said, "I must take to one who will appreciate it."

He accordingly set off for Baghdad and the palace of Haroun el-Rashid, traveling without pausing to do more than munch a few dates. Harith took two goatskins of water: one for himself, the other for the Caliph.

Days later, he reached Baghdad, and marched straight to the palace. The guards listened to his tale and, only because it was the rule, they admitted him to the public audience of Haroun.

"Commander of the Faithful," said Harith, "I am a poor Bedouin, and know all the waters of the desert, though I may know little of other things. I have just discovered this Water of Paradise, and realizing that it was a fitting gift for you, have come at once to make it as an offering."

Haroun the Straightforward tasted the water and, because he understood his people, he told the guards to take Harith away and lock him up for a time until his decision might be known. Then, calling the captain of the guard, he told him: "What to us is nothing, to him is everything. Take him, therefore, by night from the palace. Do not let him see the mighty River Tigris. Escort him all the way to his tent without allowing him to taste sweet water. Then give him a thousand pieces of gold and my thanks for his service. Tell him that he is the guardian of the Water of Paradise, and that he administers it for any traveler in my name, to be freely given away."

From *Tales of the Dervishes*

Hospitality

THE PEOPLE OF Turkestan are renowned for their generosity, their self-respect and their love of horses.

A certain Turkestani, called Anwar Beg, once owned a beautiful, fast-pacing and highly pedigreed horse. Everyone coveted it, but he refused to sell, no matter the price offered.

Time and again a friend of his, a horse-dealer named Yakub, visited Anwar, in the hope that he might buy the horse. Anwar always declined to sell.

One day, hearing that Anwar had fallen upon hard times, Yakub said to himself: "I will go to Anwar now. Surely he will part with the horse, for such is its value that the sale will restore his fortunes."

He lost no time in making his way to his friend's house.

As is the custom in that country, Anwar welcomed Yakub, and before any business was discussed there was the matter of the traditional hospitality. A meal was set before them, and they ate it with relish.

When, at length, Yakub was able to broach the subject of his visit, the penniless Anwar said:

"It is not now possible for us to have a discussion on the affair of the horse. Hospitality comes first; and, since you visited me in my poverty and I had to entertain you – know that we had to kill the horse to provide a meal, discharging in the best possible manner the obligations of host."

From *Caravan of Dreams*

9

Themes for Study and Contemplation

MEDITATION WITHOUT CONCENTRATION and contemplation is not very different from water without wetness and coldness.

From *Reflections*

THESE POINTS ARE *in fact exercises in outwitting the false self, which thrives on smaller satisfactions. The Sufi aims at Fana (passing away – of the False Self) and Baqa (remaining – of the Real). Behind the supposed "I," which is impermanent, lies the real one, which is characterized by the awareness of truth, of reality.*

And listen to the words of Junaid of Baghdad, when he said: "A good-natured sensualist is better than a bad-tempered so-called Sufi."

From *Learning How to Learn*

Sufi Study Themes
Q: IF YOU were to give a number of study themes to the people present, which ones would you stress?

A:
1. All approaches to a study or an individual may start with a desire for attention. However they start, they must never end up in this manner.
2. Study the assumptions behind your actions. Then study the assumptions behind your assumptions.
3. "Why did I do such-and-such a thing?" is all very well. But what about "How otherwise could I have done it?"
4. You have come a long way, and you do not know it. You have a long way to go, and you do know what that means.
5. In respect to some, you may have advanced. In relation to others, you have not progressed at all. Neither observation is more important than the other.
6. If your desire for "good" is based on greed, it is not good, but greed.
7. Exercise power by means of kindness, and you may be causing more damage than you could by cruelty. Neither approach is correct.
8. The man who knows must discharge a function. The one who does not, cannot arrogate one to himself; he can only try to do so.

9. Do not try to be humble: learn humility.
10. Assume that you are part hypocrite and part heedless, and you will not be far wrong.
11. To copy a virtue in another is more copying than it is virtue. Try to learn what that virtue is based upon.
12. No practice exists in isolation.
13. If you seek a teacher, try to become a real student. If you want to be a student, try to find a real teacher.
14. The more often you do a thing, the more likely you are to do it again. There is no certainty that you will gain anything else from repetition than a likelihood of further repetition.
15. At first, you are not worthy of the robes and implements of the Sufi. Later, you do not need them. Finally, you may need them for the sake of others.
16. If you cannot laugh frequently and genuinely, you have no soul.
17. When a belief becomes more than an instrument, you are lost. You remain lost until you learn what "belief" is really for.
18. When a dervish shows interest in your material welfare, you may be pleased. But it is frequently because you are not yet ready for anything else.
19. When someone asks for you to help in doing something, do you imagine that it is because he cannot do it unaided? Perhaps he is a Sufi

who wants to help you by connecting you with his task.

20. If you are lazy, count yourself lucky if someone points this out, giving you a chance to improve. Laziness is always your fault. It is the sign that a man has persevered in uselessness for too long.

From *Learning How to Learn*

Twenty-Three Study Points

IF YOU ARE not a viable unit in the ordinary world, you will not become one elsewhere. If you have a poor capacity for making human contacts, we cannot offer you the substitute of a community where "*we* understand one another." That belongs to play-life, what some, of course, generally call real life.

* * *

If you are accustomed to being supported and kept going by social, psychological and other pressures in the everyday world, there is a sense in which you do not really exist at all. The people who collapse in the often unpressured-dervish atmosphere and who slack, become tiresome to others, or seek to attract or obtain attention: they will fall to pieces and one cannot help them.

* * *

Try to remember; and, if you cannot remember, try to become familiar with this idea:

Lots of people who imagine that they are with us because they are physically present, or because by the ordinary tests (feelings of loyalty, indoctrination) are ostensibly present, lots of those people are not effectively here at all. If you are one of those people, there is nothing we can do for you. If you are like an ordinary person: that is, if you have the tendency to "be here" only for limited and primitive amusement, but have it only as a tendency and not a way of life, then we can perhaps make some progress.

*　　*　　*

Remember that the human being is so intensely standardized that an outside observer, noting his reactions to various stimuli, need not infer an individual controlling brain in each person. He would be more likely to infer the existence of a separate, outside brain, and the people as mere manifesters of its will.

*　　*　　*

Register the fact that:

Virtually all organizations known to you work largely by means of your greed. They attract you because what they say or do appeals to your greed. This is concealed only by their appearance. If you stop listening to their words and look at the effect, you will soon see it.

*   *   *

Remember that greed includes greed for being not greedy. So, if someone says: "Do not be greedy, be generous," you may inwardly interpret this in such a manner that you will develop a greed for generosity. This, however, remains greed.

*   *   *

There are some things which you have to do for yourself. These include familiarizing yourself with study-materials given to you. You can only really do this – and thus acquire real qualities – if you suspend the indulgence of desire for immediate satisfactions.

*   *   *

All members of contemporary societies, with few exceptions, are in need of graduating from primitive morality to a higher one. The primitive one is the one which tells you, like a child, that honesty will make you happy, make you successful, get you to higher things. Honesty, you may now be informed, is essential as an instrument, not to be worshiped as a seldom-attained emotion-loaded ideal.

*   *   *

Sufis have their own methods of deterring unsuitable people. You may only know one or two ways. Pay attention to the techniques which, for instance, deter by compelling people to conclude that they are worthless.

* * *

What you may take to be attractive, or even spread out by us to be attractive to you, may well not be intended in this manner at all. That which attracts you, or others, about us may be that which is laid down by us as a tool which enables us to regard you (or others) as unsuitable.

* * *

One can give or withhold in a manner far more effective, sophisticated, useful, which is quite invisible to people who think that giving or withholding is done by external assessment. If you see some mark of favor or "promotion," know that you are not ready for it. Progress comes through capacity to learn, and is irresistible. Nobody can stand between you and knowledge if you are fit for it.

* * *

Anybody or anything may stand between you and knowledge if you are unfit for it.

* * *

You can learn more in half an hour's direct contact with a source of knowledge (no matter the apparent reason for the contact or the subject of the transaction) than you can in years of formal effort.

*   *   *

You can learn and equip yourself with latent knowledge, whose development comes at a later stage. Only those who insist upon instant attention want anything else.

*   *   *

The role of the teacher is to provoke capacity in the student, to provide what there is when it will be useful, to guide him toward progress. It is not to impress, to give an impression of virtue, power, importance, general information, knowledge or anything else.

*   *   *

Systematic study or behavior is valuable when it is of use. When it is not, it can be poisonous.

*   *   *

Those who seek consistency as a major factor, in people or in study materials, are seeking system at a stage where it is not indicated. Children and savages do this, when they ask for information which will explain or make possible "everything." Consistency is, however, on offer from those people whose business it is to offer comfort and reassurance as objectives.

*   *   *

If you seek illumination or understanding when what you really need is information or rest from pressures, you will get none of these things. If you know what you want, you should go and get it.

*   *   *

If you carry the habit of judging things into an area where it does not apply, you will judge in a manner which will not correspond with your needs.

*   *   *

You cannot work on a higher level entirely with the concepts, language and experiences of a lower level. Higher level work is in a combination of manners and relationships.

*   *   *

The ultimate absurdity, incapacitating from real learning beyond the stage you have reached, is to imagine that one thing is another. If you think that a book is a sandwich, you may try to eat it, and will not be able to learn what a book can teach. If, too, you imagine that you are being "open" or "working" or eager to learn when you are only playing a social game, you will learn nothing. The people who refuse to play that game with you will also, of course, sooner or later annoy you.

*   *   *

Human organizations can take two forms: entities which are set up to express or attain the aspirations of their members; and those which exist in order to acquire or provide something which is needed. Wants and needs are not the same. The difference is in information. If people know what they need, they do not have to confuse wants with needs.

From *Learning how to Learn*

*   *   *

A Sufi Notebook: Some Contemplation-Themes

On Service

SERVICE IS THE performing of duty without either reluctance or delight. The dutiful is neither an exploited slave nor one who seeks reward. People will get out of the performing of duty what they can get out of it. If they put aside immediate enjoyment of duty and also immediate reluctance to duty, they are in a position to benefit from the other content in service. This it is which refines their perceptions.

On Seeking
SEEKING TRUTH IS the first stage toward finding it. After the seeking comes the realization that Truth is also seeking the Seeker himself. The third stage, which is the one in which the Sufi is learning from the Way, is when learning reaches a special stage: when the Seeker realizes that he is acquiring knowledge in a range beyond "seeking" and "finding," or "being sought."

On Effort
EFFORT AND WORK have many different forms. One reason for the institution of a Guide is that he knows when to direct the disciple's effort and work, and when not to direct it. He also knows the kind of effort and work which each individual should do. Only the ignorant mistake any work for useful work, or extra effort at any time they wish for even little effort at a right time.

On Idolatry
"IDOLATRY" IS WHEN attention is fixed upon some intermediary person or thing at a time and by a person when this should not take place. It is mistaking the vehicle for the content. Most institutions are, knowingly or otherwise, encouragers of idolatry. It is for this reason that potential Sufis require the constant attention of a mentor to direct their attention according to possibilities.

On Discipleship

IN THE DERVISH Way discipleship is an essential requirement. But the distinction must be made between the people who only imagine that they should be disciples – those whose greed has been aroused in disguise – and those who actually can become disciples, and where and when this stage can take place profitably.

On Mastership

THE WAY IN which a Master teaches is often incomprehensible to the students. This is generally because they are trying to understand the workings of something when in reality they are in urgent need of its benefits. Without its benefits they will never be able to understand its working.

On Companionship

THERE IS THE companionship of humanity and the companionship of transmission. Those who lack family or other forms of companionship will seek them even at times and places where associating together with others is useful for transmission. Few people know about this, partly because the one word (companionship) is generally used to denote two states, each of them quite different.

On Literature

REMARKS OF LOCAL application are often taken as being of general or universal application. When a Teacher says: "Shun literature," he is speaking about a certain audience and a certain time. It is the failures among his students who misunderstand and preserve literature as a key to understanding, or else do the reverse, saying: "The Master denied literature, therefore we will all, and always, deny it."

On Exercises

GREED IS THE dominant, though well concealed, characteristic of those who imagine that exercises are the entry to knowledge. They are as important, and as independently irrelevant, as the use of a hand without one or two of the fingers.

On Appearances

THE ORDINARY MAN judges a person not by his inner attainments but by his apparent actions and what he looks like superficially, and by what people say about him. This method is suitable, however, only for some kinds of judgment, not for others. What a person seems to be like will depend upon what one knows of him. As an example, a man carrying a spiked stick is not necessarily a murderer, he may be an elephant-driver. The elect often violate the superficial canons of appearance in order not to be affected by the behavior of the mass with its artificial criteria, and also at times in order to demonstrate, to those who can see it, that conduct alone does not demonstrate interior worth.

On Faith and Religion

THOSE WHO ARE regarded as believers or religious people, and who are incapable because of habit from behaving in any other manner, may be called religious but cannot be regarded as having faith. If, on the other hand, this is faith, then some other word should be used to convey the kind of faith which is not produced by the parents or surroundings of a person.

On Love

WHAT IS GENERALLY called love can be harmful to the lover and the object of the love. If this is the result, the cause cannot be called love by a Sufi, but must be called "attachment" in which the attached is incapable of any other conduct. Love not only has different intensities, but it also has different levels. If man thinks that love only signifies what he has so far felt, he will veil himself thereby from any experience of real love. If, however, he has actually felt real love, he will not make the mistake of generalizing about it so as to identify it only with physical love or the love of attraction.

On Study in the World

SUFISM IS A study which is not scholastic. Its materials are taken from almost every form of human experience. Its books and pens are in the environment and resemble nothing that the scholastic or enthusiast even dreams about. It is because recitations, effort and books are included in this kind of study, and because Sufi teachers are called "Teacher," that the fact of a specialized communication has become confused with academic or imitative study. There is, therefore, "Sufi Study" and "ordinary study," and the two are different. The position is as if "mouse" and "elephant" had both been given the same name. Up to a point (being quadrupeds, being grey, having tails) this inexactitude is of no moment. After that, it becomes necessary to distinguish between the two. This distinguishing takes place in a Sufi circle.

On Dervish Assemblies

SUPERFICIAL STUDENTS IMAGINE that when dervishes meet they are all of similar rank, or that any dervish can attend the meetings of any other, the difference being only in degree. In fact, it is the composition of the circle which is as important as the circle itself. Similarly, rank in the Way may hold good in one assembly and not in another. This is why teachers in one circle become pupils in another. Collections of interested parties, religious enthusiasts and would-be learners grouped together are often mistakenly called "dervish circles." These may or may not be preliminary to such circles, but they are not circles.

On Difference between Schools

MANY THINGS ARE said and written about differences in opinion, teaching and writings between Sufis. Externally there may be differences, dictated by the environment, but essentially there is no difference. To wrangle about Sufi differences is as stupid as to wrangle as to whether a coat should be spun from the bud of this or that cotton plant. That is the extent of its significance.

Parable, Idiom and Metaphor

IF YOUR TEACHER is speaking to you in your native tongue, you will have to regard the idioms which he uses as idiomatic, and not intended to be analyzed literally. When he gives you a parable, you will have to know it before you can apply it. When a thing is said metaphorically, it is meant metaphorically. Literal things are not to be taken as metaphorical.

On Higher Levels of Understanding

IF YOU USE ordinary intellect to try to unravel something which you do not understand in Sufism, you will go astray, because the intellect is too ingenious for the task. Understanding comes only by keeping the elusive within your mental grip. Many a test has been failed because it was too subtle. Be aware of subtleties.

On Annoyance and Unconcernedness

NOBODY IS ANNOYED unless there is a reason. If you annoy others it may be because they imagine you to be annoying, or it may be that you annoy them because of your speech or conduct. If you are, or anyone else is, unconcerned by a source of annoyance, this may be either laudable or depreciable. You cannot judge by annoyance.

On "States"

"STATES" ARE BASICALLY three: counterfeit or imagined, genuine and irrelevant. Like the physician, it is the sheikh who knows which is which, knows the ailment or state of health by the symptom. He also knows the desirability of the induction or otherwise of states. The height of folly is to assume that the presence or absence of a "state" is in itself indicative of something good or bad.

On Reading, Hearing, Being Present
THE MATERIALS OF study may constitute only the action of being present, without intense reactions, at an assembly of the Wise. It may at one time mean reading, at another, audition. Sometimes the reader or instrumentalist may be one of the initiated. At other times he should on no account be such. This science has been verified and only blunderers experiment with it.

On Repentance
REPENTANCE MEANS TURNING back or giving up completely something that was of powerful attraction. Pleasure gained through repentance is in most cases as bad as the original offense, and no permanent improvement can be expected by those who pride themselves in reformation. The repentance of the ignorant is when people feel strong reactions to giving something up, or seek forgiveness for something. There is a higher form, the repentance of the Wise, which leads to greater knowledge and love.

On Hope and Fear
BEING MOVED BETWEEN hope and fear (the fear of God and the hope of His forgiveness) is the earliest state of Sufihood. Those who stay in this state are

like the ball played from one part of the field to the other. After a time this experience has its benefit and after that it has its disadvantages. Following the Path without the lower qualities of hope and fear is the objective. A higher objective is when there is neither bribe nor stick. Some need hope and fear; they are those who have had it prescribed for them.

– Pahlawan-i-Zaif
From *The Way of the Sufi*

Meditations of Rumi

THERE IS NO cause for fear. It is imagination, blocking you as a wooden bolt holds the door. Burn that bar...

Every thought has a parallel action.

Every prayer has a sound and a physical form.

There are a thousand forms of mind.

If the seawater did not rise into the sky, where would the garden get its life?

A totally wise man would cease to exist in the ordinary sense.

The worker is hidden in the workshop.

To the ignorant, a pearl seems a mere stone.

If a tree could move on foot or feather, it would not suffer the agony of the saw nor the wounds of the blade.

What bread looks like depends upon whether you are hungry or not.

You may seek a furnace, but it would burn you. Perhaps you need only the weaker flame of a lamp.

Counterfeiters exist because there is such a thing as real gold.

Whoever says everything is true is a fool, whoever says all is untrue is a liar.

A great obstacle in the Path is fame.

God's mirror: the front is the heart, its back the world.

The infinite universe lies beyond this world.

They say: "He cannot be found" ... Something that cannot be "found" is what I desire.

To make wine, you must ferment the grape juice.

Water does not run uphill.

The moment you entered this world of form, an escape ladder was put out for you.

To boil water you need an intermediary – the vessel.

From *Caravan of Dreams*

Counsels of Bahaudin

YOU WANT TO be filled. But something which is full has first to be emptied. Empty yourself so that you will fill properly, by observing these counsels, which you can do as duties to yourself:

FIRST

Never follow any impulse to teach, however strong it might be. The command to teach is not felt as an impulsion.

SECOND
Never rely upon what you believe to be inner experiences because it is only when you get beyond them that you will reach knowledge. They are there to deceive you.

THIRD
Never travel in search of knowledge unless you are sent. The desire to travel for learning is a test, not a command.

FOURTH
Never trust a belief that a man or a community is the supreme one, because this feeling is a conviction, not a fact. You must progress beyond conviction, to fact.

FIFTH
Never allow yourself to be hurt by what you imagine to be criticism by a teacher, nor allow yourself to remain elated because of praise. These feelings are barriers in your way, not conductors of it.

SIXTH
Never imitate or follow a man of humility who is also mean in material things, for such a man is being proud in material things. If you are mean, practice generosity as a corrective, not as a virtue.

SEVENTH
Be prepared to realize that all beliefs which were due to your surroundings were minor ones, even

though they were once of much use to you. They may become useless and, indeed, pitfalls.

EIGHTH

Be prepared to find that certain beliefs are correct, but that their meaning and interpretation may vary in accordance with your stage of journey, making them seem contradictory to those who are not on the Path.

NINTH

Remember that perception and illumination will not at first be of such a character that you can say of them "This is perception" or "This is illumination."

TENTH

Never allow yourself to measure everything by means of the same time measurement. One thing must come before another.

ELEVENTH

If you think too much of the man, you will think in a disproportionate manner about the activity. If you think too much about yourself, you will think wrongly about the man. If you think too much about the books, you will not be thinking correctly about other things. Use one as a corrective for the others.

TWELFTH

Do not rely upon your own opinion when you think you need books and not exercises. Rely less upon your belief when you think you need exercises and not books.

THIRTEENTH
When you regard yourself as a disciple, remember that this is a stage which you take up in order to discover what your true distance is from your teacher. It is not a stage which you can measure, like how far you stand from a building.

FOURTEENTH
When you feel least interested in following the Way which you have entered, this may be the time when it is most appropriate for you. If you imagine that you should not go on, it is not because you are not convinced or have doubts. It is because you are failing the test. You will always have doubts, but only discover them at a useful time for your weakness to point them out.

FIFTEENTH
Banish doubt you cannot. Doubt goes when doubt and belief as you have been taught them go. If you forsake a path, it is because you were hoping for conviction from it. You seek conviction, not self-knowledge.

SIXTEENTH
Do not dwell upon whether you will put yourself into the hands of a teacher. You are always in his hands. It is a question of whether he can help you

to help yourself, for you have too little means to do so. Debating whether one trusts or not is a sign that one does not want to trust at all, and therefore is still incapable of it. Believing that one can trust is a false belief. If you wonder, "Can I trust?" you are really wondering, "Can I develop a strong enough opinion to please me?"

SEVENTEENTH
Never mistake training for ability. If you cannot help being what people call "good" or "abstemious," you are like the sharpened reed which cannot help writing if it is pushed.

EIGHTEENTH
When you have observed or felt emotion, correct this by remembering that emotions are felt just as strongly by people with completely different beliefs. If you imagine that this experience – emotion – is therefore noble or sublime, why do you not believe that stomachache is an elevated state?

NINETEENTH
If a teacher encourages you, he is not trying to attach you to him. He is trying, rather, to show you how easily you can be attracted. If he discourages you, the lesson is that you are at the mercy of discouragement.

TWENTIETH
Understanding and knowledge are completely different sensations in the realm of Truth than they are in the realm of society. Anything which you

understand in an ordinary manner about the Path is not understanding within the Path, but exterior assumption about the Path, common among unconscious imitators.

From *Thinkers of the East*

10

Topics

WHEN YOU REALIZE the difference between container and content, you will have knowledge.

From *The Book of the Book*

Sufi Psychology

"IN THE NEXT life, you will not be asked, 'Why did you not behave like such-and-such a person?' You will be asked: 'Why did you not behave like your real self?'"

"If you know who and what you are, you can start to be that person, instead of a copy of the ideas, the behavior or the image of someone else, or some collection of people. Then you can really *be*."

From *The Commanding Self*

IDRIES SHAH MAINTAINED *that the Sufis' psychological insights not only echo modern advances, but that they even surpass Western discoveries to date.*

He translated and adapted a huge body of material from Sufi sources, which reveals a profound knowledge of the way people think, stretching back over a thousand years.

However, he always insisted that these materials were part of a holistic system with a practical goal: human development and evolution.

Some of this material points up common patterns of thought and how these patterns allow us to be manipulated. Other materials provide analogies as to how we may break free from such thought-prisons, while still being able to live and operate in the everyday world: to acquire the knack, in the Sufi phrase, of being "in the world but not of it."

Editor's note

Sufi Psychology – A Framework for New Knowledge

AN ANCIENT TALE, among the Sufis, tells how a wise man once related a story about a remarkable tree which was to be found in India. People who ate of the fruit of this tree, as he told it, would neither grow old nor die. This legend was repeated, by a reliable person, to one of the Central Asian kings of long ago, and this monarch at once conceived a passionate desire for the fruit – the source of the Elixir of Life.

The Fruit of the Tree

SO THE KING sent a suitably resourceful representative to find and to bring back the fruit of that tree.

For many years the emissary visited one city after another, traveled all over India, town and country, and diligently asked about the object of his search from anyone who might know about its nature and where it was to be found.

As you can imagine, some people told this man that such a search must obviously only be a madman's quest; others questioned him closely, to find out how a person of such evident intelligence could actually be involved in such an absurd adventure; and their kindness in this respect, showing their consideration for him as a deluded dupe, hurt him even more than the physical blows which the ignorant had also rained upon him.

Many people, of course, told him false tales, sending him from one destination to another, claiming that they, too, had heard of the miraculous Tree.

Years passed in this way, until the King's representative lost all his hope of success, and made the decision to return to the royal court and confess his dismal failure.

Now, there was also, luckily, a certain man of real wisdom in India – they do occasionally exist there – and the King's man, having heard of him late in his search, thought: "I will at least go to him, desperate as I am, to seek his blessing on my journey homeward..."

He went to the wise man, and asked him for a blessing, and he explained how it was that he had got into such a distressed condition, a failure without hope.

The sage laughed and explained: "You simpleton, you don't need a blessing half as much as you need orientation. *Wisdom* is the fruit of the Tree of Knowledge. Because you have taken images and form, secondary names for things, as your aim, you have not been able to find what lies beyond. It has thousands of names: it may be called the Water of Life, the Sun, an Ocean and even a Cloud... But the emblem is not the thing itself."

Whoever, this Teacher continued, attaches himself to names and clings to concepts without being able to see that these derivative things are only stages, sometimes barriers, to understanding, will stay at the stage of secondary things. They create, and remain in, a subculture of emotional stimulus, fantasy and quasi-religion.

The Sufis maintain that this principle applies to everyday human life. If you belong to a community which has made certain assumptions about life and society, you will find that the community only remains stable if it does not question its basic assumptions. Members of such cultures consequently find themselves preoccupied by the search for comfort and reassurance, which they don't *need* – they are just used to it.

Sufi psychology recognizes two important elements in this situation. First, that in order to advance in knowledge or effectiveness, people have to break bonds which prevent them from reaching development and vision. You must conceive of possibilities beyond your present state if you are to be able to find the capacity to reach toward them. Secondly, the Sufis recognize that flexibility of approach is needed, not reprogramming of beliefs.

The Sufi diagnosis has for centuries been clear. It says that the world in which man finds himself is not static – but merely appears to be so. He does not live very long, he can control very little of his circumstances, and the things which happen to him may have far more effect on his life than the things which he causes to happen.

So, in order to function more effectively, he must be versatile and flexible. He must not regard transient things as constants – rather, he must treat transience as if it were the constant. Only then can he transcend limitations which otherwise paralyze or manipulate him.

So you could say that the Sufi dominates his environment by being able to stand aside from it, allowing it to have only the minimum effect on him, and by meshing with it when indicated. On the other hand, the individual (especially in the West) very often tries to dominate it by thrusting all his weight against it.

The one attitude has largely produced the Western world, the other, much of the Eastern. But in mutual usefulness they are not as far apart as one might imagine.

The Western people have specialized for some centuries in dealing with material life, yet they have arrived at a point where they are more and more interested in the non-material. They are less and less able, indeed, to distinguish the one from the other.

Similarly, after specializing in the study of man for about the same number of centuries, the Sufis long ago began to display what seemed to Westerners equally paradoxical interests in scientific matters.

Albert Einstein arrived at an interesting point when he said:

"The cosmic religious experience is the strongest and the noblest driving force behind scientific research."

And the Sufis, whom your encyclopedias are almost sure to define as Islamic ecstatics, dancing dervishes, and so on, have for at least 1,000 recorded years been discussing the most astonishingly modern things, without any technical or scientific infrastructure to explain how they knew about them. These include space travel, atomic power, time – space theory, the circulation of the blood, a fourth dimension, aviation and the transmission of pictures to panels set in walls. They do not stop at these and telepathy, telekinesis, penetrating physical objects under paradoxical circumstances, and instant learning by holistic methods are all subjects which they insist are concomitants of, but not ways to, spiritual knowledge.

Psychologists have been interested to note that Sufi tradition a thousand years ago insisted that human beliefs are frequently produced and sustained by the environment and by the culture. Moreover, historically Sufis have asserted that what people call belief may be caused by conditioning, rather than by divine or diabolical activity and, as such, is not spiritual at all.

Sufi literature, particularly the portions which I have selected and published, is designed, in part, to help show a person's real state to himself.

The great Sufi poet Hafiz of Shiraz (fourteenth century) constantly emphasizes what we would call today a psychological exercise: that man's preoccupations prevent him from making progress in the realm of a higher consciousness. He sits, as it were, surrounded by screens, blocking him off from his own potentiality.

Limited thinking, however useful for limited purposes, "veils" human potential:

Tu khud hijab i khudi Hafiz
Az miyan bar-khez!

"You yourself are your own screen Hafiz, rise from its midst!"

Jalaluddin Rumi, seven hundred years ago, wrote a poem in which he speaks of the evolution of man and the development through which he may rejoin his origins, an evolution which is a path "retraced" as one might call it, by pushing his consciousness forward by the *exclusion* of limiting factors and the *inclusion* of others, to a destiny which is generally referred to as "beyond the stars":

Above the Skies...

WE ARE ABOVE the skies and *more* than angels...

Although we have descended here, let us speed
back: what place is this?
Every form you see has its archetype in the
placeless...
From that instant when you came down into the
world as it is ("of being")
Placed before you to get out was a ladder.
First you were mineral, afterward vegetable
What you then became was animal, although this
is hidden from you.
From that you became humankind, with
knowledge, intellect and belief;
After this Earth, from then your place is the sky...[4]

Sufi psychology, then, can only function in the
presence of an awareness of the unity of all Creation,
and of Creation with all existence, and all existence
with something eternal.

The words and actions of the Sufis have always
alluded to a cosmic plan, of which humanity is a part.
Human communities are seen as a part of that plan,
religions as instruments of the plan; yet, all forms
of knowledge are admitted as related, more or less
directly, to the same plan. The role of the Sufi (and
the Sufi is the name for the realized man or woman,
not for the mere Seeker After Truth – you can't
have a Sufi who is still learning any more than all

---

4 *Selected Poems from the Divani Shamsi Tabriz*, by Jalaluddin
Rumi, Persian text ed. R.A. Nicholson, Cambridge
University Press, 1952. Translation by Idries Shah.

medical students are doctors) is seen as nothing less than an instrument of the plan: but as a conscious instrument, not as a well-wisher or hero, not as a follower or optimist, not as an idealist or even as a dedicated monk.

His role is naturally sometimes put in very dramatic form – he is the human being who is capable of being independent of fear of loss and desire for gain alike; such a person alone, it is insisted, can discharge functions which would be completely beyond the ordinary person, trapped by the stick and carrot of familiar existence. He or she has wider choices – though often in different areas – than other people.

First presented as part of a lecture by Idries Shah
Abridged from *A Perfumed Scorpion*

Manipulation of the Mind

ONCE UPON A time there were some schoolboys. They were lazy and wanted to escape from their studies. One of them suggested that they should make their teacher feel ill by telling him how terrible he looked.

Thus it was that, as soon as the master arrived at the school, one boy after another told him that he was looking ill. At first, the teacher told the boys that he was quite well, and they were imagining things; but, as more and more boys, apparently spontaneously, described him as looking ill, he began to feel it himself.

Returning to his house, he told his wife that something was wrong with him. She said that she thought that it was his imagination, but he insisted that he was near to death, and took to his bed, even accusing her of being insensitive to his sufferings.

From *The Hundred Tales of Wisdom*

The Poet and the Physician

A POET WENT to see a doctor. He said to him: "I have all kinds of terrible symptoms. I am unhappy and uncomfortable, my hair and my arms and legs are as if tortured."

The doctor answered: "Is it not true that you have not yet given out your latest poetic composition?"

"That is true," said the poet.

"Very well," said the physician, "be good enough to recite."

He did so, and, at the doctor's orders, said his lines again and again. Then the doctor said: "Stand up, for you are now cured. What you had inside had affected your outside. Now that it is released, you are well again."

– Hakim Jami
From *The Way of the Sufi*

The Oath

A MAN WHO was troubled in mind once swore that if his problems were solved, he would sell his house and give all the money gained from it to the poor.

The time came when he realized that he must redeem his oath. But he did not want to give away so much money. So he thought of a way out.

He put the house on sale at one silver piece. Included with the house, however, was a cat. The price asked for this animal was ten thousand pieces of silver.

Another man bought the house and cat. The first man gave the single piece of silver to the poor, and pocketed the ten thousand for himself.

Many people's minds work like this. They resolve to follow a teaching, but they interpret their relationship with it to their own advantage. Until they overcome this tendency by special training, they cannot learn at all.

From *Tales of the Dervishes*

That Makes Me Think Of...

SUHRAWARDI SAID:

I went to see a man, and we sat talking.

There was a camel plodding past, and I said to him:

"What does that make you think of?"

He said:

"Food."

"But you are not an Arab; since when was camel meat for food?"

"No, it is not like that," said the man. "You see, everything makes me think of food."

From *The Way of the Sufi*

Studies and Caravans

SHEIKH REWGARI WAS visited by a man who pleaded long and earnestly to be accepted as a disciple.

The sheikh talked to him about his life and his problems, and then sent him away, saying: "Your answer will be sent to you in due time."

Then the sheikh called one of his senior adherents, and said to him:

"Go to the house of such-and-such a man (the would-be disciple) and without mentioning my name offer him a secure and profitable employment in your caravan trade."

Soon afterward, a message came from the would-be disciple to the sheikh:

"I beg to be excused for not waiting upon you, since fortune has recently decreed that I be given an excellent position with one of the largest merchants in this town, and I must give all my time to this, in the interests of my family."

Sheikh Rewgari on several occasions correctly divined that visitors to his presence were there only because they had suffered disappointment in their lives. This is not a rare example of his actions in this manner.

From *The Way of the Sufi*

The Indian Bird

A MERCHANT KEPT a bird in a cage. He was going to India, the land from which the bird came, and asked it whether he could bring anything back for it. The bird asked for its freedom, but was refused. So he asked the merchant to visit a jungle in India and announce his captivity to the free birds who were there.

The merchant did so, and no sooner had he spoken when a wild bird, just like his own, fell senseless out of a tree on to the ground.

The merchant thought that this must be a relative of his own bird, and felt sad that he should have caused his death.

When he got home, the bird asked him whether he had brought good news from India.

"No," said the merchant, "I fear that my news is bad. One of your relations collapsed and fell at my feet when I mentioned your captivity."

As soon as these words were spoken, the merchant's bird collapsed and fell to the bottom of the cage.

"The news of his kinsman's death has killed him, too," thought the merchant. Sorrowfully he picked up the bird and put it on the windowsill. At once the bird revived and flew to a nearby tree.

"Now you know," the bird said, "that what you thought was disaster was in fact good news for me. And how the message, the suggestion of how to behave in order to free myself, was transmitted to me through you, my captor." And he flew away, free at last.

From *Tales of the Dervishes*

Why the Dog could not Drink

SHIBLI WAS ASKED:

"Who guided you in the Path?"

He said: "A dog. One day I saw him, almost dead with thirst, standing by the water's edge.

"Every time he looked at his reflection in the water, he was frightened, and withdrew, because he thought it was another dog.

"Finally, such was his necessity, he cast away fear and leaped into the water; at which the 'other dog' vanished.

"The dog found that the obstacle, which was himself, the barrier between him and what he sought, melted away.

"In this same way my own obstacle vanished, when I knew that it was what I took to be my own self. And my Way was first shown to me by the behavior of – a dog."

From *The Way of the Sufi*

Meaning of a Legend

Sayed Imam Ali Shah draws attention to an ancient legend which uses the Egyptian pyramids as its framework, and then explains the way in which stories were devised for teaching purposes.

The story tells how a certain pharaoh had a secret chamber built in his pyramid-tomb during his lifetime, so that all his treasures could accompany him to the next world.

The builder, however, told his two sons, saying, "I shall die poor, but you will be able to enter the treasury by this secret passage whose map I give you as your heritage, for the king is an usurper, and has accumulated the gold from poor people such as us."

When the sons had taken away some of the gold, however, one of them was caught by a hidden trap. He persuaded his brother to cut off his head, so that the family would not be caught, and could continue to enter. After some argument, the brother did this, and made good his escape.

The king was surprised to find the body without a head. He gave orders for the body to be tied to a wall, and a watch kept on it. The relatives, he reasoned, would want the body back, and if they tried to reclaim it, he would have them captured.

But the surviving brother was clever. He got some skins of wine, loaded them on a donkey, and allowed them to spill on the road near the watching guards. The guards took some of the spoiled wine and drank it. When they were drunk, the brother took the body away for burial.

The Sayed states that this tale illustrates that events are parallel with mental working. The treasure stands for accumulated human knowledge; the pharaoh is the delinquent tendency of the mind to prevent people from learning something which is to their advantage. The father is the man who knows how to obtain the knowledge; the two sons are two conditions of the human mind. The first brother represents the reckless yet imaginative function; the other stands for the surviving, active principle, which has as much inventiveness as the other.

"In this manner, as much as any other," continues Imam Ali Shah, "the service of humanity continues. Note well that the operation of the teaching takes place in an extraordinary manner.

"It is not necessary for this story to be untrue for it to be significant for teaching illustration."

From *Thinkers of the East*

The Barriers

A MAN IS anxious to free himself from a prison, and yet he strengthens the bars. Will he escape? These bars are the habits of depending only upon the secondary self, the desire for emotional stimulus and greed.

Supposing someone were to want to rise above the surface of the water but persisted in holding on to stones at the bottom of the sea. What would happen to him and what would you call him? These are the attachments to outworn and irrelevant systems, ideas and slogans.

Suppose someone were to want to grow taller, but kept himself in a box which dwarfed his growth? This box is the reliance upon cults and organizations which dwarf people's capacities.

Supposing, again, that someone were to think that he wanted to travel, but yet placed great weights on his feet so that he could not walk or even move. What would you call such a person? Those weights are the desires for attention and for getting something before the time is right.

Supposing, yet again, that some people were to aver that they wanted to be better people, yet they constantly stole what belonged to others and told lies, working against being better in any way. What would you call such people? Those actions are paralleled by believing that one will get paid twice: once by feeling good after doing something good, and once in a future life.

Supposing, finally, that there were people who said that they wanted to see around them, yet who persisted in wearing blinkers, what would you call them? Those barriers are the habit of mixing attractive but useless formulae and totems with specific teachings.

From *The Commanding Self*

Prisons of Thought
PEOPLE THINK THEY are being spiritual, when their thought is so polluted by subjective psychological

motives that they have lost all sense of what is really spiritual.

There are three major "prisons" of thought which manipulate people, instead of their being on top of them:

- Demanding sequentialism in everything: there has to be timing and stimuli within periods of time stipulated by the "prisoner";
- Expecting reward and punishment connected with spiritual ideas, irrespective of whether they are really involved;
- Thinking in terms of contract: "give me this and I'll give you that."

If you escape these, then there follows, closely behind, the curse of needing either the familiar or the unfamiliar. People seek the familiar for comfort or verification, the unfamiliar for emotional stimulus or excitement...

From *The Commanding Self*

Full Up

A MAN CAME to Bahaudin Naqshband, and said:

"I have traveled from one teacher to another, and I have studied many Paths, all of which have given me great benefits and many advantages of all kinds.

"I now wish to be enrolled as one of your disciples, so that I may drink from the well of knowledge, and thus make myself more and more advanced in the Tariqa, the Mystic Way."

Bahaudin, instead of answering the question directly, called for dinner to be served. When the dish of rice and meat stew was brought, he pressed plateful after plateful upon his guest. Then he gave him fruits and pastries, and then he called for more *pilau*, and more and more courses of food, vegetables, salads, confitures.

At first the man was flattered, and as Bahaudin showed pleasure at every mouthful he swallowed, he ate as much as he could. When his eating slowed down, the Sufi Sheikh seemed very annoyed, and to avoid his displeasure, the unfortunate man ate virtually another meal.

When he could not swallow even another grain of rice, and rolled in great discomfort upon a cushion, Bahaudin addressed him in this manner:

"When you came to see me, you were as full of undigested teachings as you now are with meat, rice and fruit. You felt discomfort, and, because you are unaccustomed to spiritual discomfort of the real kind, you interpreted this as a hunger for more knowledge. Indigestion was your real condition.

"I can teach you if you will now follow my instructions and stay here with me, digesting by means of activities which will not seem to you to be initiatory, but which will be equal to the eating of something which will enable your meal to be digested and transformed into nutrition, not weight."

The man agreed. He told his story many decades later, when he became famous as the great teacher Sufi Khalil Ashrafzada.

From *Wisdom of the Idiots*

Feeling your own Nothingness

THE SUFI SAINT Attar records the great ancient Bayazid[5] as saying: "You must feel your own nothingness."

To perceive one's own nothingness is valuable. To indulge oneself emotionally by frightening oneself with it is shallow self-amusement – all the more attractive to many people because they can pretend to themselves that it is sincerity or piety. One has to get beyond this childish state.

From *Learning How to Learn*

The Transmission of Baraka

ABDUL-QADIR CALLED TOGETHER all his adherents in Baghdad and said to them:

"I beg you never to forget what I am now going to tell you, because otherwise you will become the

---

5 In Attar's *Tadhkirat al-Awliyya*. Bayazid died in 875 of the Christian era.

source of great error. I address those of you who will remain more ignorant than the others, because the Knowers and the Attainers will never make the mistake which I shall now describe.

"During the period of Duty and Repetition [certain exercises], many people acquire the capacity to affect others with a strange experience. This produces trembling, excitement and many other feelings, and signals a stage of awareness. There may be visions of great teachers, or of divine influence.

"Acting upon the unprepared 'heart,' such experiences must instantly be stopped, because they cannot progress to real contact with the Divine until something else has been cultivated in the disciple.

"This opening of capacity, once discovered by the ignorant or raw, spreads especially among villagers and other simple people, until they indulge it regularly, thinking it to be a true state. It is in fact merely a signal, a sign of something. When it occurs, it must be reported, and those who experience it should undergo an appropriate period of preparation.

"Persistence in this practice in the past exhausted the capacities of the followers of saints and prophets, all deludedly believing themselves to be the recipients of *Baraka* (grace). Those who Attain dare not induce this state once it has appeared. Those who indulge it may never Attain.

"Follow only the practices of the Teacher, who knows why these things occur and who has to adjust the study accordingly."

From *The Way of the Sufi*

To be a Believer

YOU PROBABLY SEEM to yourself to be a believer, even if you are a believer in disbelief.

But you cannot really believe in anything until you are aware of the process by which you arrived at your position.

Before you do this you must be ready to postulate that all your beliefs may be wrong, that what you think to be belief may only be a variety of prejudice caused by your surroundings – including the bequest of your ancestors for whom you may have a sentiment.

True belief belongs to the realm of real knowledge.

Until you have knowledge, belief is mere coalesced opinions, however it may seem to you.

Coalesced opinions serve for ordinary living. Real belief enables higher studies to be made.

– Attributed to Ali
From *The Way of the Sufi*

Ali, Son of the Father of the Seeker

ALI SAID:

"None may arrive at the Truth until he is able to think that the Path itself may be wrong.

"This is because those who can only believe that it must be right are not believers, but people who are incapable of thinking otherwise than they already think."

From *Thinkers of the East*

Conditioning and Education

Q: YOU SEEM to say that people are trained by many ordinary institutions in a manner which people call brainwashing or conditioning. But if psychologists have discovered that this is the way man is trained, what can be done about it, and what is wrong with it?

A: There is no doubt that people are conditioned, and that what they call their opinions and beliefs are frequently not their own but implanted by other people and institutions. Among others, the Sufi Al-Ghazzali pointed this out almost a thousand years ago.

But assumption that all human education, training and development must be done by these methods is as unnecessary as to imagine, say, that because a tomato can be force-ripened, there is no other way for a tomato to ripen.

Conditioning is necessary, but it will function only for certain purposes.

Other purposes need other approaches.

The *Anwar-i-Suhaili* says:

The world is a hill and our actions are a shout;
The echo of the shout comes back to us.
Even though the wall throws a long shadow,
The shadow itself still runs back to the wall.

Sufi learning comes through nutrition, as it were, in the sense that Tustari answered the question "What is food?" He said:

"'Food' is the contemplation of the Living One." The community of those who have self-realization is regarded, by Ibn Arabi and others, as "organic," except that this organization is far more subtle and effective than that which gave us the analogy in the first place.

The secondary self stands in the way of learning, and it will be conditioned unless it is "polished" – another technical term, likening it to a mirror on which dust has settled, again emphasized by Ibn Arabi (in his *Fusus*) as well as by the classical and contemporary exponents of Sufism.

From *Learning How to Learn*

Attention

PEOPLE DEMAND ATTENTION. The right kind of attention at suitable times leads to the maintenance of a thriving individual. Ignorance of attention-need leads to too much or too little intake of attention.

Ignorance of the attention-factor, too, leads to mistaking attention-demand for something else. This something else is the social, psychological or other ritual which people think is the essential reason for human contact. In fact it is only one ingredient of human contact and interchange.

It is a basic error to imagine that only a human being can be involved in the attention-situation. Some of the most important attention-situations concern real or imagined sources of attention other than human ones.

From *Reflections*

Characteristics of Attention and Observation

Q: CAN YOU define characteristics of attention and observation as of importance in Sufic studies?

A: Study the attracting, extending and reception, as well as the interchange, of attention.

One of the keys to human behavior is the attention-factor.

Anyone can verify that many instances, generally supposed to be important or useful human transactions on any subject (social, commercial, etc.), are in fact disguised attention-situations.

It is contended that if a person does not know what he is doing (in this case, that he is basically demanding, extending or exchanging attention) and as a consequence thinks that he is doing something else (contributing to human knowledge, learning, buying, selling, forming, etc.), he will (a) be more inefficient at both the overt and the covert activity; (b) have less capacity of planning his behavior and will make mistakes of emotion and intellect because he considers attention to be other than it is.

If this is true, it is most important that individuals realize:

1. That this attention-factor is operating in virtually all transactions.
2. That the apparent motivation of transactions may be other than it really is. And that it is often generated by the need or desire for attention-activity (giving, receiving, exchanging).
3. That attention-activity, like any other demand for food, warmth, etc., when placed under volitional control, must result in increased scope for the human being who would then not be at the mercy of random sources of attention, or even more confused than usual if things do not pan out as they expect.

Certain Principles may be Enunciated. They Include:

1. Too much attention can be bad (inefficient).
2. Too little attention can be bad.
3. Attention may be "hostile" or "friendly" and still fulfill the appetite for attention. This is confused by the moral aspect.
4. When people need a great deal of attention, they are vulnerable to the message which too often accompanies the exercise of attention toward them. E.g.: someone wanting attention might be able to get it only from some person or organization which might

thereafter exercise (as "its price") an undue influence upon the attention-starved individual's mind.

5. Present beliefs have often been inculcated at a time and under circumstances connected with attention-demand, and not arrived at by the method attributed to them.

6. Many paradoxical reversals of opinion, or of associates and commitments, may be seen as due to the change in a source of attention.

7. People are almost always stimulated by an offer of attention, since most people are frequently attention-deprived. This is one reason why new friends, or circumstances, for instance, may be preferred to old ones.

8. If people could learn to assuage attention-hunger, they would be in a better position than most present cultures allow them, to attend to other things. They could extend the effectiveness of their learning capacity.

9. Among the things which unstarved people (in the sense of attention) could investigate is the comparative attraction of ideas, individuals, etc., apart from their purely attention-supplying function.

10. The desire for attention starts at an early stage of infancy. It is, of course, at that point linked with feeding and protection. This is not to say that this desire has no further nor future development value. But it can be adapted beyond its ordinary adult usage of mere satisfaction.

11. Even a cursory survey of human communities shows that, while the random eating tendency, possessiveness and other undifferentiated characteristics are very early trained or diverted – weaned – the attention-factor does not get the same treatment. The consequence is that the adult human being, deprived of any method of handling his desire for attention, continues to be confused by it, as it usually remains primitive throughout life.

12. Very numerous individual observations of human transactions have been made. They show that an interchange between two people always has an attention-factor.

13. Observation shows that people's desires for attention ebb and flow. When in an ebb or flow of attention-desire, the human being not realizing that this is his condition, attributes his actions and feelings to other factors, e.g., the hostility or pleasantness of others. He may even say that it is a "lucky day," when his attention-needs have been quickly and adequately met. Reexamination of such situations has shown that such experiences are best accounted for by the attention-theory.

14. Objections based upon the supposed pleasure of attention being strongest when it is randomly achieved do not stand up when carefully examined. "I prefer to be surprised by attention" can be paraphrased by saying, "I prefer not to know where my next meal

is coming from." It simply underlines a primitive stage of feeling and thinking on this subject.

15. Situations which seem different when viewed from an oversimplified perspective (which is the usual one) are seen to be the same by the application of attention-theory. E.g.: People following an authority-figure may be exercising the desire for attention or the desire to give it. The interchange between people and their authority-figure may be explained by mutual-attention behavior. Some gain only attention from this interchange. Some can gain more.

16. Another confusion is caused by the fact that the object of attention may be a person, a cult, an object, an idea, interest, etc. Because the foci of attention can be so diverse, people in general have not yet identified the common factor – the desire for attention.

17. One of the advantages of this theory is that it allows the human mind to link in a coherent and easily understood way many things which it has always (wrongly) been taught are very different, not susceptible to comparison, etc. This incorrect training has, of course, impaired the possible efficiency in functioning of the brain, though only culturally, not permanently.

18. The inability to feel when attention is extended, and also to encourage or to prevent

its being called forth, makes man almost uniquely vulnerable to being influenced, especially in having ideas implanted in his brain, and being indoctrinated.

19. Raising the emotional pitch is the most primitive method of increasing attention toward the instrument which increased the emotion. It is the prelude to, or accompaniment of, almost every form of indoctrination.

20. Traditional philosophical and other teachings have been used to prescribe exercises in the control and focusing of attention. Their value, however, has been to a great measure lost because the individual exercises, prescribed for people in need of exercise, have been written down and repeated as unique truths and practiced in a manner, with people and at a rate and under circumstances which, by their very randomness, have not been able to effect any change in the attention-training. This treatment has, however, produced obsession. It continues to do so.

21. Here and there proverbs and other pieces of literary material indicate that there has been at one time a widespread knowledge of attention on the lines now being described. Deprived, however, of context, these indications survive as fossil indicators rather than being a useful guide to attention-exercise for contemporary man.

Attention upon oneself, or upon a teacher, without the exercise of securing what is being offered from beyond the immediate surroundings, is a sort of short-circuit. As Rumi said: "Do not look at me, but take what is in my hand."

From *Learning How to Learn*

Instrumental Virtues

IF YOUR DESIRE for "good" is based on greed, it is not good, but greed.

From *Learning How to Learn*

ONE OF THE *more unaccustomed teachings of the Sufis which Idries Shah brought to the West is the view that what religious teachings regard as virtues are not important for any moral, theological or social reason. Rather, they are seen as having an instrumental function.*

If certain mental conditions – emotional cravings, assumptions, greed, envy and so on – act as barriers to perception, the conscious practice of "virtues" may enable an individual to overcome these barriers.

Editor's note

WE DISCOUNT, AND we even deride at times, the qualities upon which men pride themselves because those very qualities should be the minimum, not the maximum, attainable by man. If a man is a hero, or a patient one, or devout, or hospitable, or has any of the other qualities – this is the point from which he starts. Is he a beast, that he should be proud if he learns to conduct himself well in relation to others? Is he a fruit, that people should remember his name and always seek others of the same type? No, he is someone who should be ashamed that he has not always been worthy, and should be grateful that he is capable of great things.

From *The Magic Monastery*

Generosity and Wisdom

How are generosity and wisdom connected?

Here is one way:

A generous person may not have wisdom – but, unlike others, he has the means to gain it.

From *Reflections*

Hope

There was once a king, descended from a long and powerful line, whom adversity had driven from his position, and who was in flight before his enemies.

The king was soaked to the skin by rain and, in the middle of a desolate moor, came across a small hut used by shepherds. He thought that he would rest there for a little, and when he went inside, he found that there were two shepherds already there, wrapped in blankets against the cold.

They welcomed him kindly, and shared their only food, some cheese and onions, with him.

The king said:

"One day, when I am restored to sovereignty, I shall repay you in the coin of a king!"

Now, although both shepherds had offered the king food and were therefore equally generous, they were not both possessed of equal qualities in every way.

The first shepherd, therefore, strutted about telling everyone that he was better even than a nobleman, for he had given food to a king when there was nobody else to do so.

But the second shepherd, on reflection, said to himself: "My being in the hut, and my having some food with me, were accidents. My offering food to the king was a normal action. But the king, with truly royal generosity, chose to interpret these facts as the result of merit. Now it is for me to be inspired by this example, and to make myself truly worthy of such high-mindedness."

Two or three years later, the king returned to his rightful power, and he sent for the shepherds. Each of them was given rich gifts and both obtained powerful positions at court.

But the first shepherd, not having exerted any efforts to improve and prepare himself, soon fell a victim to an intrigue, and he was put to death for plotting. The second shepherd, on the other hand, worked so well that when the king reached a great age, he was nominated and accepted as his successor.

From *Wisdom of the Idiots*

Obedience

THE LOWEST FORM of obedience is performing actions for someone else. The high form of obedience is when one desists from behavior which one desires to carry out. The highest form of obedience is to be able to carry out no action at all. When this is possible, the other forms of obedience are also possible. Together they make up what people, ignorantly, imagine to be one single thing – "obedience."

The first thing to learn is that what you have been accustomed to call obedience is always either habit or servitude, whether it gives you pleasure or not.

– Anisa Imtihani
From *The Way of the Sufi*

The Saint and the Sinner

THERE WAS ONCE a dervish devotee who believed that it was his task to reproach those who did evil things and to enjoin upon them spiritual thoughts, so that they might find the right path. What this dervish did not know, however, was that a teacher is not only one who tells others to do things by acting through fixed principles. Unless the teacher knows exactly what the inner situation is, with each student, the teacher may suffer the reverse of what he desires.

However, this devotee one day found a man who gambled excessively, and did not know how to cure the habit. The dervish took up his position outside the man's house. Every time he left for the gambling-house, the dervish placed a stone to mark each sin upon a pile which he was accumulating as a visible reminder of evil.

Each time the other man went out, he felt guilty. Each time he came back, he saw another stone on the pile. Each time he put a stone on the pile, the devotee felt anger at the gambler and personal pleasure (which he called "Godliness") in having recorded his sin.

This process continued for twenty years. Each time the gambler saw the devotee, he said to himself:

"Would that I understand goodness! How that saintly man works for my redemption! Would that I could repent, let alone become like him, for he is sure of a place among the elect when the time of requital arrives!"

It so happened that, through a natural catastrophe, both men died at the same time. An angel came to take the soul of the gambler, and said to him, gently:

"You are to come with me to paradise."

"But," said the gambler, "how can that be? I am a sinner, and must go to hell. Surely you are looking for the devotee, who sat opposite my house, who has tried to reform me for two decades?"

"The devotee?" said the angel. "No, he is being

taken to the lower regions, since he has to be roasted on a spit."

"What justice is this?" shouted the gambler, forgetting his situation, "you must have got the instructions reversed!"

"Not so," said the angel, "as I shall explain to you. It is thuswise: the devotee has been indulging himself for twenty years with feelings of superiority and merit. Now it is his turn to redress the balance. He really put those stones on that pile for himself, not for you."

"And what about my reward, what have *I* earned?" asked the gambler.

"You are to be rewarded because, every time you passed the dervish, you thought first of goodness and secondly of the dervish. It is goodness, not man, which is rewarding you for your fidelity."

From *Wisdom of the Idiots*

Definitions

A GOOD MAN is one who treats others as he would like to be treated.

A generous man is one who treats others better than he expects to be treated.

A wise man is one who knows how he and others should be treated: in what ways, and to what extent.

The first man is a civilizing influence.

The second man is a refining and spreading influence.

The third man is a higher-development influence.

Everyone should go through the three phases typified by these three men.

To believe that goodness or generosity are ends in themselves may be good or it may be generous. It is, however, not an informed attitude – and that is the most good and the most generous we can be about it.

If someone said: "Is it better to be good, generous or wise?" one would have to reply:

"If you are wise, you do not have to be obsessed by being 'good' or 'generous.' You are obliged to do what is necessary."

From *Seeker After Truth*

The Miracle

IMAM ALI, ACCORDING to the *Durud-i-Qasimi*, admitted a barbarian stranger to his presence, in spite of the trepidation of those around him. Less than fifteen minutes had passed before the Imam said to his companions:

"This man will become a saint when he leaves this house, and his powers will seldom be excelled."

Since Hadrat Ali had done no more than raise his right hand over the newcomer's head, his disciples asked one another why they could not receive a similar blessing, so that they could instantly be transformed in a like manner.

Ali said:

"This man had humility. As a consequence I was able to impart Baraka (grace) to him. Failure to exercise humility has made you difficult to act upon, because you are your own barrier. If you want proof of this arrogance, here it is: the humble man would assume that he could not learn without great effort and much time. Consequently he will learn easily and quickly. The arrogant imagine that they are ready, and agitate for the Baraka, refusing to entertain even the thought that they are unworthy. To be unworthy is one thing; to fail to realize that it is possible is another, and worse. Even worse is to imagine that one is humble or trying to be sincere when one is not. Worst of all is to think nothing until one sees someone – such as the barbarian stranger – to whom one feels so superior that one's actions become uncontrolled."

From *Thinkers of the East*

The Cure of Human Blood

MAULANA BAHAUDIN NAQSHBAND was asked: "How is it that ignoble men or infants, as in so many stories, can be spiritualized by a glance, or in some indirect way, merely by coming into contact with a great teacher?"

He gave the following story as a reply, saying that this method paralleled the indirect route of spiritualization.

In the days of the great empire of Byzantium, one of its emperors was sick with a dreadful disease which no doctor could cure. He sent ambassadors to every country with full descriptions of the ailment. One arrived at the school of the great El-Ghazali, who was a Sufi whom the Emperor had only heard of as one of the great sages of the East. El-Ghazali asked one of his disciples to make the journey to Constantinople.

When the man, El-Arif, arrived, he was taken to the Court and treated with all honor, the Emperor beseeching him to effect a cure. Sheikh El-Arif asked what remedies had been tried, and which further ones were contemplated. Then he made an examination of the patient.

Finally he asked for a full audience of all the Court to be called, while he made his declaration of how the cure might be effected.

When all the nobles of the Empire had assembled, the Sufi said: "Your Imperial Majesty had better use faith."

"The Emperor has faith," answered a cleric, "but it does not take therapeutic effect."

"In that case," said the Sufi, "I am compelled to say that there is only one remedy on earth which will save him. But I do not want to speak it, so dreadful a thing is it."

But he was pressed, promised riches, threatened and cajoled. So he said:

"A bath in the blood of several hundred children under seven years of age will cure the Emperor."

When the confusion and alarm occasioned by these words had subsided, the Counselors of State decided that the remedy was worth trying. Some, it is true, said that nobody had any right to attempt such a barbarity at the behest of a foreigner of doubtful origins. The majority, however, considered that any risk was to be taken to preserve the life of an Emperor such as this, whom they all respected and almost worshiped.

They prevailed upon the monarch, in spite of his reluctance, saying: "Your Imperial Majesty has no right to refuse; for this would deprive his Empire of even more than the life of all his subjects, let alone a number of children."

Therefore the word was sent around that all children in Byzantium of the required age were to be sent to Constantinople within a certain period, in order to be sacrificed for the Emperor's health.

The mothers of these children in almost every case called down curses upon the head of their ruler, for being such a monster as to demand flesh and blood for his own salvation. Some, however, prayed instead that the Emperor might be healed before the time set for the slaying of their children.

The Emperor himself, after a certain amount of time had elapsed, began to feel that he could not allow such a deed as the slaughter of young children, on any pretext whatsoever. The problem put him into such a state of mind that it tortured him night and day; until he gave out the edict: "I would rather die myself than see the innocent die."

No sooner had he said this than his sickness began to abate, and he was soon perfectly well again. Shallow thinkers at once concluded that he had been rewarded for his good action. Others, as shallow, attributed his improvement to the relief of the mothers of the children, acting upon Divine power.

When the Sufi El-Arif was asked as to the means by which the disease had abated, he said: "As he had no faith, he had to have something equivalent to it. This was his single-mindedness coupled with the constructive desires of the mothers who wanted a remission of the disease before a certain time."

And the scoffers among the Byzantines said: "What a special dispensation of Divinity it was that the Emperor was healed in response to the holy prayers of the clergy, before the bloodthirsty Saracen's formula was tried. For was it not obvious that he was only trying to destroy the flower of our youth, which would otherwise grow up, and would one day fight against his kind?"

When the matter was reported to El-Ghazali, he said: "An effect can take place only through a manner devised to operate within the time allotted to its attainment."

Just as the Sufi leech had to adapt his method to the people with whom he found himself surrounded, so the dervish spiritualizer can activate the inner cognitions of the infant, or the ignoble, even in the realm of the science of Truth, by the employment of the methods known to him, given to him for this purpose. This latter was the explanation of Our Master Bahaudin.

From *Tales of the Dervishes*

"IF YOU PRAY, and feel satisfaction at having prayed, your action has made you worse. In such circumstances, cease to pray until you have learned how to be really humble."

From *Thinkers of the East*

Seekers and Gurus

IT IS A big claim, to call oneself a Sufi. Remember, anyway, that I do not call myself one.

– Hadrat Abul-Hasan Khirqani
From *The Way of the Sufi*

THE BARRIERS TO Sufi knowledge, at least initially, are almost always mistaken postures on the part of the student.

The very human desire for consistency, reassurance, certainty causes people to seek very often oversimplified formulae, not as instruments or vehicles of learning, but as "truths."

In many cases this tendency leads to a cult, sometimes literally so, sometimes in a concealed way.

Sufi studies have often deteriorated into the automatic and mimetic use of robes, beards, formulae and appurtenances.

These exterior objects and concepts have a powerful appeal for those who need reassurance or who desire something strange. But their use without an understanding of any function which they might have had and the transitory nature of formulation designed to protect and conduct from one stage to another, leads to "idolatry": the grasping and holding onto things which hamper progress because they are static. This is not the "Sufi Way" at all, but a social phenomenon.

From *Neglected Aspects of Sufi Studies*

Mistaken Identity

A CERTAIN "SEEKER after Truth" rushed into the house which had been pointed out to him as that of the Eastern sage. He grabbed the hand of the figure seated on a prayer rug and begged for advice.

"I have three things to tell you," said the other man. "First, you are too excited to understand anything. Second, you are standing on my foot. Third, I am a servant – the Sage lives next door!"

From *Learning How to Learn*

Escape

Q: I WANT to get away from "things of this world," and as a result I have immersed myself in the study of all kinds of books on occultism and experiential religion.

I feel that I am on the way to "finding myself," and wonder whether you would agree with me that this is the right thing to do?

A: Have you ever heard of the man who jumped into a river to get away from the rain?

Books on occultism and religion will merely make you think of such things in a "worldly" way, if you are a worldly person. What you have to learn is how to find the unworldly in everything. Can you do that? Obviously not, or you would not have asked the question.

It is not the immersion alone, as you call it; it is very much a question of who or what is being immersed. Some things are cleaned by immersion; others merely become waterlogged.

From *The Commanding Self*

What it is Really Like

Q: *WHAT CAN one do if one's closest friends or spouse object to one's attending study-meetings?*

A: I suggest that you tell such people the following story:

Misinterpretation

THERE WAS ONCE a man who used to go out at night to study spiritual and psychological subjects with a number of others. His wife objected, and she was always complaining that he was selfish and peculiar.

One day he managed to get her to go along, just to see what it was like. She sat there among all those strangers, listening to incomprehensible things. Finally, when they left, she said: "What a lot of ridiculous nonsense! I could hardly stand it..."

The husband said: "Well, now you know what it is like, you surely don't still think that I enjoy myself there, do you?"

This tale brings out two points. First, that things that you are not used to, or from which you are excluded, seem unpleasant or awful. The second point, which may well be true in many cases, is that a great number of these groups have an atmosphere which really does tell newcomers that they are not normal. So the test always is whether your friends in this kind of interest are acceptable to relatives or other, normal, friends. If they are, well and good. If they are not, you have to discover whether you are in a weird group, and whether your other associates might not be right, after all.

From *The Commanding Self*

Imitators

I HAVE HAD endless difficulties with people, both men and women, who purport to "give out my teachings," but get everything wrong.

In desperation, I asked a man and a woman who were terrible offenders, to come to see me and told them that they were just indulging themselves and were misleading people. I objected to their exploiting people, to their random collection of students, to their "teaching" when they understood nothing, to using the wrong materials with the wrong people, and so on.

They listened carefully to everything that I said – and then carried on exactly as before, with one difference.

The difference is that they now claim to be "personally instructed by Idries Shah"!

From *The Commanding Self*

Subjective

BECAUSE OF IMAGINATION and the lack of experience in understanding what inner developments signify, people experimenting with different states of consciousness more often than not give garbled accounts of their inward life.

One day a number of disciples were sitting around talking about their experiences. One of them said:

"As I was doing my exercises, I felt as if I had been illuminated by a shaft of light which split my brain into two equal and glowing halves..."

He was interrupted by another who said: "That reminds me of the time when my brain was split into 90,000 pieces and the greatest mystics in the world came to find out how I had done it."

There was a shocked silence. Then one of the other pupils said: "Perhaps you might care to show your humility by asking forgiveness of our friend for such levity."

"Well," said the other, "if our friend cares to do something about the glow of his brain, I shall try to reduce the number of spiritual masters who paid homage to me."

From *A Veiled Gazelle*

Wishing to be Wise

PEOPLE OFTEN MISTAKE dervishes, who are treading the Sufi path, for Sufis, who have already trodden it.

There is a tale, told by a dervish, which helps to fix this distinction in the mind.

There was once a young man, he related, who sought out a dervish, and asked him: "I wish to be wise – how can I achieve my wish?"

The dervish heaved a great sigh and answered:

"There was once a young man, just like you.

"He wished to be wise, and this wish had great strength.

"Suddenly he found himself sitting, as I am, with a youth, like you, seated before him, asking, 'How can I be wise?'"

From *Seeker After Truth*

Permission to Expound

BECAUSE OF THE special nature of Sufi writings, teachers of the Way have often issued permissions to expound and to explain their books to worthy individuals.

Not everyone, of course, has abided by this requirement, and many have been the supposed Sufis who have made a career for themselves by purporting to be able to teach through the books of Sufi masters.

It is related that a dervish was holding forth on one of the illustrious poet Jami's works one day, when a newcomer slipped into the lecture-hall and started to shake his head more and more often, as the learned one gave his interpretations of the meaning of Jami.

Everyone was looking at the stranger, and finally the dervish fixed him with a penetrating eye and cried:

"Do you presume to disagree with me?"

"Yes," said the other man.

"And," asked the dervish, "have you permission from the Great Master Jami to interpret his works?"

"No."

"Then who are you, and by what right do you behave in this ridiculous manner, challenging a man of my importance?"

"My name is Jami," said the visitor, and slipped away.

From *Seeker After Truth*

The Man who Walked on Water

A CONVENTIONALLY MINDED dervish, from an austerely pious school, was walking one day along a riverbank. He was absorbed in concentration upon moralistic and scholastic problems, for this was the form which Sufi teaching had taken in the community to which he belonged. He equated emotional religion with the search for ultimate Truth.

Suddenly his thoughts were interrupted by a loud shout – someone was repeating the dervish call. "There is no point in that," he said to himself, "because the man is mispronouncing the syllables. Instead of intoning YA HU, he is saying U YA HU."

Then he realized that he had a duty, as a more careful student, to correct this unfortunate person, who might have had no opportunity of being rightly guided, and was therefore probably only doing his best to attune himself with the idea behind the sounds.

So he hired a boat and made his way to the island in midstream from which the sound appeared to come.

Sitting in a reed hut he found a man, dressed in a dervish robe, moving in time to his own repetition of the initiatory phrase. "My friend," said the first dervish, "you are mispronouncing the phrase. It is incumbent upon me to tell you this, because there is merit for he who gives and he who takes advice. This is the way in which you speak it." And he told him.

"Thank you," said the other dervish humbly.

The first dervish entered his boat again, full of satisfaction at having done a good deed. After all, it was said that a man who could repeat the sacred formula correctly could even walk upon the waves:

something that he had never seen, but always hoped – for some reason – to be able to achieve.

Now he could hear nothing from the reed hut, but he was sure that his lesson had been well taken.

Then he heard a faltering U YA as the second dervish started to repeat the phrase in his old way...

While the first dervish was thinking about this, reflecting upon the perversity of humanity and its persistence in error, he suddenly saw a strange sight. From the island the other dervish was coming toward him, walking on the surface of the water...

Amazed, he stopped rowing. The second dervish walked up to him and said: "Brother, I am sorry to trouble you, but I have to come out to ask you again the standard method of making the repetition you were telling me, because I find it difficult to remember it."

From *Tales of the Dervishes*

1001 Days

A WOULD-BE DISCIPLE visited the home of a Sufi teacher.

He was told:

"You must try to answer a question. If you succeed, he will accept you for teaching in three years' time."

The question was put, and the Seeker puzzled over it until he had the answer.

The teacher's representative took his answer to the master, and returned with the message:

"Your answer is correct. You may now go away for the 1001 days' waiting, after which you will be allowed to return here, to receive the Teaching."

The applicant was delighted. When he had thanked the other man, he asked:

"What would have happened if I had failed to provide the correct answer?"

"Oh, in that case – you would have been admitted immediately!"

From *Seeker After Truth*

Two Gurus

THERE WERE ONCE two Gurus. They meditated and lectured, studied the lives and sayings of the ancient mystics who taught that man could control his outer life in order to attain release from the bondage of events and escape from the tyranny of the environment.

One of the Gurus knew the properties of secret herbs and had contemplated in the hermitages of the Himalayas. He had made pilgrimages and *darshan* visits to the abodes of Mahatmas great and small. He had attended the gatherings and rituals of the forests and the temples, and he was thoroughly versed in the mysteries of the sacred mantrams.

The other Guru, who lived at some distance from the first, had for many years instructed disciples. He had himself been a *chela* of several masters of high repute. He was familiar with the scriptures and the ancient classics inscribed on leaves, and he had measured his length along the ground in spiritual journeys, to countless monasteries. He had practiced posture-training and mandala-gazing, had eaten the berries of the hermit and had worn the robe of the Sanyasi. He was regarded as a perfect Master by his followers, and by many who knew him and many who did not.

One day the Second Guru was visited by the First, who said to him:

"I have a young and recent disciple who wishes to attain *moksha*. I have sat with him and chanted over him, and I have also breathed on him and recited holy words, but he still seems very restless. I have exposed him to silence and to vocational exercises. We have meditated together and rung bells. The beads are never still in our fingers, and we have kissed holy relics. What would you advise me to do with him now?"

The Second Guru asked:

"Have you had him on a bed of nails?"

"No," said the First Guru.

"Very well then, try that."

A few days later, the First Guru returned and said:

"It is with reluctance that I trouble you again, but I am in need of advice for my troublesome disciple."

"Is he still restless, even after lying on a spiked bed?"

"I regret to say that he is."

"Very well then," said the Second Guru, "I now advise a course of concentration upon secret inner sounds, hot and cold baths, and an application of holy oils and certain ancient breathing exercises."

The First Guru went away, only to appear after a few more days, to report that all was not well with his *chela*:

"He seems to lack resolution, and the course of holy efforts is not visibly taking effect."

"We must resort to even more advanced methods," said the Second Guru, "and this is what you shall now do."

He described a regime of special gyrations and calisthenics, the application of charms, a period of silence, special robes and several other secret and initiatory techniques and procedures.

Three days later, the Second Guru was sitting with his customary serenity at the entrance to his ashram when the First Guru again arrived.

"I suppose that you have come for further guidance for your disciple?" asked the Second Guru benignly.

"No," said the First Guru, "that is not now necessary, since the man is dead."

"Dead? When did he die, and how?"

"He died suddenly, in front of me, this morning. He just went limp and collapsed. When I raised his head I saw that all life had departed from him."

"But did he say nothing before he died?"

"Hardly anything. Just before he fell to the ground, he had started a sentence with the words, 'When am I going to get some food?'"

From *Reflections*

False Masters
Q: WHY ARE there so many false spiritual teachers around?

A: This is one of the most common questions, and there are almost as many answers as there are people asking. When there is a true or useful thing, there is sure to be a counterfeit. This does not mean that the original intention was bad, but things turn out bad if they are not properly organized. There is no difference between this problem and the one of the

Lovelorn Taiwanese
THERE WAS ONCE a young man of Taiwan who desperately desired that a certain girl should marry him. He wrote her letters, over a period of two years, an average of one a day, declaring his love.

This continued, says the United Press, from 1972 to 1976.

Without that effort it is unlikely that the lady would have become engaged, in the way she did, to the postman who delivered the letters.

From *Seeker After Truth*

Streaky Sand
THERE WAS ONCE a woman who abandoned the religion in which she had been brought up. She left the ranks of the atheists, too, and joined another

faith. Then she became convinced of the truth of yet another.

Each time she changed her beliefs, she imagined that she had gained something, but not quite enough. Each time she entered a new fold, she was welcomed, and her recruitment was regarded as a good thing and a sign of her sanity and enlightenment.

Her inward state, however, was one of confusion. At length she heard of a certain celebrated teacher,[6] and she went to see him. After he had listened to her protestations and ideas, he said, "Return to your home. I shall send you my decision in a message."

Soon afterward the woman found a disciple of the sheikh at the door. In his hand was a packet from his Master. She opened it, and saw that it contained a glass bottle, half-full with three layers of packed sand – black, red and white – held down by a wad of cotton. On the outside was written: "Remove the cotton and shake the bottle to see what you are like."

She took the wadding out, and shook the sand in the bottle. The different colored grains of sand mixed together, and all that she was left with was – a mass of greyish sand.

From *Thinkers of the East*

---

6 Traditionally Imam Jafar Sadik.

A Basic Pattern

IF YOU COLLECT a number of the most frequent reasons said to be given by women to explain why they want something, you might be rather surprised when comparing them with supposedly "less frivolous" desires. On the left is a list of the "reasons" or justifications advanced by women; on the right, taken from my own files, actual examples of reasons given to me why various correspondents think they should study to be Sufis:

1 It is good for my morale	1 I want to be happy/fulfilled
2 It is from Paris	2 It is from the East
3 Everybody has one	3 Everyone is entitled to knowledge
4 Nobody else has one	4 It is rare knowledge/for the few
5 It is cheaper in the long run	5 It may be harder, but it is more real
6 It is different	6 It is different
7 I have waited so long	7 I have waited all my life
8 I like it: it must be right	8 Something tells me it must be true
9 I have always wanted one...	9 The need has always been in me

There is no doubt that both – the wanting of the adornment and the wanting of the more subtle "spiritual" satisfaction – are varieties of an acquisition impulse in these cases.

Sufis are aware that this stage must be passed. To get beyond this acquisition point, it may be necessary to reach it first, recognize it and then discard it.

There are three useful reflections which apply to the description and superseding of this state:

1. If I worship You for desire for Paradise, exclude me from Paradise; if I worship You for fear of Hell, cast me into Hell (Rabia).
2. The donkey which brought you to the door is not the means by which you enter the house.
3. First repent; afterward, you have to repent your repentance.

From *Seeker After Truth*

Mystery

TALIB SAID:

"People who know nothing, or know very little and should be studying instead of teaching, are fond of creating an air of mystery. They may foster rumors about themselves and pretend that they do things for some secret reason. They always strive to increase the sense of mystery.

"But this is mystery for itself, not as the outer manifestation of inner knowledge.

"The people who really know the inner secrets generally look and behave like ordinary people.

"So the ones who increase the air of mystery may be like the spider's web, they only catch flies. Are you, like the fly, a spider's dinner?"

From *Thinkers of the East*

The Elixir

ONE OF THE great Sufi teachers was asked:

"How is it possible to comprehend the teachings of the Masters, when so much of their behavior is paradoxical and frequently so very ordinary?"

He answered:

"General rules and hypothetical approaches block the understanding as often as they assist it. But I shall tell you my own experience, for the records of experience are often the best.

"When I was a student, I approached the greatest Master of the Age, and said: 'I can only behave like an animal – consent to help make me human.' He nodded his head and I attended him at his house for two years, waiting for a sign of teaching. After this time, I went to another wise man and asked him how I could approach my teacher to learn from him.

"The wise man said: 'You seek an elixir, and I shall give you one. Take this colorless fluid and put a drop in your master's food once a day. At the same time make sure that you serve him and do everything which he says, not for the time being making any attempt to see meanings in his actions, or to trick him into conversations.'

"I did as he said, and after a month, I found that I was developing perceptions and understandings. I returned to the wise man and said: 'Blessings upon you! The elixir is undoubtedly working, for I am progressing, and can now do things formerly impossible to me.'

"He said: 'And is that why you have come?'"

"I said: 'I have also come for a little more of the magical elixir, for the quantity which you gave me is exhausted.'

"He at once smiled and answered: 'You may now stop giving your teacher drops of inert water – the "Elixir" – and continue with the special behavior which I prescribed for you.'"

From *The Magic Monastery*

At the Crossroads

A SUFI WAS sitting at a crossroads one morning when a young man came up to him and asked whether he could study with him.

"Yes, for one day," said the Sufi.

Throughout the day, one traveler after another stopped to ask questions about man and life, about Sufism and Sufis, or to beg for help – or just to pay respects.

But the Sufi wanderer merely sat in an attitude of contemplation, his head on his knee, and he made no answer at all. One by one, the people went away.

Toward evening, a poor man with a heavy bundle approached the pair and asked the way to the nearest town. The Sufi immediately stood up, took the man's burden on his own shoulders and conducted him a part of the way along the right road. Then he returned to the crossroads.

The young disciple asked:

"Was that man, miserable peasant though he looked, really a saint in disguise, one of the secret wanderers of high rank?"

The Sufi sighed and said:

"He was the only person whom we have seen today who really sought the object which he claimed to want."

From *The Magic Monastery*

Sure Remedy

A MAN WENT to visit his physician. "My trouble is," he told him, "that I fall asleep during the very long lectures given by my spiritual guide."

The doctor handed him a bottle of pills: "One, three times a day," he said.

"Thank you, doctor – do I take them with water?"

"No, you don't take them – in *his* food, you fool!"

Cheetahs and Awarts

A CERTAIN MAN had read many books on the Sufi way and after some time said to himself:

"This reading is useless. I must find someone who can teach me by direct methods."

So he presented himself before the man who, he had been told, was the Master of the Age, generally known as Gilgun.

Gilgun received him in a kindly manner, asking why he had come without first writing to him.

"I am tired of reading and writing, I want something real," said the student.

"Very well," said Gilgun, "I shall show you the relation of reality to comparative reality."

He gave orders that a cheetah was to be brought into the room. When it appeared, he said:

"Why do you not fear this animal?"

The student said:

"I have read that cheetahs are harmless to humans."

"Know," said Gilgun, "that we had a man here the other day who did not have this information. When the cheetah came in, he fled in alarm. It was a pity, because he was thus prevented from enjoying the advantages of cheetahs. So your reading has been of use to you, whether you are tired of it or not."

Then Gilgun said:

"Have you ever read of the Awarts?"

"No," said the other man, "I have no idea what an 'Awarts' might be."

"Call the 'Awarts,'" said Gilgun.

At that moment a frightful apparition, shaped like a man but with colored stripes and fearsome head, rushed into the room. The would-be disciple cowered in the corner, terrified.

"Let this man go, and do not let him come into my presence ever again," instructed the Master of the Age, "because although anxious for real experience, he is unable to discern that an 'Awarts' is a name for a man with paint and a mask on him."

From *The Magic Monastery*

Sufism and Islam
"ANGELS ARE THE powers hidden in the faculties and organs of man."

– Ibn al-Arabi
From *The Sufis*

THROUGHOUT THE DERVISH *literature you will find us saying repeatedly that we are not concerned with your religion or even with the lack of it. How can this be reconciled with the fact that believers consider themselves the elect?*

Man's refinement is the goal, and the inner teaching of all the faiths aims at this. In order to accomplish it, there is always a tradition handed down by a living chain of adepts, who select candidates to whom to impart this knowledge.

Among men of all kinds this teaching has been handed down. Because of our dedication to the essence, we have, in the Dervish Path, collected those people who are less concerned about externals, and thus kept pure, in secret, our capacity to continue the succession. In the dogmatic religions of the Jews, the Christians, the Zoroastrians, the Hindus and literalist Islam, this precious thing has been lost.

We return this vital principle to all these religions, and this is why you will see so many Jews, Christians and others among my followers. The Jews say that we are the real Jews, the Christians, Christians.

It is only when you know the Higher Factor that you will know the true situation of the present religions and of unbelief itself. And unbelief itself is a religion with its own form of belief.

– Ahmad Yasavi
From *The Way of the Sufi*

SUFISM IS BELIEVED by its followers to be the inner, "secret" teaching that is concealed within every religion; and because its bases are in every human mind already, Sufic development must inevitably find its expression everywhere. The historical period of the teaching starts with the explosion of Islam from the desert into the static societies of the Near East.

Toward the middle of the seventh century, the expansion of Islam beyond the borders of Arabia was challenging, and was soon to overthrow, the empires of the Middle East. Each one had a venerable tradition in the political, military and religious spheres. The armies of Islam, originally composed mainly of Bedouins, but then swollen by recruits of other origins, struck northward, eastward and to the west. The Caliphs fell heir to the lands of the Hebrews, the Byzantines, the Persians and the Greco-Buddhists; the conquerors reached the south of France in the West, and the valley of the Indus in the East. Those political, military and religious conquests form the nucleus of the Muslim countries and communities of today, which extend from Indonesia in the Pacific to Morocco on the Atlantic.

If is from this background that the Sufi mystics became known in the West, and they maintained a current of teaching which links people of intuition from the Far East to the farthest West.

The early Caliphs had possessed themselves of more than millions of square miles, uncounted riches and the political supremacy of the known world of the Middle Ages. The centers of learning of the ancients, and particularly the traditional schools of mystical teaching, had almost all fallen into their hands. In Africa, the ancient communities of Egypt, including Alexandria; and farther west, Carthage, where St Augustine had studied and preached esoteric, pre-Christian doctrines. Palestine and Syria, the homes of secret traditions; Central Asia, where the Buddhists were most firmly entrenched; and northwest India with its venerable background of mysticism and experiential religion – all were within the empire of Islam.

To these centers traveled the Arab mystics, anciently known as the Near Ones (*muqarribun*), who believed that essentially there was a unity among the inner teachings of all faiths. Like John the Baptist, they wore camels' wool, and may have been known as Sufis (People of Wool), though not for this reason alone. As a result of these contacts with the Hanifs each one of the ancient centers of secret teaching became a Sufi stronghold. The gap between the secret lore and practice of Christians, Zoroastrians, Hebrews, Hindus, Buddhists and the rest had been bridged. This process, the confluence of essences, has never been grasped by non-Sufis as a reality, because such observers find it impossible to realize that the Sufi sees and contacts the Sufic stream in every culture, as a bee will suck from many flowers without becoming a flower. Even the Sufic usage of "confluence" terminology to denote this function has not penetrated far.

Sufi mysticism differs tremendously from other cults claiming to be mystical. Formal religion is for the Sufi merely a shell, though a genuine one, which fulfills a function. When the human consciousness has penetrated beyond this social framework, the Sufi understands the real meaning of religion. The mystics of other persuasions do not think in this manner at all. They may transcend outer religious forms, but they do not emphasize the fact that outer religion is only a prelude to special experience. Most ecstatics remain attached to a rapturous symbolization of some concept derived from their religion. The Sufi uses religion and psychology to pass beyond all this. Having done so, he "returns to the world," to guide others on the way.

It was not always safe, in the face of vast numbers of enthusiastic and victorious Muslim zealots to claim, as the Sufis did, that human realization came only from within and not through just doing certain things and not doing certain other things. At the same time, the Sufic attitude was that mysticism must be taken out of its utterly secret character if it were to become a force which would penetrate all humanity.

In their own tradition, the Sufis saw themselves as inheritors of one single teaching – elsewhere split into so many facets – which could be made to serve as the instrument of human development. "Before garden, vine or grape was in the world," writes one, "our soul was drunken with immortal wine."

The groundwork for the wide diffusion of Sufic thought and action was laid by the masters of the classical period – which may be taken as the first eight hundred years after the appearance of Islam – between about 700 AD and 1500 AD. Sufism was based upon love, operated through a dynamic of love, had its manifestation through ordinary human life, poetry and work.

Because the Sufis recognized Islam as a manifestation of the essential upsurge of transcendental teaching, there could be no interior conflict between Islam and Sufism. Sufism was taken to correspond to the inner reality of Islam, as with the equivalent aspect of every other religion and genuine tradition.

The great Sufi Khayyam, in his *Rubaiyat*, stresses this interior experience, which has no real connection with the theological version of what people consider, by default, to be real religion:

In cell and cloister, monastery and synagogue, one lies
In dread of hell: one dreams of paradise.
But none that know the divine secrets
Has sown his heart with suchlike fantasies.

It is sometimes difficult for a conventionally minded person to grasp how far-reaching the rule of essential Sufic action really is. Since Sufism was bound to exist in Islam as elsewhere, it could easily be taught through Islam. It is instructive to note that two legalistic and theological compendia, obviously straining to present Sufism publicly as religiously orthodox, were written by Sufi giants – the *Taaruf* of Kalabadhi of Bokhara (died 995) and the first public Persian treatise, the *Kashf* of Hujwiri (died 1063). Both authors are of the highest Sufi rank, yet each often speaks as if he were an observer, not an initiate, as Omar Khayyam also frequently does, to the mystification of some of his trustingly literalist commentators. These authors are full of hidden meanings, never reproduced in translation, and it was precisely in this way that many of the Orders of medieval Sufism proceeded. They continued their work, which was entirely valid within the Islamic world. Yet, as some Sufis note, "Sufism was even taught at one time exclusively by signs." The end product, the Completed Man, is the same in both cases. The symbolism and chain of experience whereby Islam and other systems are reconciled through Sufi practice is another matter, vouchsafed only to practitioners and concealed in the dictum: "He who tastes, knows."

The recognition of the climate established by Islam as a suitable one for projecting Sufi wisdom is easy to trace. In spite of the development of an unauthorized clergy in Islam, those narrow-minded scripturists who stuck to a dogmatic interpretation of the religion, Islam provided better conditions for propagating an inner doctrine than any of its precursors in the same area. Religious minorities were guaranteed freedom from persecution – an immunity which was rigidly adhered to during the period when the Sufis were becoming visibly active. Islam itself was a matter of legal definition. What was a believer? At the minimum, a person who would repeat the phrase *La-illaha-illa-Allah, Muhammad ar-Rasul-Allah* – "Nothing worshiped but the divinity, the Praised one the messenger of the worshipful" – which is generally understood as, "There is no God but Allah, and Muhammad is His Prophet." The unbeliever was a person who actively denied the words of this creed. Nobody could see into the heart; so belief could not be defined, only inferred.

Provided that a person could assert that he subscribed to this formula, he could not be proceeded against for heresy. No dogma as to the nature of this divinity and the relationship with the Prophet was fixed; and there was nothing in the phrase of affirmation which could not be subscribed to by a Sufi. His interpretation might be more mystical than that of the scholastics, but no power existed, no ordained priesthood, for instance, which could finally establish the ascendancy of the clerics. Ultimately, Islam as a community was regulated by the interpretations of the doctors of law. They could not define Allah, who was beyond human definition, nor could they precisely interpret Messengership, a unique relationship of deity and man. Before very long, Sufis were able freely to say such things as: "I am an idol worshiper; for I understand what idol worship means, and the idolater does not."

The breakup of the old order in the Near East, according to Sufi tradition, reunited the "beads of mercury" which were the esoteric schools operating in the Egyptian, Persian and Byzantine empires into the "stream of quicksilver" which was intrinsic, evolutionary Sufism.

The Sufis even established the principle, often to be accepted by Islamic courts of law, that seemingly irreverent statements made in a state of mystical ecstasy could not be taken at their face value for penal purposes. "If a bush can say, 'I am Truth,'" said a famous Sufi, "so can a man."

There was, too, a well-established belief among the general public that Muhammad had had a special relationship with other mystics, and that the devout and highly respected "Seekers of Truth"[7] who surrounded him during his lifetime might have been the recipients of an inner doctrine which he imparted in private. Muhammad, it will be remembered, did not claim to bring any new religion. He was continuing the monotheistic tradition which he stated was working long before his time. He inculcated respect for members of other faiths, and spoke of the importance of spiritual teachers of many kinds. The Quran itself was revealed by mystical methods, and provided many indications of mystical thinking.

In the religious sphere, the Quran maintains the unity of religions and the identical origin of each – "Every nation had a Warner." Islam accepted Moses, Jesus and others as inspired prophets.

---

7 *Tulab el Haqq.*

Again, it is authoritatively on record that the name "Sufi" was in use before the declaration of his prophetic mission by Muhammad.[8] It is essential to grasp this sense of continuity of inner teaching, and also the belief in the evolution of society, if the Sufis are to be understood to any real extent.

But perhaps the greatest contribution of Islam to the spread of Sufic thinking was its lack of exclusivism and its acceptance of the theory that civilization was evolutionary, even organic. Islam, unlike any of its predecessors, insisted that truth became available to all peoples at specific times in their development; and that Islam, far from being a new religion, was no more and no less than the last in the chain of great religions addressed to the peoples of the world. In stating that there would be no prophet after Muhammad, Islam in its sociological sense reflected the human consciousness that the age of the rise of new theocratic systems was at an end. The events of the succeeding fifteen hundred years have shown this to be only too true. It is, for reasons of the development of society as we have it today, inconceivable that new religious teachers of the caliber of the founders of world religions should attain any prominence comparable to that achieved by Zoroaster, Buddha, Moses, Jesus and Muhammad.

After the full development of the Islamic civilization in the middle ages, Sufism began to

---

8 *Kitab el-Luma.*

spread in a number of different ways. Adapting their teachings to the needs of society, Sufi poets and singers created masterpieces which were to become a part of the classical heritage of the East. In circles where entertainment and frivolity prevailed, the Sufi techniques adjusted themselves in music and dance, in teaching through romantic and wonderful tales, and especially in humor. The concentration on the theme of love, and the separation of the human being from his goal, was early introduced into military spheres, where chivalry and the theme of the quest of the beloved and of an ultimate fulfillment produced further literature and the formation of chivalric orders, subsequently significant in East and West.

Abridged from *The Sufis*

Sayings of the Prophet

Trust
TRUST IN GOD – but tie your camel first.

The World
TREAT THIS WORLD as I do, like a wayfarer; like a horseman who stops in the shade of a tree for a time, and then moves on.

Objects
IT IS YOUR attachment to objects which makes you blind and deaf.

Sleep
SLEEP IS THE brother of death.

Reflection
THE FAITHFUL ARE mirrors, one to the other.

Women
WOMEN ARE THE twin-halves of men.

Privacy
WHOEVER INVADES PEOPLE'S privacy corrupts them.

Wives
A VIRTUOUS WIFE is the best treasure any man can have.

Oppression
WHEN OPPRESSION EXISTS, even the bird dies in its nest.

Love
DO YOU THINK you love your Creator? Love your fellow-creature first.

Distribution
GOD IT IS who gives: I am only a distributor.

Helping Others
I ORDER YOU to assist any oppressed person, whether he is a Muslim or not.

Monkishness
NO MONKERY IN Islam.

The Pious
MY BACK HAS been broken by "pious" men.

Cursing
YOU ASK ME to curse unbelievers. But I was not sent to curse.

Teaching
ONE HOUR'S TEACHING is better than a whole night of prayer.

Day and Night
THE NIGHT IS long; do not shorten it by sleep. The day is fair; do not darken it with wrongdoing.

Humility
HUMILITY AND COURTESY are themselves a part of piety.

Envy
ENVY DEVOURS GOOD deeds, as a fire devours fuel.

The Learned
WHOEVER HONORS THE learned, honors me.

Poverty
MY POVERTY IS my pride.

Death
DIE BEFORE YOUR death.

The Tongue
A MAN SLIPS with his tongue more than with his feet.

Desire
DESIRE NOT THE world, and God will love you.
Desire not what others have, and they will love you.

Pride and Generosity
PRIDE IN ANCESTRY is really a property-investment.
Generosity is a variety of piety.

Practice
WHO ARE THE learned? Those who put into practice
what they know.

Kindness
WHOEVER HAS NO kindness has no faith.

Princes and Scholars
THE BEST OF princes is one who visits the wise. The
worst of scholars is one who visits princes.

Anger
YOU ASK FOR a piece of advice. I tell you: "Do not get
angry." He is strong who can withhold anger.

The Judge
A MAN APPOINTED to be a judge has been killed
without a knife.

Struggle
THE HOLY WARRIOR is he who struggles with himself.

Ink and Blood
THE INK OF the learned is holier than the blood of
the martyr.

Contemplation
AN HOUR'S CONTEMPLATION is better than a year's
worship.

Understanding
SPEAK TO EVERYONE in accordance with his degree of
understanding.

Food
NOBODY HAS EATEN better food than that won by
his own labor.

Work
I AM A worker.

Accusations
ANYONE REVILING A brother for a sin will not himself
die before committing it.

Paradise
I WILL STAND surety for Paradise if you save yourself
from six things: telling untruths, violating promises,
dishonoring trust, being unchaste in thought and
act, striking the first blow, taking what is bad and
unlawful.

Tasks
WHOEVER MAKES ALL his tasks one task, God will help him in his other concerns.

Poetry
IN SOME POETRY there is wisdom.

Lies, Promises, Trust
HE IS NOT of mine who lies, breaks a promise or fails in his trust.

Thoughts
GOOD THOUGHTS ARE a part of worship.

Vision of the Faithful
THE FAITHFUL SEE with the light of God.

Some Behavior
I AM LIKE a man who has lighted a fire, and all the creeping things have rushed to burn themselves in it.

The Quran
THE QURAN HAS been revealed in seven forms. Each verse has inner and outer meaning.

Obligation to Learn
THE PURSUIT OF knowledge is obligatory on every Muslim.

The Young in Paradise
OLD WOMEN WILL not enter Paradise: they will be made young and beautiful first.

A Journey
ON A JOURNEY, the lord of a people is their servant.

Recognition
SOULS WHICH RECOGNIZE one another, congregate together. Those which do not, argue with one another.

Truth
SPEAKING THE TRUTH to the unjust is the best of holy wars.

Knowledge
JOURNEY EVEN AS far as China seeking knowledge.

The Time Will Come
THE TIME WILL come when you are divided into seventy-two sects. A group among you will be my people, the people of Salvation.

The Bequest
I HAVE NOTHING to leave you except my family.

Motives

THE MESSENGER OF Allah said:

A martyr will be brought before God on resurrection day and the man will say: "I fought for your cause, even to martyrdom."

God will say: "You are a liar. You fought in order that you should be called a hero, and people *have* called you such."

He will be taken to hell.

Then a man learned in the Quran will be brought and he will say: "I studied and read the Quran for Your sake."

God will say: "You are a liar. You gained learning, in order to be called learned by men. They *have* called you learned."

He will be taken into hell.

Now a rich man will be brought forward, and he will say: "I have given liberally for that to which You desired generosity to be extended."

God will say: "You are a liar. You did what you did in order to be called generous by men. They *have* called you generous."

He will be taken into hell.

From *The Mishkat*

The bier of a Jew was carried past. The Messenger stood up in respect. Someone said: "It is the body of a Jew." The Prophet answered: "Is it not a soul?"

Abu Musa records

THE PROPHET SAID: "Feed the hungry, visit those who are sick, free the captive."

If anyone seeks learning to argue with the wise or to dispute with the foolish, or to attract attention to himself, Allah will deliver him into hell.

Men will come from every part of this earth to understand the Faith.

When they come to you, give them right advice.

Whoever is without gentleness is devoid of good.

Aisha relates
WHEN GIVEN A choice, the Messenger always took the lesser of two objects.

The Emissary patched his own sandals, did his own work, behaved in the house like anyone else.

Abdulla, son of Harith states
I HAVE NEVER seen anyone who smiled more than the Envoy of Allah.

Anas testifies
I NEVER SAW anyone more kind to children than the Messenger of God.

Mu'ad recalls
THE LAST WORDS I had from the Messenger were: "Treat people well, Mu'ad."

The Parable of the Rain

THE PROPHET MUHAMMAD said of his knowledge that it was like a heavy rain falling upon the earth.

One part of the earth received the rain, and from that nourishment and what was in the earth produced plants and life.

Another patch of ground, not far away, took the water and collected it, making it available for mankind to drink.

A third area of the earth neither accepted the

rainwater to keep it, nor did it absorb it to produce herbage.

In the second it takes and gives, but does not use it. In the first stage, the ground takes and also gives.

In the third, the land is unaffected by the rain, it neither takes nor uses, nor does it give.

The Son of a Camel

A MAN WENT to Muhammad and asked him for a camel.

"I will give you the child of a camel," said the Prophet.

"How can the child of a camel bear the weight of a huge man such as me?" asked the man.

"Quite easily," said the Prophet; "I will grant your wish and mine. Have this fully grown camel – is it not the son of a camel?"

Knowledge

THE PROPHET SAID: "There will be a time when knowledge is absent."

Ziad, son of Labid, said: "How could knowledge become absent, when we repeat the Quran, and teach it to our children, and they will teach it to their children, until the day of requital?"

The Messenger answered: "You amaze me, Ziad, for I thought that you were the chief of the learned of Medina. Do the Jews and the Christians not read the Torah and the Gospels without understanding anything of their real meaning?"

From *Caravan of Dreams*

Hunger

PEOPLE SATED WITH themselves are so because of their hunger for something else. They are therefore hungry. Those who turn back from wrongdoing, they are the ones who are at prayer; not those who merely seem to bend in prayer. Prayer is an activity.

– Sanai, *Hadiqa*
From *The Way of the Sufi*

The Being of God

NO HUMAN MIND can attain an understanding of the form of being which is called God.

– Sanai, *Hadiqa*
From *The Way of the Sufi*

Bayazid Bistami

A FIRE-WORSHIPING MAGIAN was asked why he did not become a Muslim.

He answered:

"If you mean that I should be as good a man as Bayazid, I lack the courage. If, however, you mean that I should be as bad a man as you, I would detest it."

From *The Way of the Sufi*

A DEVOUTLY RELIGIOUS man, who was a disciple of Bayazid, said to him one day:

"I am surprised that anyone who accepts God should not attend the mosque for worship."

Bayazid answered:

"I, on the other hand, am surprised that anyone who knows God can worship him and not lose his senses, rendering his ritual prayer invalid."

From *The Way of the Sufi*

Service

I WILL NOT serve God like a laborer, in expectation of my wages.

– Rabia el-Adawia
From *The Way of the Sufi*

To Reach the Degree of Truth...

NONE ATTAINS TO the Degree of Truth until a thousand honest people have testified that he is a heretic.

– Junaid of Baghdad
From *The Way of the Sufi*

One of Ours

A THEOLOGIAN FOUND himself at the entrance to the Gardens of Paradise. He had a pious look, and the angel on duty asked him a nominal question or two and then said:

"Pass, friend, enter the Garden."

"Not so fast, my boy," said the cleric; "I am a noted Believer, impeccable in faith and renowned for my intellect, accustomed to making up my own mind, and not to people making up their minds about me. How can you prove that this *is* Paradise, and not a snare and a delusion; think carefully before you answer."

The angel rang a bell and angelic guards appeared.

"Take this one inside, will you? He's one of ours all right."

From *The Dermis Probe*

11

Table Talk

IF YOU ARE uninterested in what I say, there's an end to it.

If you like what I say, please try to understand which previous influences have made you like it.

If you like some of the things I say and dislike others, you could try to understand why.

If you dislike all I say, why not try to find out what formed your attitude?

From *Reflections*

EVERY SATURDAY NIGHT, for many years, Idries Shah held dinner-meetings for around twenty or thirty people at a time.

After the meal, he would talk. The range of subjects he covered was astonishing; in common with many historical Sufi figures, Shah was a polymath and there seemed no limit to the things that interested him. Sometimes he would discuss a topic from the newspapers, or advances in psychology, anthropology or scientific understanding; at others, he would recount anecdotes, tales from history or from the lives of the classical Sufi masters.

Sometimes people would ask questions and these, as often as not, would spark more stories and illustrations.

The following excerpts are intended to give a flavor of those evenings.

Editor's note

Letters and the Charitable King

PEOPLE ARE ALWAYS asking why I correspond with them so seldom.

Here are two answers to that.

The first is that there was a king who asked a dervish why he did not come to see him more often. The dervish answered: "Because the words 'Why have you not been here lately?' are sweeter to my ear than 'Why have you come again?'"

The second is that there was once a king who developed a charitable outlook and decided to distribute all his wealth equally among the people of the world. When all the necessitous ones had been counted, however, it was discovered that there was no coin small enough to give an equal amount to each, quite apart from the fact that the smallest coin had by itself no purchasing power.

Merely to reproduce one's words and circulate them to all interested people may appear to be keeping in touch with them; but, unless the occasion is suitable, it is only of social value, not of informative usefulness, let alone of knowledge value.

If we are to admit that it is strictly social needs which are fulfilled by writings and meetings, then I will insist all the more upon a proper social relationship, not a false one produced by modern methods of multiplying copies.

Without Comment

I WAS INVITED one day to the home of a distinguished psychiatrist.

He received me in his study. There was another guest present.

While we were in the study, this man talked very volubly. We went into another room to listen to some tape recordings. The other guest interrupted them frequently with his opinions.

When the dinner was served, the same man monopolized the conversation.

After the meal, he talked and talked over coffee in the drawing-room.

Eventually he left, and I stayed behind to finish some discussions with our host.

I said to him:

"That man talked a great deal in the study."

"Yes," said the psychiatrist, "that was because he did not know you, and he was nervous."

"But he talked a lot while we were playing the tapes."

"Yes, that was because he felt that they were competition for him."

"And he talked all through dinner."

"Yes, that was because, with my wife present, he felt more at ease."

"And then there was all that talk after dinner, while we were having coffee."

"Yes, that was because the drawing-room was rather large for him, and he felt that he had to fill it with his voice to compensate."

"I suppose that he would talk a great deal in a very small room, because he would feel hemmed in," I said.

"Yes, that's a fair assumption," said the psychiatrist.

Q: Why is my life so miserable? I am often in despair, and then things seem to happen to me to make me even more worried. I feel that other people do not have anything like the problems which beset me.

A: Anyone who had your attitude would probably have similar problems to yours. Has it not occurred to you that, conversely, other people do not have your difficulties because they do not react as you do to what happens?

Have you heard the account of the experience of Farisi and the snake?

Thirst and Snake
THE SUFI KALABADHI was told by Farisi:[9]

---

9   Abu'l-Hasan al-Farisi, in Abu-Bakr al-Kalabadhi's *Kitab al-Taaruf.*

"I was going through the desert when I became so thirsty that I could not walk. I sat down and, recalling that it had been said that just before someone dies of thirst, the eyes start to water, I waited for this to happen.

"All at once I heard a sound and saw a silvery white snake slithering toward me. I was so frightened that I leaped up and fled, in spite of my feebleness, with the snake just behind, hissing as it went.

"Eventually I arrived at a place where there was water, and I could not hear the snake hiss. When I looked back, I saw that the serpent had disappeared. I drank, and my life was saved."

Farisi, when he sat down, was not helpless, although he thought he was until the snake approached. And the snake, the second calamity, was the means of his deliverance.

From *Seeker After Truth*

Coercive Agencies

MAKE IT YOUR business to study in your life and in your surroundings:

The growth, development and activity of informal coercive agencies, not often recognized as such because of the poorly delineated identification and measurement tools in current use.

Such tyrannies seldom have guns, clubs, centralized propaganda machines, uniforms and recognizable officials.

If you set up an experiment in any expectation, this expectation becomes a coercive agency whose attempts to lead you to certain conclusions you will have to take into account. Certain customs, social pressures, personal predilections, even individual decisions, can become coercive agencies in your life.

One of the reasons why man struggles against what he takes to be undesirable is that he unconsciously recognizes the coercive influences in the surroundings and in himself. He then chooses a measurable form of them, to satisfy and therefore "abolish" his need to resist or frustrate them.

He has in so doing, of course, only begged the question.

Thoughts, circumstances, the social milieu, a hundred and one things, can provide as powerful coercive agencies as anything that the human being can point to as a "despotism," or "tyranny."

If you are against tyranny, you must be against all tyranny in order to be consistent: not just an aunt-sally tyranny.

A set of misunderstood ideas or practices may become such a tyranny. A group of people who deal with each other with the greatest kindness yet who perform practices or carry out other activities unsuitable for their development are such an agency.

The tyranny of ideas or practices is far subtler and more effective than the avowed repressive institution because the participants are not aware that they are being constrained. The extreme case, the man who spends all his time shouting "I'm free, I tell you!"

is not free, because of lack of time, to do anything other than shout "I'm free!"

Certain coercive agencies have become indispensable to the victims. People with closed minds or small ranges of thought and action depend for their pleasures upon the rewards offered by obedience to the coercive agency. If this obedience is couched in the form of "disobedience," they feel that they are not coerced.

Such people cannot make progress toward their mental liberation at one bound. Their world has to be made larger, and to be seen to be larger, before they can take any step beyond their narrow life.

There is no repression like that of the man who causes his own, in the name of freeing himself. Since he cannot attribute it to any outside source, and since he cannot see himself suppressing himself, he may very well be lost. He is already under the duress of "Slavery is freedom." It is interestingly indicative of his state that he fears loss of freedom while he has already lost it. He does this because – like a child – if he has lost something and merely pretends that he might lose it, this implies that he has still got it.

We need not talk of social action, politics nor economics, nor even sociology in this matter. The individual, and groupings of people, have to learn that they cannot reform society in reality, nor deal with others as reasonable people, unless the individual has learned to locate and allow for the various patterns of coercive institutions, formal and also informal, which rule him. No matter what his reason says, he will always relapse into obedience to the coercive agency while its pattern is within him.

This is one reason why you see people converted from one system of belief or practice to another – they are aware of the shortcomings of the first; they can pretend that the second, because it does not have the outer defects to which they take exception, is "true," when the former was "not true."

The Study of Coercive Agencies and Man is what I would call this effort.

Social and Psychological Elements in Sufi Study

Q: ARE YOU reducing metaphysical and spiritual studies to the level of sociology and psychology?

A: No, I am, on the contrary, trying to show the contaminants and confusions from socializing and popular psychology in these studies. If people think that they are worshiping God when they are in reality seeking emotional excitement, this can hardly be to everyone's advantage. If the sensations aroused by transfer of emotions from one person, or one system, to another are thought to be "special," when they are extensively described and illustrated as normal social actions and developments, what harm is there in affirming the truth?

Q: It is often said that it is better to leave people with their beliefs, rather than to disturb them.

A: If the belief is equivalent to believing that an appendix pain is the work of the devil, it is wrong to leave the patient with it, for he is likely to die.

The Man who Fell off a Mountain

IT MAY NOT be our role to do anything for him, but on the lower level, we can't be prevented from alluding to his state. People like this sometimes resemble the man who fell off a mountain. When he had reached halfway down, he said to himself: "Five thousand feet and nothing has happened yet – in fact it is quite pleasurable."

We may have to leave such a man alone, but we can't help noting his real situation. Such people are often those who turn up and say: "I am following the X Path, and I find it rewarding, but I would like to add a little of your wisdom..."

What Religion Is

THE BELIEF THAT something which is really, for instance, a selfish self-absorption in religious activity is anti-religion in effect. Sheikh Ibrahim Gazur-Ilahi truly says: "That which takes you to God is religion/ whatever stands between you and God is 'the world.'" How many pious people realize that?

The levels of sociology and psychology, which your question regards as a "reduction" are, in fact, essential to examine at the learning how to learn stage, because unless the psychology is correctly oriented, there is no spirituality, though there can be obsession and emotionality, often mistaken for it. Those who trade in such things, mistaking them for spirituality, have of course – knowingly or otherwise – a vested interest in discouraging interest in the psychological and sociological levels. Those interested in truth, however, cannot afford such luxuries. As for the social level, this and the psychological are dealt with by this quotation from one of the greatest of all Sufis, who is not dealing in spirituality, if you define this term narrowly:

Sheikh Abdullah Ansari says:

What is worship?
To realize reality.
What is the sacred law?
To do no evil.
What is reality?
Selflessness.

This is the Sufi approach – not the other way about. There can be no spirituality, according to the Sufi masters, without psychology, psychological insight and sociological balance.

So, if you are looking for spirituality which requires such insights, you have to look at the "reduction" by the great classical Sufi masters, not by me, for I am no innovator in this respect. If, too, you imagine that the Sufis are not to be regarded as "spiritual" because of their insistence on psychology and sociology, you are out of luck again; not only Islamic authorities but scholars from all faiths continue to regard the Sufis as among the greatest exponents of the spiritual among humankind.

There is no wisdom where there is no common sense; it cannot under those conditions find any expression.

They say: "Seek wisdom while you have the strength, or you may lose the strength without gaining wisdom."

From *Learning How to Learn*

General Gordon

THE STORY IS told of a celebrated statue of General Gordon mounted upon a camel which was one of the sights of Khartoum.

This statue became a great favorite with a three-year-old boy, and his nursemaid used to take him every day as part of his walk, to "see General Gordon."

The day came when the family was leaving the Sudan, and the nurse took the little boy to say goodbye to General Gordon.

He stood for a long time looking at the statue, and said: "I shall not be seeing you again for a long time, so goodbye General Gordon."

Then he turned from the man on the camel to the young woman and said to her:

"Nanny, who is that sitting on General Gordon's back?"

This tale could very well be true. It illustrates as well as would any other the manner in which people assume things about knowledge without ever imagining that their view may be inconsistent with real circumstances. Sometimes it is almost by accident, as in this case, that one knows exactly what it is that the person has seen awry, although it may be evident that he is not clear about it.

Like the camel of General Gordon, people often imagine that the means of transportation of a teaching is the teaching itself. For this reason they carry on reversing the externals of individuals, or mere words, or exercise or theories. What counts is the effect, not the appearance, of a thing.

Like our little boy, the student may see something which prompts him to ask a question which could clear everything up. And the information that he has been attached to something in the name of something else may be unwelcome.

From *Caravan of Dreams*

Man and Hero

MAN REALLY IS a hero. Everywhere you will find him struggling for freedom and opposing its curtailment.

Yet, very often he is obviously struggling for his own enslavement at the same time and with equal force.

To be obsessed by the idea of freedom, for instance, is itself a form of slavery. Such people are in the chains of the hope of freedom, and are therefore able to do little else than struggle with them.

From *Reflections*

Teachers and Pupils

Q: THERE ARE a lot of people who claim to have studied under you who have now become "Sufi Teachers," both in the East and in, for instance, the USA. How do we know whether they are genuine?

A: The number of people who claim to have studied under me and to be teaching what I communicated to them will soon, I fancy, equal the number who say that they taught me. They, in turn, may be as numerous as those who say that they have improved on what I am doing, and those who insist that they would not have anything to do with me at any price. This is a sociological phenomenon, common among people who know very little about something but imagine that they know a lot. This is the kind of person who thinks in "transactional" terms: he accepts, rejects, "improves," avoids things, treating all things from cornflakes to Sufi knowledge, with the same low-level lack of perception.

Q: Then how are we to know which of these people to heed?

A: You will instantly know as soon as you get rid of your own transactional mentality. Until you do, you cannot know; you have to depend on opinion and what you can evaluate of what you are told.

From *Knowing How to Know*

Human Development

MANY PEOPLE IMAGINE that any higher human development, if it exists at all, must follow a pattern whose form (or at least whose beginning) is instantly perceptible to them as such.

In making this assumption these people expose themselves to control by any system which can take advantage of this expectation. And systems do take advantage of this.

Many aspects of higher human development can only take the form of communicating knowledge and experience in a disguised manner – rather as we teach our children by involving them in activities which they consider to be amusements rather than lessons in (say) counting, or coordination, or manners.

One method of accustoming people to a "higher pattern" is to involve them in activities and enterprises which are equivalences of higher things.

Another procedure of great worth is also comparable to one employed in teaching children. It is to surround the pupil with data which he absorbs piecemeal until the "penny drops."

I Know that Already

ONE OF THE commonest defenses against really learning something is to believe that one knows it already.

If you say "I know that!" when someone who knows your interests and how to teach says something, you are indulging in this almost unconscious activity.

12

Travel Writing

My leg is not lame, Allah's earth is not small.

From *Caravan of Dreams*

Idries Shah's travel writing should not be taken as literal autobiography, as some commentators have tried to do.

Rather, it is a way of presenting experience to his readers in a form intended to be accessible to them. In the following extract, he picks a position that is somewhere between his own and that of the reader, to show how one can, in the Sufi phrase, "learn about life through life."

Editor's note

Sorcerer's Apprentice

Everyone has heard of Yoga; people are prepared to believe that Tibetan divines can sit for weeks stark naked in the snow, and derive some spiritual advantage therefrom, or, at least, suffer no lasting harm from the experience. The witchcraft of Africa is an established fact. But how many people in the West know anything much about Sufism?

The mystical philosophy of the Muslims is one of those things which is an open secret to the people of the East, yet as impenetrable to a Westerner as anything you can imagine. It is practiced by perhaps ten to twenty million people. In some places, such as Muslim India or Afghanistan, almost every adult male is affiliated to a greater or lesser degree to one of the four main Orders. True, there are books on the subject in English; certain Western Orientalists (ridiculous term) have even made a special study of it. Some of the East's greatest literature has been written by Sufi mystics, and this has formed the source of material for the plausible but useless books "explaining" Islamic mysticism to the West.

Writing, as I do, in English, and for a Western public, I can understand some of the problems that Orientalists have to face in trying to describe something for which there are no precise parallels in European thought. It is easy to simplify, easy to get a general idea of Sufism, possible to put down on paper general remarks which seem to have authority, but merely scratch the surface. This is the temptation to which too many of the otherwise highly respected professors of oriental studies have succumbed. For I would rather go on record as saying that these sages understand more than they write but find it hard to write it, than to hold that they understand it not at all.

Perhaps the difficulty can in part be likened to the task of an outsider studying freemasonry. Those who want to go further into Sufism will have to seek elsewhere than in these pages for a deep presentation of the cult.[10]

All that I can hope to do here is to give a general outline of some of the main features of the system and then plunge into my story; for this, after all, is a travel book, even if it does not dwell upon every moment of my journeyings, and deals with my search for the unusual, and the highlights of what I actually saw and heard in the Middle East.

Sufism is organized mainly into four schools, or semi-monastic Orders, each deriving from a Teacher who developed a rigidly organized system of recitations, exercises and studies. The object of this effort is the refinement of the soul, and the unification of the mind of man with that of God. Sufism is Islamic, and for that reason it is held to be impossible for a non-Muslim to become a Sufi. A staggering number of miracles are attributed to Sufis, including foreknowledge, levitation, power over trees, plants and other natural things, curing of disease, flying from one place to another – and supernatural power in most of its aspects.

Time, as we know it, is of little interest to Sufis. They claim to be in contact telepathically with one another irrespective of time and distance. Long-dead saints are believed to be in active contact with living divines. These are the people known as Dervishes

---

10 Details are given in my *Oriental Magic* (Rider, London, 1956; ISF Publishing, London, 2016).

in Turkey and elsewhere, and many of those who have the name *fakir* (i.e., "humble") in India. A son generally joins the *Halqa* (circle) to which his father belonged. There is no celibacy in Sufism, and no set time for the transition between one stage of power and the next. All depends upon individual progress. The Sufis, incidentally, do not believe in reincarnation, but rather in the unreality of death.

Now Sufis do not preach the cult. It is up to the inquiring youth – for such he generally is – to seek out a Sufi circle and apply for admission. No fees are charged, and once a candidate is accepted, he is under an absolute vow of obedience stricter than any military code that I know. The purpose of the development of the Sufi himself is to become a perfect man, and hence to be of the greatest possible value to the community.

I had been present often enough at the gatherings of Sufis in various places, taken part in their recitations and listened to their discourses. Now, in Syria, I decided to see whether I could penetrate further into the actual active side of Sufi life. I wanted to get a clearer, firsthand view of the whole thing.

At Yeniburj (whose locating was difficult, since its very existence was denied by some), I made my way up the steep slope of the hillside, where the ancient monastery – a collection of weathered former fortifications – stood out against the late afternoon sky. I had a letter to the *Wali* (saint) of the place, whom I shall call Sheikh Ibrahim. The "lay brethren" whom I passed on the incline were pious-looking men, wearing the patched cloak of the dervish, carrying water, tending vegetable gardens, milking goats. I was taken into the largest building to await the arrival of the Sheikh.

This community, it seemed, was composed mainly of refugees from the Kemalist regime in Turkey, where the Republic had dissolved the monasteries in the nineteen-twenties, and the practice of Sufism became illegal.

Filtering southward into Syria, these Sufis had taken up their abode in the ruined fortress, added a number of smaller buildings to it, and now carried on the cult free of any interference.

The hall of the castle where I sat was high, arched and surrounded with cloisters, after the fashion of the Middle Eastern caravansary. In one corner of the huge courtyard, food was being cooked over a brazier. A Sufi-cook turned *shashlik* meat on a skewer over the sullen flames, and watched a soup cauldron simmering over a slow, sullen charcoal fire. Ranged beside him were the communal soup-bowls of the community, for nobody is allowed to have private property, and there is one famous (probably apocryphal) story of a venerable Sufi being "drummed out of the Order" for having indicated a preference for one bowl over the others.

The corner of the courtyard facing Mecca was decorated by a painted niche, with the word ALLAH written upon it. I was seated on one of the rugs which were arranged in horseshoe form around the southern part of the arena. From the fort itself came the monotonous rhythm of the *halqa* in action –

there must have been some three hundred voices intoning the chant: *La-illaha-illa-lah!* (no God but Allah), and I could imagine the circle of worshipers swaying backward and forward to the beat of the syllables. This is a familiar Sufi exercise (*dhikr*) in all Muslim countries.

A young member of the Order, dressed in a cotton mantle of subdued Sufi orange, brought me a copy of the Quran, and I immersed myself in reading it. Suddenly, from the very top of the castle's tower, the long-drawn-out, thin and appealing cry of the Muezzin echoed forth: "*Hayya alaessalah...*" ("Come to Prayer, Come to Success!"). It was time for the afternoon devotions, for Sufi exercises are additional to the five obligatory prayers of established Islam.

I hurried to the fountain in the middle of the courtyard, and performed my ablutions: washing hands, arms, face and feet. As I looked round, the whole place seemed suddenly full of hurrying figures, heading for the interior of the fort. I followed them into the Mosque. This, in the very center of the building, was an enormous chamber without windows; bare except for matting on the floor and the names of the Prophet and the Four Caliphs inscribed upon medallions high upon the walls.

After the congregational prayers were over, and we sat silent for a few minutes in private contemplation, I looked around to get some idea of my companions. They were a very assorted-looking lot. About half of the five-hundred-odd were dressed in long orange robes. Others wore common garments covered with patches – both varieties of the Sufi "uniform." Each one had hair reaching to his shoulders, and most had beards. There was something very monkish about them. They seemed to come in all sizes, and ranged in age from perhaps about twenty to the Sheikh himself, who could have been a hundred, with his white hair and staff. There was not much light, for the oil lamps were low and flickering.

I presented myself to the Sheikh. He was tall, thin and serious of face. "Welcome, brother, stay as long as you will..."

Slowly, in twos and threes, the congregation broke up. I was told that for the purposes of study the community was divided into sections, each under a leader. Between the hours of prayer, each leader took his section into one or other of the rooms set aside for their use, and gave them instruction. At certain times the whole community assembled in the *Zawiya* (assembly-hall) and carried out physical and religious exercises under the guidance of the Sheikh or one of his five assistants. These assistant sheikhs were the most developed spiritually after the Sheikh, and one day one of them would take over the saffron robe of leadership of the monastery, while the others would go out into the world to form their own communities.

We returned to the courtyard where the *Diwan* of the Sheikh was assembling. Each Sufi has his own rug or mat, and his own position in the horseshoe. These are factors which are determined by the Sheikh, and none may occupy another's seat. The arrangement of the places denotes the degree of spiritual enlightenment which the individual has attained.

Because my Persian was better than my Syrian Arabic, and possibly due to the fact that Persian is a classical tongue of Sufism, the Sheikh and his "cabinet" carried out their deliberations in that language. Their linguistic ability was considerable. The session was divided into three parts. First came secular matters. One by one, the lay brethren in charge of various activities came and presented accounts and reports. The Sheikh adjudicated upon small matters, and gave general administrative instructions.

Then the uninitiated were dismissed, and the Sheikh gave an interpretation of one of the works of Al-Ghazzali. For over an hour he held forth on the meaning of one passage of the *Renaissance of Religious Sciences*, while the assembly sat mute and relaxed, allowing every word to sink in. There was no doubt that he was a man of the most profound knowledge. Speaking without a note, and without even the text before him, he interpreted an obscure part of the most difficult work of Islamics, with profuse literal quotations from the Quran, which he knew by heart.

Up to this point silence had been obligatory upon all. No questions might be asked.

Now, however, came the debate. One of the Sufis had challenged another to a debate upon the reality of existence and the meaning of time. First one spoke, then the other. Then the first was allowed to reply.

Poems and passages from classics were recited to embellish and elucidate points. A number of works of vast erudition unfamiliar to me were quoted *in extenso*. Then the others were asked as to whether anyone wished to comment upon the debate. One by one, three of the more important Sufis spoke for and against the motion, as it were.

Then silence. The Sheikh summed up the entire range of the arguments and gave his verdict, rather after the fashion of an appeal judge in England. This was probably my most absorbing experience of all during that Middle Eastern journey. This seemed standard-enough procedure here, but the range and depth of the proceedings – entirely extemporaneous – were amazing.

Now, as the evening shadows were gathering, we lined up for food at the "kitchen" on the other side of the square. Each man was issued with a bowl filled with vegetable soup, in which pieces of roast meat had been included; a large, round unleavened loaf was added, and a bottle of water from the well. We sat round in a circle, eating – as is the custom – in complete silence. There was no order of precedence in meals, and the Sheikh sat next to a beardless youth, while I was flanked on the one side by one of the superior sages, and on the other by the cook himself.

When we had finished, and washed our hands, faces and bowls, we performed the evening prayer in congregation at the Mosque.

As I was leaving, the Sheikh took me aside and asked me whether I would join his *halqa* at their special devotions that night. Trying not to show too much delight, I agreed. He told me to be in the Mosque at midnight. I had about four hours until then, which I spent exploring the monastery. In one room, three dervish tailors sat, repairing the garments of their fellows with bone needles, by the light of oil lamps. Clothes were, it seemed, communally owned. Next door was the weaving shop, where material was made from goat-hair for sale locally. In the library, twelve copyists sat laboriously illuminating manuscripts of the Quran and the Traditions of the Prophet. As each page was finished, it was checked for accuracy five times, and then passed to the Chief Librarian – an elderly Yemenite – to be finally pitted against his memory.

My guide, Abdullah, had been with the monastery only two years, before which he had been a doctor who had taken his degree in Berlin. He told me a remarkable story about the Librarian, which I give here just as I heard it.

"Last year, a wandering dervish came this way, and asked if we would lend him one of the manuscripts. It was the only copy we had, and normally it would not have been lent under any circumstances. But the Sheikh agreed, because the wanderer was known for his piety and complete indifference to things of the world. It was not thought possible that he would lose it or sell it. Unfortunately, we miscalculated. When he reached Damascus, the dervish met a man who he thought would benefit more by the book than he himself would. So he lent it to him. This man died on a pilgrimage to Mecca, and his effects were dispersed. Nobody knew where the book was.

"When the news came to the Librarian, he simply sighed and wrote out the book from memory!"

I believe that this may be possible, because the practice of committing to memory is not uncommon, and very many children are schooled in this technique by having learned the Quran by heart. This takes two to four years. The Quran being in rhymed Arabic, the task is easier than it would otherwise be.

There were about thirty dervishes in the Mosque when I arrived just after midnight. After a few minutes, the Sheikh appeared, and led us across the courtyard into a subterranean chamber about a hundred feet long and half as wide. The ceiling was low, the floor was thickly carpeted with Persian rugs, the walls were whitewashed, and quite bare. We removed our sandals at the door, where several Sufis stood as if on guard.

The congregation formed up in a circle, facing inward, seated cross-legged. I sat beside the Sheikh. For a moment all was silence.

Then the Sheikh intoned the words *Allahu!* about six times, in rapid succession. From the other side of the circle the cry was taken up. Soon every one of us was repeating the phrase (God Exists!) as fast as we could, still maintaining a rhythm. Then, slowly at first, edging into the recitation, about ten of the dervishes added the word Akbar, Akbar, *Akbar*, *AKBAR*, AKBAR, *Akbar!* The phrase now ran: God Exists, Greater than All Else! As the rhythm was established, the bodies of the devotees swayed backward and forward in time to the syllables. I noticed that a few of them seemed to be more affected than the rest. Some had their eyes closed, others had a fixed, wide-eyed expression. There were small beads of perspiration appearing on every face. Then, as if in response to a signal, half of them started to clap, in monotonous time, and the shouting grew in volume, thrown back by the bare walls, seeming to reverberate through one's entire frame ... All*aho*-A*k*bar, All*aho*-A*k*bar, Alla*hu*, Alla*hu*... Then it faded, and finally there was silence again.

I looked around me. Three of the dervishes seemed to be in trances. One lolled forward, eyes closed, head on his chest, arms clasped before him. The other two, with eyes wide open, were directly facing me, and such was the intensity of their stare that I could not face it. There was something uncanny about the whole thing. Even the room seemed to have become uncomfortably hot, though I knew that it should be cool, at this time of night, underground... I began to feel that my own senses were being affected, I thought I could see something standing beside me; a man with a beard, towering, surely far too tall for a real human being? He wore long robes, and had a staff – no, a snake – or something, in his hand.

I was shaken out of my reverie by a touch on the arm by the Sheikh. He beckoned me closer, and I turned toward him. Into my ear he said: "Remember this: you are going to be a big man, an important man. I see you walking about in a large garden, there are roses, and there are tulips. You are going into a huge palace, there is a red carpet on the steps, you are asking for something, and it will be granted..."

He stopped, his voice becoming so slow that it sounded almost funny. I whispered in his ear: "You are speaking of the past, Great Sheikh, these things have happened. I am a poor man now, and probably will remain so. I have no hopes of being great or powerful."

The Sheikh had described, in a rather garbled form, things which had happened to me. He spoke again. "I make no mistake, they may have happened, but they did not happen like that. Your life is a set pattern, and I want you to know that this pattern will come round again, but slightly different. Here is a watchword: 'Build to the Sea!'"

"I do not understand you."

"Never mind. Stop thinking. There is fear in your heart. Nothing is going to happen to you. Why should you worry?"

I still do not know what Build to the Sea means; or whether the Sheikh snatched some images from my memory and retold them to me – or if so, why... This is in any case not the main point of the story.

I decided just to let the whole thing roll over me, as it were, and sort out impressions the following day. I knew that Sufis are not dangerous, and anyway I had little to lose.

Suddenly, one of the dervishes stood bolt upright and shouted something which I did not understand. Immediately, he was followed by three more, and then another. Together they drew apart from the rest, and started to whirl counterclockwise at first slowly, then faster and faster. These were the actual Dancing Dervishes – of the Bektashi Order – in action!

I would have given anything to have had my camera with me. This thought brought me fully alert again. I decided to think of secular things, to clear the brain. I thought of the smoky lighting. Not much good, even for a fast lens and hyper-sensitized film. At that speed of movement, too, it would have been impossible to get a picture without flash. Flash would not be allowed...

Then, as if he had been struck a heavy blow from behind, the tallest of the whirling dervishes collapsed in a heap on the ground. Then the one next to him, then a third. They rolled over where they lay, eyes open, glazed, faces turned toward the ceiling. The other two continued their dance. This time they were circling one another, repeating HY HY, H, H, HU HU, HY, ALLAH, at the tops of their voices, with arms outstretched like so many birds in mime. None of them seemed to go into a trance. After a few more circles, they came and sat down quietly outside our squatting circle.

Then another, who had been sitting quietly passing the beads of a rosary through his fingers, gave an unearthly shriek, and fell forward flat on his face. Gently, the Sheikh turned him over. His eyes were shut, and his breathing was so shallow that it was imperceptible to me.

We sat for what seemed only a few minutes more, when the door opened and one of the brethren called the summons to the Dawn Prayer. The session had lasted all night.

The recumbent figures came alive at this. All the Sufis then shook hands and greeted each other with salaams, as if they had been separated for some time. It was at this time that I felt an almost overwhelming urge to stay at the monastery, and to take part in their ceremonies.

The Sheikh knew it, for when he took my hand he said: "Your time is not yet. You have places to see and people to meet. Remember what I have told you."

I asked him, later, about the state of the dervishes whom I had seen in a trance. He told me that according to their belief they were in a state of nearness to the Supreme Power, and that in order to commune with it this state of ecstasy required that all connection with the physical body should cease: a sort of short-circuiting of the nervous system.

I told him that I had seen such things in hypnosis and also in mediumistic trance. "Yes, I know about these things. They are called *ruhaniyyat*, and are against Islam. Our trance is different, and each time the person achieves it, he becomes more powerful in the spiritual sense. You cannot say the same for *ruhaniyyat*.

"You must remember," he went on, "that our exercises have little to do with ordinary, mundane magic. In a sense we are cultivators of a divine form of magic. But the normal and worldly magic is to be found elsewhere. If you want to see that, why not amuse yourself by visiting Musa the Jew who lives in Damascus?"

I asked him whether he did not think that magic of that kind was dangerous or deceptive, or perhaps diabolical?

"Everything is bad in accordance with the use to which it is put. Sufism cannot be put to evil uses, simply because its power comes from God. Mundane magic can be put to evil or good uses, just as any other non-spiritual thing can be put to such uses. If you want to achieve an evil end by magic, you can, and if you want to accomplish good, you can do so. What you do not understand is that you do not yet understand – except very approximately – what is evil and what is good. That is why it is best to stick to Sufism, which is entirely and essentially good."

From *Destination Mecca*

Now that I am Dead

Now THAT I am dead, you may read something of the truth of the Sufi. Had this information been given to you, directly or indirectly, when I was perceptibly among you, you would all, except for a few, have fed your acquisitiveness and love of wonder alone from it.

Know, then, that what the Sufi master is doing for the world and for its people, great and small, is often not seen by the observer.

A Sufi teacher uses his powers to teach, to heal, to make man happy and so on, according to the best reasons for using the powers. If he shows you no miracles, this does not mean that he is not doing them. If he declines to benefit you in the way you wish, it is not because he cannot. He benefits you in accordance with your merit, not in response to a demand by you. He has a higher duty – this is what he is fulfilling.

Many among you have had your lives transformed, have been rescued from perils, have been given chances – none of which you have recognized as benefits. But you have had these benefits just the same.

Many of you, though you are looking for a fuller life, would have no life at all were it not for the efforts of the Community of the Friends. Many of you who are poor, would be cursed if you were rich. Many of you are still rich because of the presence of a Man of Wisdom. Many of you who have been at my school think that you have been taught by me. In actuality, you have been physically present in our assemblies, while you were being taught in another assembly.

All these things are so foreign to your customary thoughts that you are not yet in a position to recognize them.

My task has been to benefit you. The task of making that benefit perceptible to you is that of others.

Your tragedy is that, while waiting for me to vouchsafe miracles and make perceptible changes in you, you have invented miracles which I did not perform, and have developed a loyalty to me which is of no value at all. And you have imagined "changes" and "help" and "lessons" which have not taken place. The "changes," the "help," the "lessons," however, are there. Now find out what they really are. If you go on thinking and doing what I told you to do and think, you are working with yesterday's materials, which have already been used.

> – Mirza Abdul-Hadi Khan of Bokhara
> From *The Way of the Sufi*